IT'S THE PICTURES

A SERIES FROM WESLEYAN UNIVERSITY PRESS
EDITED BY JEANINE BASINGER

The new **Wesleyan Film** series takes a back-to-basics approach to the art of cinema. Books in the series will deal with the formal, the historical, and the cultural—putting a premium on visual analysis, close readings, and an understanding of the history of Hollywood and international cinema, both artistically and industrially. The volumes will be rigorous, critical, and accessible both to academics and to lay readers with a serious interest in film.

Series editor Jeanine Basinger, Corwin-Fuller Professor of Film Studies at Wesleyan University and Founder/Curator of the Wesleyan Cinema Archives, is the author of such landmark books as *The World War II Combat Film: Anatomy of a Genre*, *A Woman's View: How Hollywood Spoke to Women, 1930–1960*, *Silent Stars*, and *The Star Machine*.

ANTHONY MANN
New and Expanded Edition
By Jeanine Basinger

IT'S THE PICTURES
THAT GOT SMALL
*Hollywood Film Stars on 1950s
Television*
Christine Becker

THE FILMS OF SAMUEL FULLER
If You Die, I'll Kill You!
by Lisa Dombrowski

PHYSICAL EVIDENCE
Selected Film Criticism
by Kent Jones

ACTION SPEAKS LOUDER
*Violence, Spectacle, and the American
Action Movie*
Revised and Expanded Edition
by Eric Lichtenfeld

HOLLYWOOD AMBITIONS
Celebrity in the Movie Age
by Marsha Orgeron

To: ~~████████~~

Good friends are met in the most unlikely places!

IT'S THE Da

PICTURES

THAT GOT

SMALL Hollywood Film Stars

on 1950s Television

CHRISTINE BECKER

Best wishes to my dad's friends + neighbors!

Christie Bell

WESLEYAN

UNIVERSITY

PRESS

Middletown,

Connecticut

Published by Wesleyan University Press

Middletown, CT 06459

www.wesleyan.edu/wespress

© 2008 by Christine Becker

Printed in United States of America

5 4 3 2 1

Parts of chapters 1 and 4 were first published in "Televising Film Stardom in the 1950s," by Christine Becker in *Framework: The Journal of Cinema and Media* (vol. 46 no. 2: Fall 2005): 5–21, and are presented here with the permission of Wayne State University Press. Parts of chapter 2 were first published in "Glamour Girl Classed as TV Show Brain: The Body and Mind of Faye Emerson" by Christine Becker in *The Journal of Popular Culture*, Volume 38, Number 2 © Blackwell Publishing, and are reprinted by permission from Blackwell Publishing.

Library of Congress Cataloging-in-Publication Data

Becker, Christine, 1971–
It's the pictures that got small : Hollywood film stars on 1950s television / Christine Becker.
    p. cm. — (Wesleyan film)
  Includes bibliographical references and index.
ISBN 978-0-8195-6893-9 (cloth : alk. paper)—ISBN 978-0-8195-6894-6 (pbk. : alk. paper)
  1. Television programs—United States—History. 2. Motion picture actors and actresses—United States—Biography. I. Title.
PN1992.3.U5B37 2008
791.4502'8097309045—dc22   2008029056

Wesleyan University Press is a member of the Green Press Initiative. The paper used in this book meets their minimum requirement for recycled paper.

To Mom and Dad,

who supported me when

I changed my major to film,

and to Christopher, who

supported me when I

started watching so

much TV.

CONTENTS

ACKNOWLEDGMENTS

I am certain that I am neglecting here many people deserving of thanks. To those people, I say: please blame my faulty memory across the lengthy period it took to complete this project, not a lack of appreciation for your assistance.

All authors should be as fortunate as I have been to have had editors as thorough and knowledgeable as Jeanine Basinger and as responsive and encouraging as Eric Levy and Suzanna Tamminen. The book is immensely better than it would have been without their help. Thanks also to the anonymous readers for providing such helpful feedback.

To all of the librarians and archivists who have helped me, I thank you. The fields of film and television studies are so much richer thanks to the service of those at the Margaret Herrick Library in Los Angeles, the UCLA Film and Television Archive, the Warner Bros. Archives and the Cinema-TV Library at the University of Southern California (special thanks here to Ned Comstock), the New York Public Library for the Performing Arts, the Library of American Broadcasting at the University of Maryland, the Museum of Television and Radio in Beverly Hills and New York, the Russel B. Nye Popular Culture Collection at Michigan State University, Photofest in New York, and the Wisconsin Center for Film and Theater Research and Wisconsin Historical Society (special thanks here to Dorinda Hartmann, Maxine Fleckner Ducey, and Harry Miller). I am also grateful to those who assisted my research in a variety of ways, including Susan Murray, Madelyn Ritrosky-Winslow, Jim Jennewein, Linda J. Alexander, Burt Rosen, Ethel Winant, Carl Bruno, Ben Carbonetto, and Skitch Henderson. A special thanks goes to Morleen Getz Rouse at the University of Cincinnati, who not only gave me a place to stay during my research trip there but also set up an interview for me with the legendary Frederic Ziv. The research in this book is built out of myriad kindnesses like this.

This project began at the University of Wisconsin–Madison. The professors there provided immeasurable guidance and encouragement, and I am happy to be able to thank them here: Lea Jacobs, Tino Balio, Vance Kepley, David Bordwell, J. J. Murphy, James Baughman, Stephen Vaughn, and especially Michele Hilmes, whose work inspires me so much. Fellow graduate students helped me survive and thrive, particularly Wendy

McPherson, Katherine Spring, Jason Mittell, Michael Newman, Derek Kompare, Ron Becker, Scott Higgins, Sally Ross, Paul Ramaeker, Jonathan Walley, Jane Greene, Dale Murray, and most especially Jennifer Fay, without whom I would never have cared enough to wonder what's wrong with gum disease.

I completed the book at my current home, the University of Notre Dame. Here, the support of Pam Wojcik, Aaron Magnan-Park, Jim Collins, Jill Godmilow, Peter Holland, and Chris Sopczynski has been so valuable. I've also greatly appreciated the financial support of the College of Arts and Letters, Dean Mark Roche, and the Institute for Scholarship in the Liberal Arts. Finally, I give special thanks to Susan Ohmer and Donald Crafton, the best colleagues a junior faculty member could hope for.

To my wonderful family, whose help and support I can never truly repay, I hope that your being able to hold this book in your hands and realize the part you played in its completion is adequate reward. I am forever grateful to Anne and Dan Becker and Robert and Madeline Gloss, whose support has meant everything to me. And to Art, Michele, Joel, and Derek Becker, who helped to refuel me with food and fun during my many visits. And to Mabel Becker, whose inspirational spirit is ever part of me. And to Christopher Sieving, without whom I wouldn't want to get up in the morning, let alone write a book.

Finally, to anyone who ever assured me that I could finish this project, I thank you for your encouraging words. You were right.

INTRODUCTION

During a two-week period in April 1955, a television viewer could have sat in her living room and watched Ronald Reagan hosting *General Electric Theater* and presenting Jimmy Stewart in his small-screen acting debut, James Mason hosting *Lux Video Theater* and introducing Claire Trevor as guest star, Gary Merrill starring in the dramatic series *Justice*, Groucho Marx hosting *You Bet Your Life*, Lon Chaney, Jr., unmasked on *Masquerade Party*, Claudette Colbert featured on *Climax*, James Cagney touting his new film on *The Ed Sullivan Show*, Charles Boyer acting on *Four Star Playhouse*, Ray Milland starring in *The Ray Milland Show*, Ann Sothern featured in *Private Secretary*, Rock Hudson and Cornel Wilde guest-starring on Lucille Ball's *I Love Lucy*, and Judy Holliday and Frank Sinatra performing in the special *Kaleidoscope*.

It is commonly presumed that only dethroned film stars and minor character actors would ever consent to appear on television, but the wide range of stars listed above certainly complicates this assumption. From television's earliest days, even as it developed in significant distinction from the film industry, it utilized one of Hollywood's most bankable assets: its stars. The result, however, was not a duplication of theatrical filmmaking on the small screen; rather, early television borrowed elements from film, as well as radio and theater, and adapted them to serve the new medium's unique industrial and cultural needs. This book argues that film stars were key participants in this adaptation.

The trajectory of the corporate relationship between Hollywood and television in this period is already well known to media historians. In brief, after being shut out by the FCC from significant station ownership, and after failing to compete via independent strategies (such as pay TV and theater television), the major Hollywood studios began to participate in the production of TV shows in the mid-1950s; indeed, they came to dominate television production by the early 1960s. Most histories of these circumstances focus on uncovering the roles of sponsors, ad agencies, networks, critics, the FCC, and Hollywood and independent film producers; they predominantly ignore the role of actors in general and film stars specifically. This omission is crucial. After all, TV audiences might not have even known who David O. Selznick and Pat Weaver were, but they did know and love Lucille Ball, Loretta Young, Groucho Marx, and Ronald Reagan. These figures were essential vehicles for the institutional aims of everyone from television stations to talent agents, and we can understand the nature and impact of those aims more precisely by analyzing these actors and their careers on television.[1]

It's the Pictures That Got Small reassesses early television's history in light of the activities of film stars, exploring the industrial circumstances that made possible the evident marriage between Hollywood film talent and television programming in TV's first commercial decade and the ways in which early television presented this plethora of film talent. It also delineates which film stars chose to appear on the new medium and which didn't, the factors that influenced their decisions, and the reasons behind the successes and failures of those who attempted the crossover. Moreover, each chapter considers how a new medium struggling for financial stability and cultural credibility could rely on the star power of film performers yet navigate the possible negative implications surrounding their very decision to appear on TV—especially the assumption that such a star was "washed-up."

This predominant assumption is presumably responsible for the cursory treatment of the topic in many television histories, as it spawns a subsequent hypothesis that such stars had minimal influence on the new medium. Indeed, given the gap between the mature eminence of Hollywood cinema and the fledgling nature of television in the early 1950s, one can easily conclude that (1) only those actors whose film careers had dried up were willing to appear on TV in this period, and (2) by making such appearances, any remaining credibility of their star status was damaged considerably. As a result, the hypothesis assures us, television merely circulated nostalgic, tired versions of these actors' film images, meaning that their television careers and any resulting effects of their appearances were quite limited. With such suppositions firmly entrenched, few have interrogated the topic more closely: why investigate the presence of an insignificant number of washed-up actors? Why bother to analyze the status of static, low-culture star images? Why pretend to explore multiple motives for film actors to move to television when there was really only one: the end of their feature film careers?

The problem is that these very questions are hasty and misdirected. Is it true that across the 1950s only film actors with declining careers appeared on television? Is it true that the only motivation to appear on

2

TV was the desire to resurrect a moribund career? Is it true that a film star's credibility was always negatively affected by an association with television? Is it true that a star's image was merely recycled on television rather than reshaped in some notable way? On the contrary, I show here that a significant number and range of Hollywood film actors, from bit players to legitimate stars, appeared on early television, that the reasons for their moves into television went well beyond sheer popularity decline (indeed, were as varied as the stars themselves), and that the imprint of a television appearance on a film star's image could be considerably more complex than a mere diminished aura or recycled persona.

Chapter 1 explores the industrial conditions of film star appearances on 1950s television in detail. With the breakdown of the classical studio structure across the 1950s, stars were progressively cut loose from their contracts. Although the biggest stars prospered in a new milieu of freedom in Hollywood, featured players and character actors were hurt substantially by the subsequent slowdowns in film production. Television provided a saving grace for many of their careers, as the new medium yearned for nationally recognizable and visually dynamic talent both to attract audiences, sponsors, and financiers and to fill its voluminous production schedules. Only minor Hollywood film actors filled this role during the early years of television, but higher-level stars with still-viable film careers made frequent appearances by the middle of the 1950s, for such reasons as publicity, production control, and money. In a sense, this demarcation represents a parallel with the studios themselves: minor studios (such as Columbia) participated in television early on, and major studios (such as Warner Bros. and Fox) only got involved by the middle of the decade.

This parallel ends by the early 1960s, however. As the major studios substantially increased their production involvement into the new decade, film star participation in television actually declined due to changes in the industrial and programming landscape of television, including the demise of the anthology program, a major outlet for film star talent. Further, as the Hollywood studios eventually came to control the majority of television programming, they and the networks found it more prudent for a variety of reasons to develop young talent on television rather than to feature film stars. Across most of the 1950s, however, film stars did have a significant impact on the new medium: they shaped the configuration of particular genres, enabled substantial financial investments in production, fostered the rapid growth of talent agencies, and helped to sell television sets, consumer products, and the medium itself to audiences and sponsors.

Besides extensive overviews of these industrial conditions, I shall also present here a variety of case studies to clarify how these circumstances worked on the individual level. In addition, I shall investigate what alterations these crossover appearances brought to the traditional mechanisms of the star system and to star images. Only a handful of studies have addressed the concept of television stardom, and they generally suffer from a lack of historical grounding. Most build upon the pioneering work of Richard Dyer—who established the theoretical concept that film stars present a combination of the extraordinary and the ordinary, the inaccessible and the attainable—and try to drape his ideas onto television. For instance, in *Visible Fictions*, John Ellis extends Dyer's ideas and argues that a star is both present in the cinematic image but absent in a material sense, and this paradoxical meshing— "[t]he star is tantalisingly close and similar, yet at the same time remote and dissimilar"—results in a spectator's fascination with the star. Consequently, because of its foundation of intimacy, immediacy, and the ordinary, television does not truly produce stars.[2]

Problematically, these ideas remain on a theoretical level and ignore the industrial mechanisms and historical catalysts that define how actors are utilized on both film and television, thereby denying the very context within which stardom is created. Rather than addressing film stars as theoretical products of spectatorial fantasy, I shall in this book instead follow the lead of star studies scholar Paul McDonald and treat stars not just as images but also as labor and capital operating within particular industries and historical contexts. The star's identity is considered primarily as an industrial factor circulated within a particular institutional framework and affecting the material conditions of the actor's career in film and on television.[3]

As a result of ahistorical theories such as Ellis's, the predominant tendency in star studies has been to denigrate the stature of stardom on television, to argue that television does not produce stars of the complexity, depth, and cultural value that film does, largely because of the medium's lesser cultural status and its essential familiarity and intimacy. Susan Murray, author of a foundational text on early broadcast stardom, rightly denounces these theories and their lack of analytical rigor: "[I]t would appear as though, while the cinema's star system was

4

delineated by a complicated aesthetic, industrial and economic history, the television star is simply a fall from grace." Such assumptions have traditionally forestalled deeper critical investigation into the generative mechanisms of television stardom and, by extension, the consequences of film star appearances on television.[4]

Scholars such as Murray, Denise Mann, Diane Negra, and Mary Desjardins have more recently supplied concrete historical explanations for the early development of broadcast stardom and its evident contrasts with classical film stardom. Murray argues that the seeming "ordinariness" of the 1950s television performer was not inherent to the medium but instead was part of a strategy constructed from the specific industrial, cultural, and programming catalysts that shaped the medium. The development of a commercial basis for television particularly required that a star be perceived as natural and authentic in order to cement trust with viewer, thereby guarding the credibility of any commercial pitches associated with the star or program.[5]

Similarly, and specifically in reference to film star appearances on television, Denise Mann assesses the tensions resulting from mixing the perceived glamour of Hollywood stars in variety and talk shows with the commercial and domestic complexion of early television—especially given the ambivalence of 1950s society to representations of material excess and the desire for sponsors to connect with middle-class viewers. Mann offers the example of Martha Raye, who left her film career to host a television variety program: *The Martha Raye Show* (NBC, 1955–56), which through parody of and outright separation from its filmdom guest stars definitively set its star apart from connotations of Hollywood and filmdom glamour in order to bolster Raye's integrity as a television performer and commercial pitchwoman. Thus, this account contends, early television favored the genuine "personality," as opposed to the extravagant "movie star," and negatively associated glamour with the film world.[6]

While this account is compelling, it is also narrowly prescriptive, and both Mary Desjardins and Diane Negra provide more varied portraits of film stars on 1950s television. Negra looks at Hedy Lamarr's television appearances and argues that her ethnicity, exotic persona, and declining celebrity made for an uneasy fit on the new medium. For instance, Lamarr's 1956 stint on *The Perry Como Show* mobilized her star image in conflicting ways, including both reverent nostalgia for her past Hollywood glamour and self-conscious mockery of her status as the "monstrous," aging female star. Mary Desjardins finds similarly heterogeneous star presentations on 1950s television, from the celebratory combination of glamour and authenticity wrapped around stars presented on *This is Your Life* to the clash between old and new conceptions of Hollywood stardom evident in the 1960 television special *Hedda Hopper's Hollywood.* The latter's schism in particular revealed a decline in the power of classical Hollywood's traditional signs of glamour—but also a certain ambivalence about what would come to replace them.[7]

Both Negra's and Desjardins' accounts indicate that Mann is correct in claiming that television often strategically manipulated connotations of authenticity relative to filmdom glamour. Yet their case studies also indicate that the glamorous and the ordinary were not always mutually exclusive, nor were they always clearly split between film and television stars (especially because these representations were in flux across the 1950s). Chapter 2 of this book confirms these conceptions in its analysis of talk show host Faye Emerson, commonly known in the early 1950s as the "glamour girl of the television screen." The careful enmeshing of Emerson's glamorous image with the generic codes of authenticity engendered by television talk show conventions resonates with these established accounts.

Nonetheless, one key condition has not been fully explored by previous studies: that the majority of film actors appearing on TV, such as Hedy Lamarr and Faye Emerson, were not elite stars; more frequently, they were figures from the margins of that world, whether due to secondary status or declining careers. Although this marginality might have made the construction of the everyday in their images less complicated, it also potentially reinforced the suggestion of the "fall from grace," the television personality as failed film star, and thus television as an inferior medium in comparison to film. Therefore, it was essential for early television, in its struggle to compete economically and culturally with its long-established rival, to find ways to boost the images of such minor stars and elude connotations of inferiority and failure. Stars themselves had similar goals, as the preservation of their entertainment careers depended on sustaining the audience's admiration for and fascination with their images. Thus, yet to be accounted for is how 1950s television and its crossover film stars could capitalize on their relationship without diminishing the industrial and cultural value of the products

that resulted from this synthesis.

Close analysis of programming and publicity reveals myriad strategies to negotiate these tensions. Foremost was the reliance on connotations of authenticity and the implication that television's ability to transmit unfettered reality into the home was superior to Hollywood's version of constructed glamour. By draping film stars with markers of authenticity and continually underscoring these as values superior to filmdom's artificiality, television underscored its unique ability to rediscover or uncover the genuine capabilities of the film world's indigenous talent. This strategy was overwhelmingly evident in publicity and programming, even beyond the variety and talk show appearances that Murray, Mann, Negra, and Desjardins primarily focus on, where it seems quite likely that a star appearing as his or her "real" self in a publicity context would raise issues of genuineness. For example, as chapter 5 illustrates, anthology fiction programs like *Playhouse 90* drew on notions of authenticity in casting and publicizing their film star guests. By presenting such actors as Mickey Rooney in roles that contrasted in key ways with their established film images and then publicizing those performances as evidence of both the true acting talents of the star and the true art of television drama, producers of these anthology programs marked their work as superior to other television genres and to Hollywood film. It must be noted that this technique purposefully separated the preexisting star persona from the actor and then characterized that persona as a contrived representation determined by Hollywood's economic demands.

Accordingly, chapter 1 proves that film stars were a significant presence on 1950s television, and subsequent chapters show that, as a result, the traditional mechanisms of the film star system could not function without being substantially altered for TV. Studios developed film stars during the classical era by identifying appropriate starring roles for actors and subsequently matching publicity about their personal lives to those roles in order to create unified star identities with a balanced mix of the extraordinary and the ordinary. For film stars moving to television in the 1950s, their star identity was already established, but the intimate and routine quality of early television, as well as its small visual dimensions, presentational genres, overt commercialism, and lesser cultural standing in relation to film, enforced a recrafting of that identity away from the extraordinary. The preformed star image, and even glamour itself, was thus reconstituted as a more ordinary and personal construct. This familiarization of stardom produced performers who were neither solely film stars nor only television personalities. They were intermediary figures of celebrity, a new kind of star for a new medium still in flux. As numerous examples in this book show, television borrowed from the star power of Hollywood quite readily, but the new medium neither merely transplanted it nor merely diminished it. Instead, television meshed this star power with the unique aura of liveness and intimacy that the medium was fostering as a strategy of distinction and took strategic advantage of these altered star images to lend prominence and prestige to the programs and their stars.

By presenting star images in this manner, television also helped to expose the very mechanisms behind the creation of star images across the 1950s. Aroused in significant measure because of appearances by film stars on television and the resulting questions of what this might mean to their star images, the popular press began to interrogate what stardom actually was, to what extent it was a contrived phenomenon, and whether television could construct it (or, of course, weaken it). Television programming and publicity then took advantage of these discussions to portray its featured film talent as set free from the restrictions of Hollywood's star-making machinery, thereby helping to break apart some of the carefully manufactured illusions that the classical star system had relied upon for decades.

Admittedly, such overt recognition of the artificialities of stardom was not necessarily new. Some of these changes were rooted in radio and in postwar trends toward realist representations. One could even look all the way back to silent films such as Colleen Moore's *Ella Cinders* (1926) or at contemporaneous films such as *Sunset Boulevard* (1950) to see the explicit deconstruction of stardom's facade on the theatrical screen. In fact, television emerged at a time when many were already questioning the authenticity of the images and identities produced by Hollywood. As Samantha Barbas discusses in *Movie Crazy*, a dissection of movie star fandom in classical Hollywood's heyday, fans had long searched for markers of authenticity associated with their favorite film stars, yearning for the personal truth behind the distanced screen images yet often skeptical of the accounts provided by studio publicity. Barbas argues that public discussion of this mentality of fandom culminated in the late 1940s in outward criticism of gullible, "drooling" fans who accepted "the whole Hollywood myth" and confused fantasy and reality. Television was in a prime position to insert itself into this debate by capitalizing upon its unique aesthetic

8

and institutional codes of informality and intimacy (as well as the very stars that the Hollywood dream factory had created) to suggest that on this new medium, fans and critics alike could finally find the meaningful truth about screen idols.[8]

Additionally, numerous scholars have established that reflexive acknowledgment of the insincerity of star publicity was a common method for engendering audience trust in a star's genuineness during the studio system era. As Joshua Gamson writes, the skepticism about "the connection between celebrity and authenticity was . . . largely muted . . . through studio control," especially via publicity features that professed to reveal the real person behind the contrived star image. However, rather than its past incarnation as a strategy used to mute skepticism about film's manipulation of star image, this professed authenticity was now being taken up by television to *create* skepticism about film's manipulation of star images in order to bolster the new medium's credibility. The skeletons of the constructed star image had never been laid so bare as they now were in living rooms across the country.[9]

Indeed, the new medium continuously streamed a parade of multiplied film star images in diverse contexts, from lowly sitcoms to exalted spectaculars, from representational anthology dramas to presentational quiz shows, and from contemporaneous personifications to pre-1948 feature film portrayals. And no longer was the studio system apparatus in place to control and mold all of these star images into a seamless portrait. Now a plethora of decentralized, often shifting, and sometimes even conflicting sites of authority competed to depict and define stars: networks, sponsors, talent agents, gossip columnists, television critics, and the stars themselves. In this respect, even television's claims to authenticity and the ordinary could increasingly be recognized as constructed ideals across all of these competing discourses. Thus, this period was not solely where the authentic was weighed against the glamorous but one where the construction of those very standards, the fusion of extraordinary and ordinary that had created the film star image, was exposed, questioned, and challenged through television and its corresponding discourses.

Hence, the title of this book and its reference to Norma Desmond's famous quote from *Sunset Boulevard*—"I am big. It's the pictures that got small"—is fitting in multiple ways. Just as *Sunset Boulevard* indicts the artificiality and decadence of classical filmdom glamour through the character of Norma Desmond, 1950s television presented itself as a valuable alternative to its competitor's contrivances through its presentation of film stars as their genuine, unaltered selves. Of course, Norma constructs a delusional belief that it is contemporary film, not her own aura, that has declined in stature. Similarly, 1950s television's use of the authentic film actor to combat connotations of inferior stature was no less a construction than the most glittering of Hollywood's manufactured film stars. Further, the shifting industrial situation implied by Norma Desmond's comment and depicted by *Sunset Boulevard* was central in making the film-to-television crossover phenomenon possible. Without the decline of the classical Hollywood studio system, film stars would not have had so pervasive and varied an influence on early television. Thus, the title reflects this book's primary goals: (1) to outline the transformative economic and institutional conditions in both the film and television industries that influenced how film stars would be used as labor and capital on 1950s television, and (2) to assess the ways in which star images were both products and shapers of early television's developing representational and programming standards.

To maximize the study's analytical depth, I established specific parameters. First, the book is limited to prime-time television, as this arena was by far the most substantial for participation by Hollywood actors. The primary years of focus are from 1948 to 1961. Television had existed prior to 1948, but that year brought the true dawn of commercial TV: prime-time programming schedules were nearly full, a significant number of stations were in operation across the nation, sets were selling in sizable numbers, and the limited network structure that came to rule the industry took root. By 1961, the medium had established the primary production trends and general structure that would sustain it throughout the network era of the 1960s and 1970s.

In terms of performers, the book focuses primarily on what I have termed "established film actors"; that is, those actors who had already cultivated a career in Hollywood film prior to the commercial establishment of network television. This designation rules out those who attained Hollywood success simultaneous to or after their television appearances, thus omitting such actors as James Dean, Audrey Hepburn, and Paul Newman. This latter area is undoubtedly worthy of study, and I do make occasional reference to such examples, but its specificities put it primarily outside of the scope of this book. Instead, the "established film actor" delineation provides a clear window on the intermixture of the two separate industries: because the actors made a choice to move into a new medium from a set presence in film, program producers had each actor's prior film career and persona to consider when selecting and presenting talent. And, of course, audiences had had some measure of exposure to these actors during their film careers and thus possessed preceding knowledge of their star images. The phrase should also make clear that the book is not focused exclusively on "movie stars": I account for a range of experiences by film performers, from box office kings to minor character actors. The abundance of accessible historical material on top-level stars did lead me to focus most of the book's in-depth case studies on actors who at some point in their careers were legitimate A-listers. Of course, the status of these stars made the exploration of their crossover decisions more richly complex, as well.[10]

Chapter 1 surveys the first half of the 1950s decade and establishes why it became relatively common for film star talent to appear on television by the middle of the decade. The chapter begins by outlining the conditions of star employment within the classical studio system and the changes that resulted once that system began to crumble. It then turns to the principal reasons why film actors were initially hesitant to appear on television and subsequently illustrates why those obstacles were less constraining as the decade continued, prompting a significant influx of credible Hollywood talent into a variety of core television genres. A primary purpose of this chapter is to illustrate how television activities of film stars reflected both the positive and the negative effects of the burgeoning labor freedom from the studio system. This theme is reflected in the chapter's closing case study of Four Star Productions, which was founded in 1952 by Dick Powell and co-owned by three film actors, Powell, David Niven, and Charles Boyer. These actors had each bristled under or completely avoided studio control over their careers in the 1940s; through the new opportunities for independent production, however, they became become media moguls in television. As such, the Four Star actor-owners used the new medium to bring a wider industrial and representational range of circumstances to the traditional star system.

Subsequent chapters focus on genre-specific conditions for crossover stars. All of the featured film actors had forged their public identities through feature-length, fictional theatrical films and attendant publicity. Now they had to transfer those identities onto the small screen via a vast range of programming types and through a varied set of performance contexts, and genre would be a major factor in determining the paths that established film actors would follow. The anthology drama proved to be the ideal format for welcoming A-list stars and the so-called spectacular was essentially created to showcase them, while continuing-character dramas and sitcoms gave Hollywood character actors the opportunity to become featured players. Further, variety shows allowed these actors to reveal their "real" selves to television viewers and potential filmgoers, and the quiz and panel show transformed many from accomplished actors into professional wags. These chapters cover a broad range of performers and programs, from lesser-known to more eminent actors and from the nadir of the low-budget syndicated film series to the heights of the lavish spectacular. The approximate chronology of the case studies also helps to highlight progressive changes in how film stars were presented, as well as concurrent industrial changes in both the television industry and Hollywood film across the 1950s—all of which affected the decisions and strategies of actors, networks, and producers.

Chapter 2 looks at performances within a set of definitive early television genres. Variety, talk, and quiz shows were dominated by the "television personality," an entity publicized as distinct from the contrived "film star." Even so, many of these personalities came from the world of film, and an analysis of the negotiation of their images across these moves into presentational television genres affords a glimpse into the performative principles of both media in this transitional era. This negotiation is especially illustrated by a case study of Faye Emerson. As the popular host of a string of self-titled interview programs in the early 1950s, Faye Emerson was touted by author Cleveland Amory as "the first television star created by television." This television stardom followed a period of failure in the film industry for Emerson; a comparison of these two phases of her entertainment career allows for both an assessment of the circumstances leading minor film actors to television in its early days and an interrogation of the concept of broadcast stardom in indigenous genres like the talk show. This section also emphasizes a cardinal tenet: although film stars principally avoided television in this early period, those actors who did cross over had to fit within the new medium's exhibition standards. These standards, which put particular demands on a star image, actually facilitated Emerson's television stardom; they allowed her to find success playing a version of "herself," rather than continuing to fail at establishing a character-based persona in Hollywood film.[11]

Chapter 3 examines another presentational role, though one tied to a very different type of programming. Hosts of anthology drama programs were also presented as "themselves," but these identities had to be matched to the elevated, cultured standing of the well-respected anthology genre and the particular nature of the stories being told. These factors favored participation by film stars, as an elevated status relative to ordinary television fare was often inherent to their images. Nonetheless, the intricate meshing of persona and program that was required to naturalize an anthology hosting role could be tangled by a complexity of factors: the diminished status of a cast-off film star, gendered social formations that mitigated against placing women in authoritative roles, and the necessity of weaving commercial pitches into this supposedly artistically pure format and around the prestige of film stars. This chapter's case study—Adolphe Menjou—throws these complexities into relief. After the dramatic decline of his film career, Menjou found himself hosting a syndicated anthology program, *Favorite Story*, in the early 1950s. Syndication programming carried a negative, secondary image in comparison to network programming, which meant that an actor such as Menjou was an ideal host: he was not successful enough to be "above" syndication, but his prior film stardom still lent needed credibility and stature to the show. In detailing how *Favorite Story* successfully resurrected elements of Menjou's refined film persona and married them to the anthology-host role, this chapter shows how even a marginalized film star's personality could be central in shaping television programming.

This theme also resonates in chapter 4, which looks at the role of established film actors in the continuing-character series, particularly the situation comedy. Because of the career commitment dictated by the ongoing series format, no true film star would deign to affiliate with these shows, leaving them as a space largely for character actors and faded stars to occupy. But star image was still central here, as these performers parlayed the primary elements of their film personae into television characters, basically molding versions of their own identities to series standards. This arena, more than any other, was where Hollywood's supporting actresses thrived; Eve Arden, Ann Sothern, and their like created popular characterizations that drew from their filmic pasts to varying degrees. In fact, this chapter argues that only *with* such filmic pasts could these actresses have found the success that they did on early television. This claim buttresses the chapter's case study of Ida Lupino, who portrayed a movie star married to a fellow star (played by her real-life husband Howard Duff) in a 1957–58 sitcom called *Mr. Adams and Eve.* Lupino's movie star–character actually manifested many of the complexities embedded in the actress-director's own star image, especially in terms of her potentially disruptive status within the male-dominated entertainment industry. This section argues that both Lupino's constructed identity and the high volume of film star appearances on television to this point helped to spawn this uniquely self-conscious representation. Therefore, chapter 4 highlights the extent to which film stars on television had affected the medium and the nature of stardom by the latter half of the 1950s.

The final chapter focuses on two genres in which top-tier movie stars did perform regularly: anthology shows and spectaculars. Following a period of development, these genres provided ample attractions for stars: periodic appearances with no long-term commitments, a variety of roles, a big paycheck, and prestigious frameworks that appeared commensurate with a star's eminent status. As a result, Hollywood film stars frequented anthologies and had considerable impact on the complexion of the genre. Especially representative of this impact was *Playhouse 90.* This show's producers relied heavily on what was termed "stunt casting"; that is, featuring the show's filmdom guest stars in unconventional roles. They then publicized this strategy as artistically superior to the typecasting allegedly prevalent in Hollywood, thereby elevating the creative status of the program in relation to film. The subsequent demise of *Playhouse 90* in 1961 echoed the advancing decline of the anthology drama, which eliminated a key site for film star participation on television, and the chapter concludes with a consideration of the principal reasons behind the genre's disappearance. This denouement leads into the conclusion, which assesses why the relatively common movement of established film actors to television came to a close by the early 1960s and which summarizes the industrial and cultural influence that this crossover phenomenon had on film, television, and stardom alike.

Through detailing each actor's circumstances and experience and each program's objectives and characteristics, this book illustrates how the use of established film actors on 1950s television both fit within and helped to shape the development of television in its formative decade.

Each chapter closely analyzes the activities of film stars at the discrete historical moment when television developed into a nationally popular mass medium, borrowing programming formats, corporate methods, and talent from film while simultaneously forging a unique institutional and cultural identity. This material will thereby expand our understanding of how the conditions of entertainment stardom shifted across the waning days of the classical studio system and the budding years of early television, as well as augment our knowledge of how television grew as an entertainment industry and an aesthetic medium. While television developed from numerous economic, technological, and cultural conditions, the active involvement of movie stars and their impact on the industrial and aesthetic framework of the medium is unheralded in television history. As television scholar William Boddy argues, "The often-proclaimed importance of television in our daily lives and political culture makes imperative a fuller understanding of how the program forms and social institutions of American television came about." Because film performers were so crucial to the early development of television, this missing piece of broadcast history must be put back into place.[12]

CHAPTER I
THE PRODUCTION
OF NEW CAREERS
HOLLYWOOD FILM
ACTORS MOVE TO
TELEVISION

1946 was Hollywood's most lucrative year. Never before had Americans gone to the movies in such numbers, with some ninety million people settling into theater seats every single week. Hollywood kept these theaters full by releasing nearly four hundred films across the year, and the studio system worked at maximum efficiency to maintain this volume. Studio complexes were brimming with busy soundstages and acres of active backlots, while hundreds of contract employees, from screenwriters to painters, were at their stations, ready to mobilize at a moment's notice.

Sprinkled across these soundstages, backlots, and offices were movie stars at work: acting in films, posing for publicity shots, and taking orders from studio executives about future professional and personal endeavors. More than seven hundred actors were locked into studio contracts in 1946, and those who qualified as stars were the most valuable assets the studios had. It was mainly the stars who lured those ninety million people out to theaters on a weekly basis. Their bankable names helped to set rental and ticket prices for films, their popularity sold fan magazines and fashions, and their images supplied the raw material with which marketing campaigns and feature film scenarios could be rapidly—and repeatedly—formulated.

At the time, it was likely difficult to envision anything significantly altering this incredibly efficient operation, which generated nearly $120 million in profits in 1946. The Justice Department had filed suit against the studios in 1938, accusing the industry of violating antitrust laws with their distribution and exhibition practices, but minor concessions, legal stalling tactics, and World War II had kept this potential disruption at bay. Television might also have given the film industry pause, but a mere six television stations were in operation in 1946, and only eight thousand living rooms (that is, .02 percent of total households), contained television sets. Even 20th Century–Fox studio chief Darryl F. Zanuck was not concerned about broadcasting's encroachment, at least not publicly. He reportedly said in 1946: "Television won't be able to hold on to any market it captures after the first six months. People will soon get tired of staring at a plywood box every night."

A decade later, Zanuck had undoubtedly revised his viewpoint. By 1956, television had spread to 72 percent of all households, and audiences stared at their plywood boxes for an average of about five hours each day. Meanwhile, only forty-six million Americans attended movies on a weekly basis, annual studio profits plunged to $30 million, and the Justice Department's mandated dismantling of the studio system was complete. As a result, soundstages were increasingly empty, backlots were clearing out, and contract employees were being cut loose. Not even stars were spared. Fewer than 250 actors were under contract in 1956, while the rest were left to fend for themselves. In some ways, this freedom was preferable to the restrictions of the previous era; stars now had more power to shape their own careers and images. This power was undercut, however, by the increasing volatility of the new media landscape and the unpredictable consequences of myriad decisions, foremost among which: to do or not to do TV?[1]

To answer this question, actors had to weigh a variety of factors, from the roles that television offered, to the financial benefits available, to a small-screen appearance's possible impact on a star image. Above all, stars had to consider how a crossover to television would affect the future viability of their acting careers. As with all things related to stardom, there was no single formula for success; every star confronted with this decision faced a unique set of questions. In turn, when considering how to incorporate these established stars into their operations, early broadcasters had to determine the functions that movie stars could fill, the economic value that they could bring to programming and advertising, and the ways in which star images could enhance the medium's stature—all at a time when television's economic and cultural status was still in flux. While there were more questions than answers for both film stars and the television industry in this period, when the dust kicked up by television's arrival finally started to settle by the mid-1950s, established film actors stood among the most important catalysts to have shaped the medium to that point and television had become a viable career option for countless film actors.

STAR EMPLOYMENT DURING THE STUDIO SYSTEM ERA

The linchpin of studio dominance within the classical-era film industry was oligopolistic vertical integration that limited competition. The five major studios (MGM, Warner Bros., Fox, Paramount, and RKO) during much of the 1930s and 1940s tightly controlled the most lucrative components of production, distribution, and exhibition, and along with the three minor studios (Columbia, Universal, and United Artists), they participated in collusive business practices that ensured their ongoing collective power over both independent producers and their own contracted talent. Given their centrality to all of these facets of industry operation, film stars had the potential to command the most influence, but even they were rarely able to overcome studio supremacy.

The most visible realm of value for stars was in exhibition, where star names were used to draw patrons to studio-owned first-run theaters in the early weeks of a film's release, during which time the highest ticket prices were charged and the most money ended up in studio coffers. This box office popularity similarly affected distribution, where the film rental prices charged to exhibitors could be based upon a featured star's track record and movie marketing campaigns were orchestrated around the promotion of star identities. This relative predictability of profit also allowed for the rationalization of production around stars. Investment in a big-budget picture was guaranteed if a star with proven marquee value was attached, while lesser featured players provided reliable support to stars and could carry B movies and so-called programmers (films that could fill either the top or bottom of the bill of a double feature depending on the theater and the film with which it was paired). Alongside genre components and continuity principles, stars enabled efficiencies in production that allowed the studios to maintain a full production schedule and thereby keep their first-run screens occupied year-round. A certain type of star translated into a certain type of film, allowing for economical reuse of story ideas, resources like sets and costumes, and even other personnel such as cinematographers and character actors. These circumstances also enabled stars to act as identifiable brands for a studio; the exoticism of Greta Garbo marked MGM as distinctly as the grittiness of James Cagney defined Warner Bros.

Thus, film stars afforded the studios myriad ways of reducing financial risk, enhancing profits, and regularizing business practices at all three levels of industry operation. To reward them for these valuable services, the studios supplied top-rank stars with a great deal of wealth and prestige based on their box office popularity. Even midlevel players enjoyed a certain degree of financial and job security because of the need to cast so many parts in so many films. While one might assume that the studios' dependence would also translate into creative autonomy, such was not the case. Actors essentially had to grant the studios total control over their images and careers in exchange for economic prosperity, and it is in these areas that stars lost the true battle for industry power.

First, the studios tried to develop singular identities for each of their prominent actors in order to maximize the value of a star at all levels, whereby an audience was drawn to the theater by a star image, a promotional campaign would be oriented around a star image, and studio personnel could easily produce narratives structured around that image. As Thomas Harris defined it in his 1957 study of star promotion: "The star system is based on the premise that a star is accepted by the public in terms of a certain set of personality traits which permeate all of his or her film roles. The successful stars have been those whose appeal can be catalogued into a series of such traits, associations and mannerisms." A studio could work through many strategies for constructing a workable persona for a star, from drawing on performers known from other media (such as theater), to trying out unknowns in a variety of film roles until finding one that resonated with studio practice and with audiences. Once successfully devised, a star's persona would be replicated in subsequent films, and the studio's publicity machinery would shift into high gear, constructing connections between a star's screen image and his or her apparent personal life. Intent on convincing audiences that what they were seeing onscreen in a performer was not far removed from what they would see offscreen, the studios found publicity a reliable way to engender continuing fascination with screen star images.[2]

This is not to say that a star would appear only as one simplistic character type in every single film and publicity text. Granted, to maximize their investment in a star, the studios put actors to work in as many films as they prudently could. Yet overexposure could weaken audience interest in a star. Thus, off-casting—that is, unconventional casting—lent variation and allowed a star to display performative range. Further, complicating a star image through contradictory roles or countering nuggets of publicity could encourage fans to grasp for even more information and images in their yearning to understand the real person beneath the star image, thereby perpetuating box office and fan magazine sales. But in the long run, for a performer to become a true star and pay off financially for a studio, a singular persona had to be identified and exploited. If the studio was unable to develop an efficiently repeatable and popular star image for an actor, that actor would never become a star.[3]

Also, if actors refused to cooperate in the studio's efforts to shape their image, they would never become stars, and therein lay the studios' most substantial power: a combination of collusion and contracts. To ensure that the star system worked in their favor, studios tied most of their performers to term contracts. The most common was the seven-year option contract, which operated on biannual increments. After a six-month period, if the studio deemed the actor's career to be moving forward acceptably, the contract would be renewed for another six-month period at a salary bump. If the studio did not see future potential, the actor would be cut. The option was entirely in the hands of the studio; stars could not opt out of any component of the deal without renegotiating with the studio. These contracts also granted the studios nearly total control over a star's image and services, from what roles they performed in to what clothes they wore to whom they could be seen in public with. The penalties for not cooperating could be severe. Studios had the power to punish actors with inferior assignments, suspend them without pay, or drop their contracts outright. Because of oligopolistic cooperation among the studios, banished performers could then find employment at any of the other studios difficult to come by—especially given the legion of unemployed actors just begging to sign an option contract and replace them. Thus dissension among the ranks from the biggest star to the most minor extra was relatively limited.

Nonetheless, some stars did win their battles against restrictive studio rules. The Supreme Court decided in favor of Olivia de Havilland in a landmark suit against Warner Bros., which ceased the practice of adding suspension time onto a seven-year contract. James Cagney also legally broke from Warner Bros. and formed a series of independent production companies. A measurable number of actors operated on a freelance status during the studio system by signing only limited-film or nonexclusive contracts. Stars like Fredric March, Cary Grant, Irene Dunne, and Barbara Stanwyck utilized a combination of star status and shrewd business tactics to make this possible. Even so, it remained essential for the studios to contain such power and autonomy in order to ensure their ability to govern film industry operations. They were largely successful in doing so with the majority of performers in Hollywood.

STARS ON THE LOOSE

Such studio control over stars diminished across the 1940s and 1950s courtesy of two primary catalysts: the legal dismantling of the studio system apparatus and declines in theater attendance. The former resulted from the Paramount Case decision of 1948, which spawned consent decrees between the studios and the government that ended the classical studio system's antitrust business practices. In addition to banning practices like block booking (in which inferior films were packaged along with crowd-pleasers to ensure that nonaffiliated theaters would rent them all), the Paramount decision forced the major studios to cease their ownership of theaters. These provisions dealt a blow to the industry, as exhibition control had enabled the studios to operate at a high level of production and a low level of risk for many years. With the safety net of theatrical supremacy removed, the studios could no longer guarantee a lucrative market for their voluminous roster of films. A simultaneous hit to the health of the studio system was the decline in attendance. In the wake of suburbanization, the baby boom, and the arrival of television, families increasingly stayed home or spent their money on leisure pursuits other than moviegoing. The studios could no longer rely on a consistent mass audience coming out to theaters.[4]

Therefore, the studios were forced to adapt their production and distribution tactics to this new economic and social landscape. One solution was to release fewer films; the elimination of guaranteed theatrical outlets, compounded by fewer people filling theater seats, made the production of a high volume of films inefficient. Accordingly, compared to a wartime high of 379 films in 1942, the eight primary studios released only 225 features in 1954, and the seven film companies remaining after RKO's cessation distributed a mere 167 features in 1961. Having lost their past exhibition clout, the studios leaned more heavily on their competitive advantages in distribution. The studios were still the only entities who controlled the national pipelines necessary to get a film slotted into mainstream theaters across the country. Because of the substantial leverage that position afforded them, the studios were not so damaged by the Paramount decision as they could have been had the government separated them from their distribution assets.

Thus, the studios progressively turned away from their classical-era tactics of producing a large slate of films on their own lots. Instead, they focused primarily on the financing and distribution of a more limited number of films initiated by others. In this new mode of production, later termed "the package-unit system" by industry historian Janet Staiger, an independent producer, director, talent agent, or star offered to the studio a pre-production package (which might consist of a script and committed principal talent), for financing in exchange for distribution. Rather than the previous system of costs being amortized across a studio's yearly output, financing was now developed on a film-by-film basis. Coupled with the abolishment of practices like block booking, the result was that much more attention had to be given to each individual film, both in terms of formulating packages and marketing films to exhibitors and audiences.[5]

A final move for the studios was to jettison contracted talent. The decline in production and the rise in packaging dictated cuts in overhead commitments and eliminated the need to keep crew and talent under extensive long-term contracts. The decline substantially affected star employment; two-thirds of all actors were dropped from their contracts by the mid-1950s. Even stars still aligned with particular studios were usually put on short, limited-film deals with looser, nonexclusive contractual arrangements. Once set free from exclusive option contracts, actors became free agents, able to sell their services to individual studios and packagers on the open market or to develop their own independent film projects (though often with the assistance of a talent agency). Free agency heralded a new era of star power in Hollywood. Stars could become entrepreneurs rather than mere employees, and they could now compete with the studios, rather than be beholden to them.[6]

The stars' new power, however, was simultaneously tempered by the declines in overall film production and the studios' precarious financial stability. While the package-unit system extended stars the advantage of freely choosing employment, the more limited number of productions led to a shortage of available roles, and jobs became more difficult to find—especially for the lesser-caliber stars who were more likely to be dropped from their studio contracts than were A-listers. Thus the lack of a contractual safety net could be more of a hindrance than a help. Such was the impression given by actress Ann Blyth, when asked by *Screenland* magazine in 1948 if young actors should head for Hollywood: "It has always been a bad idea but it's even worse now with the studios cutting down in production and good actors being out of work." Further, stars could now willfully control their own images, but many found it yet another challenge. Though the studio system publicity machine had been restrictive, it was also expert at successfully shaping star images to be fed to the hungry maw of the publicity press. With this authority increasingly decentralized, stars themselves now had a bigger part of the privilege but also the pressure to present themselves such that suburbanites would happily leave their TV sets and baby cribs behind just to see them at the movies.[7]

Thus, along with new freedoms for film actors in the 1950s came a daunting set of uncertainties. The more diffuse and decentralized operation that progressively supplanted the studio system made it such that stars' survival would be based more heavily on their own decisions and actions than those of an external controlling force. At the same time the potential range of conflicting influences on a star's career, from agents to managers to publicists, expanded greatly.

Of course, the industry did not change overnight nor did it change uniformly, especially for performers. Some A-list actors thrived under the new labor conditions. James Stewart, for instance, reached new heights of popularity and wealth in the 1950s, thanks largely to the shrewd exploitation of his freedom from the studio system. After his wartime service, Stewart declined to renew his expired contract with MGM and took full advantage of his new leverage in selecting film roles and maximizing his earning potential. He and Lew Wasserman, the most powerful executive at the MCA talent agency, negotiated an uncommon deal with Universal for director Anthony Mann's *Winchester '73* (1950), wherein Stewart would forgo his standard $200,000 salary in exchange for profit participation in the film. The decision reportedly netted him as much as $600,000 in the end. This film and subsequent features by directors Mann and Alfred Hitchcock also allowed Stewart to complicate his screen persona in ways MGM had never granted, and the result was the golden era of Stewart's career. He appeared in twenty-three films for six different studios in the 1950s and was nominated for Oscars twice. At the midpoint of the decade, he was the top money-earner in Hollywood.

Not all stars found studio freedom so beneficial, as Mickey Rooney's experience would indicate. By the late forties, Rooney had grown out of his Andy Hardy character, and he perceived that his home studio, MGM, was not sufficiently committed to extending his career. Thus, he negotiated freedom from his $5,000-a-week contract with the studio in 1948 and launched his own production company, Mickey Rooney Enterprises. This company, however, failed to produce anything of note, and most of the feature films Rooney subsequently appeared in were low-budget failures. He also saw his name featured in countless gossip articles in the 1950s, most of which volunteered disparaging accounts of his marital failures and mounting debts. Thus, Rooney came to lament not only the loss of income and career stability that his MGM contract had supplied, but also the absence of its publicity machine. As he regretfully told *Cosmopolitan* in 1966, "My press clippings were never better than when MGM was keeping the reporters happy."[8]

One star who recognized some of the advantages of staying on with a major studio, and who also maintained a high-enough status for that studio to want to keep him onboard even as it cut most others loose, was Robert Taylor. The famed "Man with the Perfect Profile" remained a principal contract player at MGM from 1934 to 1958, one of the lengthiest contracted tenures in Hollywood history. Taylor's heyday was largely behind him by the 1950s, but his face had matured into a elegantly weathered look that fit well into the big-budget period epics that MGM was producing in the fifties. He thus supplied a reasonable rate of return on his high studio salary.

Other aging stars were not so prosperous. Errol Flynn's hard-driving lifestyle and scandalous publicity caught up to him by the late 1940s, as his heroic swashbuckler persona faded along with his regally handsome features. Warner Bros. released him in 1951. He subsequently moved overseas, both for adventure and economics, and wallowed in a number of undistinguished features, which continued upon his return to the States in 1956. Mary Astor found her career similarly stagnating; in her autobiography, she described this period of her career as between stages 4 and 5 in the classic joke about the development of a star's career: "1. Who's Mary Astor? 2. Get me Mary Astor. 3. Get me a Mary Astor type. 4. Get me a young Mary Astor. 5. Who's Mary Astor?" She also lamented the motherly roles she was largely relegated to, especially because there was not a sufficient number of them available to keep her satisfactorily active. She therefore turned down a contract renewal offer from MGM in 1949 and, owing primarily to subsequent personal problems, she temporarily disappeared from the screen.[9]

While industry upheaval played some role in these actors' struggles, one can presume that Flynn and Astor would have run into career declines whether the studio system had crumbled or not. But these new industrial circumstances did have very direct effects, both positive and negative, on the course of many careers. Prolific character actors saw their workload decline precipitously. For example, Thomas Mitchell had averaged three films per year since the mid-1930s and appeared in five in 1944 alone. Yet from 1948, when he exited MGM, until 1951, he made only four features in total. Further, new stars found themselves with more options than aspirants of the past had enjoyed. Celeste Holm, who signed with Fox in 1946 on the basis of theatrical success, struck Hollywood gold right away, winning a Best Supporting Actress Oscar for *Gentleman's Agreement* (1947), followed by nominations in the same category for *Come to the Stable* (1949) and *All About Eve* (1950). Despite such acclaim, Holm felt limited by the roles Fox was supplying and came to realize that she preferred live stage work. Thus, she proposed a contract buyout, and Fox studio chief Darryl F. Zanuck relented. Here was a definitive sign of a new era; only a decade earlier Zanuck probably would not have so readily allowed such a proven, marketable star to leave.

Of course, as noted earlier, Zanuck apparently did not foresee what a competitive force television would become only a decade later. Indeed, television quickly became key to the evolution of the entertainment industry, and all of the above-named actors and their colleagues would have to determine for themselves how to adapt to the new conditions. For some, TV would end up as merely a sidelight in their careers, little more than a convenient tool for publicizing their feature film work. For others, TV would represent a lifeline, an indispensable outlet for the prolongation of a lucrative performing career. Along the way, questions about how television's upstart status and overtly commercial nature would affect a star's established image had to be addressed. Also, options regarding job security, creative control, and competitive potential had to be weighed. Could a highly successful star like Jimmy Stewart gain anything of value from television? Would MGM even allow Robert Taylor to appear on the new medium, and would he want to if they did? Would a television appearance be more likely to help or to hurt a struggling star like Mickey Rooney, who was searching desperately for financial stability and acting credibility?

In turn, from the perspective of television's producers, guesswork abounded in regard to performers. Early on, no one was certain what the medium would become or what kind of talent could best be utilized; until techniques for developing indigenous stars could be identified and systematically implemented, it was natural for television to poach talent developed in other media. Radio placed at television's disposal a logical and affiliated talent base, whereas the theatrical stage offered proximate performers with the necessary skills to adapt to early TV's live, largely New York–based productions. But especially in the medium's early years of flux, when the future and quality of television was still in question and when Zanuck's prediction of audience indifference to the small screen still had some validity, the need to carve out a unique space within popular entertainment was paramount. The network executives who were quickly taking control of the medium had to give audiences, sponsors, and ad agencies a reason to take notice. Would a faltering Errol Flynn or an aging Mary Astor provide such a reason? Would the chance to see a character actor like Thomas Mitchell or an Oscar-winning supporting actress like Celeste Holm in the living room be worth the price of a TV set or a program sponsorship? Such figures at least furnished a proven visual allure that would set television apart from radio, and the living room intimacy of television could supply a privileged view of these stars that neither theater nor films could match. Therefore, from television's earliest years, the potential value of film stars on television was recognized by many in the new industry. But first they would have to convince them to appear.

FILM ACTOR AVOIDANCE OF THE "STEP DOWN"

While television was new at this time, broadcasting was not, and many film stars had been actively involved with radio for more than a decade. In *Hollywood and Broadcasting: From Radio to Cable*, media historian Michele Hilmes questions the long-accepted historical account that the major Hollywood studios instituted a ban on film star appearances on radio in 1932 and proves that this ban was never fully implemented. A ban was publicly announced, but it was actually a duplicitous ploy launched by the studios to court favor with two groups in direct competition with radio—movie theater owners and the newspaper industry—without having to follow through on the ban in actuality. In fact, film stars flooded to radio across the 1930s in everything from variety shows to anthology dramas, and they were encouraged to do so by the studios, who appreciated the publicity value of these appearances and the economic benefits of fostering a relationship with radio. Most of these stars were under contract to studios and were thus following studio orders, while free agents like Loretta Young and Ann Sothern made their own choices to perform on radio shows in the late 1940s.[10]

There was a much greater reluctance on the part of stars and studios to develop a similarly coextensive relationship with early television, however, and a very real ban was both instituted by the major studios and internalized by many stars early in TV's life. Except for limited appearances on interview shows and during news hours, certain established film stars completely avoided television in its first commercial decade. Marlene Dietrich, Clark Gable, Rita Hayworth, Cary Grant, Olivia de Havilland, Vivien Leigh, Gregory Peck, Tyrone Power, Katharine Hepburn, and Spencer Tracy simply would not do television. The list of stars willing to make at least a few guest appearances is longer: Marilyn Monroe, Ann Miller, Ava Gardner, Glenn Ford, Kirk Douglas, Laurence Olivier, Gary Cooper, Lana Turner, Susan Hayward, Randolph Scott, Ingrid Bergman, Cyd Charisse, William Holden, Robert Mitchum, and Gene Tierney. But most of these appearances were cursory variety show turns for publicity purposes. Even certain film stars who in later decades would be associated with television, such as Rock Hudson and Doris Day, made only brief publicity stops in the 1950s.

The reasons why most of the biggest stars largely avoided TV during its early years were myriad. For the most important screen performers in 1950s Hollywood, television was considered well beneath the stature of a true star. Radio had reached a certain maturity by the time most film stars began appearing on it in the mid-1930s. TV's incubating identity, on the other hand, as a chaotic, low-culture operation was surely not attractive to high-level Hollywood talent. Television's reach was also quite limited in its early years; in 1951, only a quarter of America's households even owned a TV set. As a result, early programs had to subsist on shoestring budgets until the medium took hold across the nation, which meant that money was not going to be an incentive for a star to appear. Partly for these reasons, while Dean Martin and Jerry Lewis initially parlayed their 1940s nightclub fame into both a Paramount film contract and hosting duties on *The Colgate Comedy Hour* (NBC, 1950–55), when the time commitment required for the variety series forced them to specialize in only one medium, they chose film over television's requirement of more work for less pay.

Stars and their publicists also eyed the commercial economic base of television with heavy suspicion—a prejudice that carried over from the radio era, as explained by Susan Murray:

> The discourse surrounding commercialism and film stars versus radio stars reasserted a hierarchical relationship between these forms of stardom. It asserted the preeminence of film in the production of "high-quality" stardom and placed broadcast stardom in a secondary position. This not only affected the broadcast industry's ability to attract Hollywood talent to the medium but also set up the assumption (still at work in star theory today) that television stars were not as culturally worthy or potent as their filmic counterparts.

How exactly commercialism on radio compared with commercialism on television in terms of a rationale for avoiding participation calls for more extensive investigation than the scope of this book allows. But stars certainly painted TV's version of commercialism as a corrupter of the dramatic arts and thus as perhaps the most salient reason to avoid the medium. In that vein, Dana Andrews related the following to columnist Hal Humphrey:

> TV is controlled by bookkeepers who don't care about the quality of their shows as long as they reach the people and sell merchandise. . . . I particularly dislike the practice of having the actors do the commercials. It is a prostitution of their art, and they must lose the respect of the audience. If an actor is going to pitch commercials, he may as well be working in a store.

Ronald Colman told the press that he would never again agree to a regular series after appearing in CBS's *The Halls of Ivy* during the 1954–55 season because he was exasperated with sponsor and ad agency interference. In contemplating this rhetoric, one wonders if Colman and Andrews were ever frustrated with studio and producer interference during their film careers. After all, the economic imperatives of mainstream Hollywood filmmaking could produce pressures similar to those of television commercialism. The creative process in the film industry could be burdened by economic pressures just as easily, if not so overtly, as in television. But Hollywood worked hard to elevate its cultural status above television by branding its competitor as a medium for crass commercialism, and so successful was the branding that television had to battle to draw film talent to the small screen.[11]

A related antipathy against television was the fear that a small-screen appearance signaled the death of a star's film career. After all, who would sacrifice "high-quality" Hollywood success for a dalliance elsewhere? Such was exactly the impression left by *Daily Variety*'s review of a Henry Fonda anthology hosting job: "In his day on the screen he was big stuff but of recent years his artistry has been restricted to the theatre. It must then follow that he's just another erstwhile lost in the cinema shuffle." Robert Young echoed this notion in commenting, "When we had the chance to take [*Father Knows Best* from radio] to TV, I thought it was a step down, a sign that you couldn't work anywhere else." And Humphrey Bogart reportedly declared in 1954, "I won't go into TV until I find myself slipping." Bogart actually did appear on *The Jack Benny Show* (CBS, 1950–64) in that year, but he did so primarily to plug his most recent film, *Beat the Devil*, a palpable signal to his fans that his film career was not over. In the following year, Bogart acted in his first—and only—television program, a live production of his breakthrough hit, *The Petrified Forest*, and he reportedly angered many in the film industry as a result. Bogart at least had enough star clout that the studios would still work with him; lesser stars had no such leverage. Jack Larson spoke of how he and George Reeves were shunned by the major film studios for starring in the syndicated program *The Adventures of Superman* (1951–57): "You were a leper who had betrayed the studios by joining that new thing called television." As the major studios fought off the competitive force of television, they used threats and contractual bans to ensure that many stars would steer clear of television.[12]

Even if actors were not influenced by studio prohibitions against television, they had many personal concerns about how television could affect the length of their careers. Van Heflin shared exhibitors' fears that regular television appearances for a movie actor could "very easily mean the complete destruction of his career in movies. The audience gets used to getting something for nothing, and then does not want to turn around and pay for it." Bing Crosby expressed a related apprehension that performing too frequently on television would cause all audiences to tire of him, so he limited his participation to a handful of specials. As in the studio system era, stars rightly feared diluting their commodity value by appearing too frequently in their established star personae. Television compounded this fear of overexposure not only by requiring a more frequent appearance schedule than film—as well as a visual component that radio lacked—but also by featuring genres that entailed weekly repetition of the exact same characters. Despite his freedom from a studio contract, Henry Fonda repeatedly rejected continuing-character series for this reason, commenting, "These TV actors are better known by their character names than by their real names. Even when they appear as the guest of another show, doing something different, they're identified as the series' characters." In this sense, film stars were worried about having one-dimensional character images replace their multifaceted star images, thereby limiting the scope, depth, and distinction of their performing careers.[13]

Finally, the modes of production and transmission customary to early television also proved problematic for some film actors. Production schedules were exponentially shorter for telefilms (films made specifically for television) in comparison to feature film work. Character actor Keenan Wynn furnished an apt summary:

> The purely movie-trained actor doesn't always fare too well in a world of television. . . . You do twenty-six minutes of a finished TV film, a normal half-hour show, in three days of shooting. In a movie studio that would take three weeks. . . . You can see some of the big names from movies try it, and they damage their reputations in the attempt. When that happens, they swear they'll never expose themselves again to the trials of TV.

Also problematic was the relatively poor quality of television images. Most early sets could only deliver a grainy black-and-white picture. Especially inferior were kinescoped programs, or filmed copies of live shows that enabled subsequent airings of the otherwise fleeting productions. Kinescopes were created basically by setting up a film camera in front of a television monitor, and the end product was a fuzzy and distorted image. *Variety* noted the film studios' "fear that the [kinescope] process would not show off their properties to best advantage," and the actors themselves voiced similar concerns, often mockingly so. Producer Walter Wanger said of wife Joan Bennett's early 1950s dramatic appearances, "She looks eighty on television."[14]

Further, the predominance of live productions presented an appreciable challenge for actors used to working in the more piecemeal methods of Hollywood film production. Owing to constant production cycles, television performers were given limited preparation time, with only a day or two generally available for camera rehearsals. The immediacy of live production also made some actors apprehensive, because errors could not be refilmed or edited out. As *Variety* observed in late 1950, this potential for embarrassment was a major reason for studios to prohibit star appearances on television: the fear that "some film stars might appear ludicrous on television through inability to memorize lines or to ad lib a sustained conversation." Joan Crawford, for one, was reportedly terrified of live performance, and accordingly turned down offers from Steve Allen, Dinah Shore, and Ed Sullivan to appear on their shows; when she did finally perform in variety television, in 1958, she opted for a filmed Bob Hope special. Radio and television talk show host Tex McCray stressed this issue when asked why film stars like Crawford would avoid television in the late 1940s: "I wonder if she'll be able to sustain the emotion she's famous for while being telecast? . . . It seems like a silly question, but I know how difficult a lot of stars would find it if they have to extend emotion without being saved by 'CUT'!"[15]

Significantly, the rhetorical undertone to these descriptions represents an impression opposite to the stars' expressed concerns about commercialism. The subtle implication within these contrasts between Hollywood filmmaking and television production is that one had to be a genuinely talented actor to succeed on television. Substandard acting skills could not be elided through a retake or via post-production manipulation and looks alone supposedly could not sustain a performance. Stars with marginal performative skills could find themselves exposed by the television camera. While these impressions might have raised concerns for film stars and their studios, television gladly perpetuated and capitalized upon this inference of performance authenticity as a marker of the medium's superiority to cinema—and thereby as a counter to its culturally derided commercial identity. As we shall see throughout this book, this claim of authenticity was absolutely central to the image that television attempted to develop for itself across the 1950s; it offered a way to resolve the tension between the supposed "high quality" of film stardom and the apparent "step down" that television thereby required.

While the top stars were for the most part skirting TV in the early 1950s, it was becoming quite common for film's supporting players and character actors to work on television. Put bluntly, many of them needed the work: they were some of the first actors trimmed from the rosters during the studio system's breakup. Although the major studios did not want the film industry's biggest stars appearing on television and potentially diluting their box office drawing power, they were not so particular about what lesser actors did. Some had little chance of working again in feature film regardless of whether they appeared on television or not. Writer Hal Kanter expressed such dour sentiments when commenting on filmdom guests like Buster Keaton who were booked for *The Ed Wynn Show* (CBS, 1949–50): "[they] came on the show only because it was the only job offered to them that month." From television's standpoint, the new medium had insatiable needs for programming and for competent, experienced talent to appear in that programming. These actors fit the bill. For instance, a 1954 issue of *TV Guide* featured an article on Randy Stuart, a former Fox contract player who subsequently appeared as a guest star on hundreds of television shows. The title of the article, "TV's Bread and Butter Girl: It's the Randy Stuarts Who Keep the Camera Rolling," indicated the importance of character actors drawn from the film industry.[16]

Higher-caliber stars did begin to surface on television in the 1953–54 season, and this migration prompted a series of cynical adages from television critics, including "movie stars don't fade away, they just go on television" and "TV has done more for old movie stars than plastic surgery." As expressed here, advancing age was openly discussed as a major reason for film stars to turn to television. *New York Times* critic Val Adams described Robert Montgomery as "now past Hollywood and pushing 53," implying that he no longer had the proper romantic, leading-role qualities for an ongoing Hollywood career. Hal Humphrey identified a parade of aging female film stars in particular as a trend by 1957: "A lot of TV viewers, male and female, must be getting pretty tired of seeing comediennes who are on the short end of a battle to keep the wrinkles from showing." Most of the actors, however, found television much more forgiving of age than the movie industry was. Citing the examples of Joan Blondell, Joan Crawford, Irene Dunne, and Ann Sothern, each of whom had graced the small screen by the mid-1950s, Humphrey claimed that these were not "has-beens. It might be more apt to describe them as mistakes made by the movie industry and rectified by television."[17]

Rhetoric such as this is rife in television publicity from the period. *TV Guide* and the fan magazine *TV* framed their respective profiles of actors June Allyson and Dan Duryea in this manner, crediting television with unearthing their true acting talents, which supposedly had been obscured by Hollywood's tiresome stereotyping. Similarly, *TV Revue* magazine presented a lengthy article in 1954 entitled "They Shocked Hollywood," focusing on dethroned film stars who rekindled their fame on television. Noting that "TV has an embarrassing habit of pointing out to it just how gross has been the waste and neglect of [Hollywood's film] talent on its own doorstep," writer Alyce Canfield indicted the studios for ignoring Lucille Ball's pure talent for comedic pantomime and blindly shoehorning her into pedestrian glamour-girl roles. The sheer volume of such articles suggests a concerted effort by the television industry and its publicity branches. Television needed these recognizable star names in order to draw in viewers and sell television sets, but the fledgling medium also had to resolve the tension created by the heavy reliance on so many actors whom the film industry apparently had rejected. Thus the claim that only television could expose these stars' true talents and reward their legitimate popularity—a strategy neatly aligned with the intimate nature of the medium and its presence in the home.[18]

For those stars hesitant to appear on television out of fear that it would brand them as washed-up, perhaps only the proven success of fellow reputable actors, some of them even close friends, could allay their worries. Early precedent-setters included Ralph Bellamy (*Man Against Crime*, CBS, NBC, and DuMont, 1949–54), Robert Montgomery (*Robert Montgomery Presents*, NBC, 1950–57), and Groucho Marx (*You Bet Your Life*, NBC, 1950–61). Lucille Ball's breakthrough role in *I Love Lucy* (CBS, 1951–61) spawned a Hollywood star influx. *Variety* cited this effect of peer influence in 1952, noting that film actors "have seen some of their top-name colleagues take the plunge into the medium and come out not only unscathed but with fine audience reception and good pay." As Robert Ryan commented about his friend Dick Powell's television ventures: "When Dick entered TV, he made it possible for the rest of us to follow his example without the industry thinking we were hard up." Beginning in 1953, spurred on by the success of *I Love Lucy*, there was a significant rise in the number of situation comedies featuring established Hollywood talent in leading roles. The many examples include *Private Secretary* (starring Ann Sothern, CBS and NBC, 1953–57), *The Ray Milland Show* (CBS, 1953–55), *Dear Phoebe* (Peter Lawford, NBC, 1954–56), and *December Bride* (Spring Byington, CBS, 1954–61). In addition, numerous film stars transferred their radio sitcoms to television. Robert Young (*Father Knows Best*, CBS, NBC, ABC, 1954–63), Ronald Colman (*The Halls of Ivy*), and Eve Arden (*Our Miss Brooks*, CBS, 1952–56) all followed this path, which was made easier by the proven value of their prior broadcast experiences.[19]

In addition to peer association and the bridge provided by radio, another catalyst for the escalating migration of film stars to TV was the increase in major studio involvement with television that began in 1953. The studios had initially resisted allowing their films and contract actors to appear, which would supply television with ratings luster at the potential expense of studios and exhibitors. Such restrictions could even affect feature filmmaking. As a case in point, MGM had initially agreed to lend Arlene Dahl to Columbia for *Cyrano de Bergerac* (1950); however, when Louis B. Mayer noticed that part of the contract included the right to show clips of the film on television, he pulled Dahl back.

It was the smaller studios, Columbia and Universal, that led the way in allowing publicity appearances by their contract stars, beginning in 1951. The major studios generally forbade such appearances; it was not until 1953 that the two staunchest holdouts, Warner Bros. and MGM, relented.[20] In January, MGM allowed Robert Taylor to appear on Ed Sullivan's *Toast of the Town* (CBS, 1948–71) to tout his recent film *Above and Beyond* (1952), and Warner Bros. permitted star appearances on Sullivan's program three months later. Warners announced that the studio would no longer prohibit televised appearances by contract talent, as long as the stars received the opportunity to plug the studio and its recent releases. *Toast of the Town* subsequently become a standard destination for film stars on the publicity trail. For example, James Cagney, Henry Fonda, and Jack Lemmon appeared live on a June 1955 episode and acted out two scenes from their upcoming Warner Bros. release, *Mister Roberts* (1955).[21]

Edward R. Murrow's *Person to Person* (CBS, 1953–61), in which Murrow conducted live fifteen-minute interviews from a New York studio with personalities in their actual homes, also became a frequent stop for film stars eager to publicize their work and to charm television audiences. The stars appeared on this show as "themselves," the real people behind the star images, chatting with Murrow about their life and work. In line with the long legacy of star image construction, these "real" identities often matched components of the stars' filmic identities. For instance, in their appearances, Humphrey Bogart and Lauren Bacall were charmingly combative, Marilyn Monroe was sultry and alluring, and Harpo Marx did not speak. The latter appearance was obviously intended as a comical one; few in the audience could have believed that Harpo Marx did not speak in real life.

In a similar manner, it was customary for variety-sitcom hybrids like *The Jack Benny Show* to have their guest stars extend the skeletons of their star identities into comedy sketch routines. In this context, there was no mistaking the fact that the stars were, in effect, impersonating their identities: the comedic style of the sketches plus the stage settings and star introductions utilized at the beginning and ending of the routines clearly marked them as theatrical representations. Given that these performances also contained threads of the stars' iconic images, the acknowledgment of the artificiality of these images was heightened. These appearances thereby granted the stars the opportunity to come across to audiences as down-to-earth, good-natured people, not aloof celebrities. Much as Jack Benny framed jokes around his frugality and poor violin playing, traits that his audience had recognized as contrivances back in his radio days, these guest stars too held up their entrenched film personae for mockery. During his October 1953 *Jack Benny Show* appearance, Humphrey Bogart performed in a skit as a one-dimensional version of his gangster persona, a vicious killer named Baby Face Bogart, complete with Brooklynese patter and an entrance reminiscent of his legendary *Petrified Forest* (1936) arrival but augmented with comically excessive applause from both the audience and the sketch performers. Gary Cooper's lone *Jack Benny Show* appearance, on a September 1958 episode, was in a similar vein. Cooper was predictably stoic and taciturn in a Western sketch and in the interview segment with Benny. In the latter, Cooper performed with a guitar and "sang" a song that consisted of just a few spoken lines and ended with an obligatory "yup."

This level of reflexivity had existed in television since its earliest days as a way to engender audience trust in the medium. It was common for early variety-comedies like *The Burns and Allen Show* (CBS, 1950–58)

A star-studded 1954 jam session on The Jack Benny Show: *Jack Benny, Fred MacMurray, Tony Martin, Dick Powell, Kirk Douglas, and Dan Dailey.*
CBS/Photofest.

to self-consciously reference the conventions of their productions and for variety show hosts such as Jack Benny to openly mock the necessity of placating sponsors. This mockery was not transgressive, however; Benny would never disparage a sponsor's product, either overtly or covertly, or truly denounce the commercial framework of television. Instead, the playful acknowledgment of this framework was intended to pacify viewer resistance to these imposed conceits, allowing the audience to laugh at the construction while still ensnaring them in it. Similarly, film star guests' mockery of their own images was largely innocuous, and it glorified them as "real" folks with a sense of humor. These episodes might have toyed playfully with Hollywood's myths, but they did not fundamentally attack or dismiss them. Instead, they allowed the featured stars to acknowledge certain artificialities of screen stardom and thereby extend audience fascination with their personae, such that viewers would still be driven to theaters to see them perform in features.

Such an outcome was essential for the studios to greenlight these appearances, and the ample opportunities for film publicity yielded by variety shows made these guest shots worthwhile. Independent producer Robert Fellows commented, "It's not only cheaper, but we can reach 10 times the number of prospective ticket buyers than if these stars just appeared at theaters." The movie studios accordingly exploited variety shows to such an extent that *Variety* characterized one *Ed Sullivan* episode as "trailerizing" Paramount's *The Girl Rush* (1955) throughout the hourlong show. This free marketing grew controversial, and advertising industry trade papers regularly debated whether or not producers should let such publicity occur without charge. While some sponsors grumbled that the networks were forcing them to pay for what was basically the same service Hollywood was getting for free, a common argument in favor of these arrangements was that the Hollywood guest star helped to boost a show's ratings and a sponsor's image, thus making the concessions worth any double-standards involved.[22]

The stars themselves became embroiled in controversies in regard to these shows. First, MGM and Fox both developed deals with *Toast of the Town* in March 1953 allowing for frequent use of their stars and film clips on the show. The studios, however, were much more forthcoming with clips than stars, and Sullivan complained that his audiences disapproved, telling *Variety* that "[viewers] tune in to see performers, not movies." This led him to cancel the deal, claiming that he would only allow studio publicity when a star was actually present to perform. This refusal did not stem the tide of studio plugs, though: Sullivan continued to present such publicity fests as specials on the histories of MGM, Warner Bros., and Columbia, as well as a retrospective of producer David O. Selznick's career—all of which included both clips and stars.[23]

Second, a number of prominent stars were part of a Screen Actors Guild controversy over unpaid appearances on variety shows. One of the first stars to speak out publicly against so-called cuffo shots, Frank Sinatra, demanded payment for his *Ed Sullivan* appearances, telling *Variety*, "I'm a businessman, and get paid when I'm on TV. . . . They can use film clips but when you make a special appearance you're entitled to compensation." The controversy culminated in an April 1955 SAG edict that banned free appearances on commercially sponsored filmed shows. The controversy and subsequent ban at the very least indicates that variety show appearances had become relevant to enough film actors by this point to call for union involvement.[24]

Television had also become relevant enough for the film industry to agree to offer their most prestigious event for airing. *Variety* accordingly cited the decision to allow the March 1953 Academy Awards ceremony to be aired on NBC as a sign of the film industry's acceptance of television's visibility and credibility. This meant that even those stars who had previously never appeared on television could now be captured by its cameras at this affair, regardless of any contractual restrictions. Master of Ceremonies Bob Hope made sure to draw audience attention to this unprecedented circumstance in his monologue:

> This is a marriage between two great entertainment mediums. It's a child bride, but the kid is loaded. But isn't it exciting to know that all of these glamorous stars are going to be in your home tonight? All across America, housewives are turning to their husbands and saying, "put on your shirt, Joan Crawford is coming."

Joan Crawford and countless other top stars also began to appear in living rooms via old feature films airing on television in this period. The minor Hollywood studios started leasing their lesser B films to television in the late 1940s, but the major studios held their libraries back until the 1953–54 season, when the competitive and financial benefits were more favorable. Even then, a Screen Actors Guild provision prohibited the release of post-1948 films to television until fair residual rates could be determined for recent films. Given the extensive time they needed to fill, many television stations gladly accepted these older films to run during non-network scheduling periods, and after 1955, all of the major studios profited handsomely from distributing their back catalogues to television. As a result, viewers could easily find 1940s stars on 1950s television, though they would have to look before 8 P.M. and after 11 P.M., as the networks rarely programmed features in prime time prior to the 1960s. TV audiences could now revel in "old Hollywood" appearing on their home screens—although this nostalgia may have tarnished as many star images as it burnished. Dick Powell lamented the reminder of his age that features on TV brought, joking that viewers might turn from his *Four Star Playhouse* (CBS, 1952–56) program to an airing of one of his 1930s musicals and assume they were now watching his son, not him. For actors already fighting against the

38

impression that they moved to television only because they were past their cinematic primes, this constant reminder of their youth was hardly helpful.[25]

The next stage of the film industry's relationship with television signaled more than just profit extraction. The studios shifted to actively participating in small-screen production, an option they embraced especially in order to survive their post–Paramount Case struggles. Declines in theatrical production and the switch to the package-unit system resulted in empty studio lots and soundstages, and the available facilities and equipment could easily be adopted for telefilm production. Columbia revived Screen Gems, a subsidiary company originally created for animation production, and in 1954 became the first nonindependent Hollywood studio to produce filmed series for television with *The Adventures of Rin Tin Tin* (ABC, 1954–59) and *Father Knows Best.* During the following year, a set of shows produced by the major studios appeared, including *Warner Brothers Presents* (ABC, 1955–56), *20th Century–Fox Hour* (CBS, 1955–57), and *MGM Parade* (ABC, 1955–56). Each of these publicity-heavy programs featured plugs for current theatrical films and included appearances by their stars. This direct studio association brought more contract stars to television screens and presumably helped to legitimate television in other non-contracted stars' eyes.[26]

In addition to having increased film industry involvement in TV, the television industry had stabilized enough by the mid-1950s to be taken seriously by legitimately successful movie actors. First, the annually rising profits (TV surpassed radio in revenue in 1954) meant that money could finally be a major incentive for a television appearance. Said Henry Fonda, "I wasn't too interested until I saw the dollar sign at the end of the telegram [offering a hosting job]." Only the top tier could draw anything near the $150,000 that was directed to Fonda for hosting an anthology program, but decent pay was widely available. The *New York Times* reported in 1954 that the going rate for two to three days of television work for a film star was $10,000, and for stars cut loose from the assurance of a multiyear contract with the film studios, a regularly paying TV job could be quite a comfort. When asked why she turned to TV after being shunned by the film studios in the 1950s, former Paramount star Betty Hutton responded with one word: "Money." Additionally, television had spread into well more than half of American homes by the mid-1950s, which translated into audiences exponentially bigger than one could expect at a movie theater. Loretta Young took this as a great incentive to host a show: "I don't have the exact figures to back it up, but on nights when our show reaches 45,000,000 people at a single crack, that's probably more people than have seen all the pictures I've made put together. You get an actress who's a ham and that's reason enough to go on doing television forever."[27]

As a result of these catalysts, television employment became more than just a side job for many Hollywood actors. A 1955 Screen Actors Guild survey of its members found that whereas theatrical films provided 54 percent of employment days for actors making up to $7,500 a year, telefilms supplied 46 percent, up from 38 percent the previous year. Obviously, for smaller-scale actors, television was quickly becoming vital to their livelihoods. Not surprisingly, this percentage dropped as salaries increased; for those making $7,500-$15,000 annually, TV films supplied 33 percent of employment days, and for those in the $15,000–$25,000 range, the figure was 24 percent. These numbers, however, only include telefilms, not live programs; considering that higher-level stars were more likely to appear on prestigious live anthologies and spectaculars than in telefilms, these percentages would likely be higher if the study had factored in all types of appearances. Regardless, even the lesser percentages indicate that many actors were juggling both television and film at this time.[28]

This juggling act could be a challenge, as stars feared the perils of being attached to a single television character and in all likelihood sapping their film futures. Some creatively navigated these hazards while still gleaning money and positive exposure from television by allowing only limited exploitation of their images in series. Henry Fonda, the most famous film star cast in a continuing-character series during the 1950s, narrated and played a Western marshal on NBC's *The Deputy* (1959–61). His previously cited concerns about excessive character attachment were soothed by the show's premise: although Fonda narrated every episode, the character he played usually delegated assignments to the titular deputy, played by TV actor Allen Case. Fonda only took the lead role in nineteen of the show's seventy-six episodes despite being billed as its star. Doubtless, the network's presentation of this as a Henry Fonda vehicle resulted from a desire to use the drawing power of his star name and the potency of his dignified image, regardless of his limited involvement.

Given the potential positives and negatives of appearing on television, it is not surprising that the anthology program became the most common place for many film actors, especially noted stars, to start and carry on their television careers. Here, the presumption that only aging film actors with declining film careers appeared on television is shown to be drastically reductive: many of the period's bigger stars, including Humphrey Bogart, John Wayne, Gene Tierney, and Ingrid Bergman, *did* appear on anthology programs. The anthology drama, which presented self-contained plays with a different cast of characters each week, was viewed as a prestige format by critics and journalists, and critics placed anthologies (especially those that originated live from New York) well above continuing-character dramas in terms of quality and cachet. Hence, these dramas were attractive to stars who feared that appearing on the smaller medium of television would dilute their star aura. As the live anthology drama in particular took on connotations of high-culture entertainment, critics defined the genre as akin to Broadway theater. Top-level stars could thus make guest appearances on these shows while remaining true to their star status and retaining acting credibility. The pervasive critical attention given to anthology dramas also meant that star performances were likely to earn journalistic reviews, thereby granting stars more substantial publicity than they were likely get from any other program format.

Fears of overexposure would also have made anthology drama appearances more attractive than continuing-character series commitments, as they required only periodic visits rather than extended attachment to a single show or character. Further, actors appearing regularly on anthologies had the potential to explore a wide range of roles, allowing diverse opportunities for those who professed to have been pigeonholed into a singular film persona. Anthology producer Martin Manulis described why A-list stars would be so attracted to these qualities: "We got actors to do the show for a pittance compared to their movie salaries, but we also offered them parts that they might not normally get."[29]

Simultaneous to the rise in series appearances by film actors during the 1953–54 season was an increase in the frequency of anthology roles filled by film stars. In the 1954 article "Stars in Your Eyes: Whole Constellations Gleam in TV Dramas This Season," *TV Guide* noted, "Time was, not long ago, when a single authentic stage or screen star in a TV show inspired furious fanfare. Times change. This season, two 'name' players seem par for an hour-long script. Some TV dramas have enlisted 3, 4, even more." Also important, the period from 1953 to 1955 witnessed the growing credibility of the anthology program, due especially to an increase in the use of original teleplays written specifically for the unique properties of the medium. Historian Erik Barnouw heralds the 1953 broadcast of "Marty" on *Goodyear TV Playhouse* (NBC, 1951–60) as a landmark in the development of the anthology as a prestige form, and such acclaim drew in a better class of writers, further boosting the genre. Said film actor–turned–anthology producer Dick Powell, "Once we were able to get 'name' movie and magazine writers to turn out scripts for the TV medium, the next step of attracting stars was almost academic."[30]

Additionally, the television networks and primary shows began moving to Hollywood for production by the mid-1950s. Most early television shows had been produced in New York and were simply not so accessible to Hollywood talent already tied to motion pictures on the West Coast. Not surprisingly, some of the first major film actors to do television shows were active on Broadway too, including Ralph Bellamy, Paul Muni, and Fredric March. Rosalind Russell's 1951 television debut on *Schlitz Playhouse of Stars* (CBS, 1951–59) coincided with her return to the New York stage. As television production increasingly moved westward, however, this circumstance began to shift. The industrywide transplant began as early as 1952, when CBS completed its Television City studios in Hollywood. *Variety* predicted that moves west would become commonplace, as advertisers preferred Hollywood names over Broadway ones, and "since the Hollywood stars would still rather remain by their swimming pools, most top-spending sponsors are turning to Hollywood-produced vidfilms to plug their wares." Subsequent years did see an increasing number of shows moving to the West Coast; by the 1956–57 season, about 70 percent of prime-time network programming originated from the Los Angeles area, up from 54 percent the previous season. As a revealing case of art imitating industry, and based on the same logic of the lure of the Hollywood milieu, *I Love Lucy* presented Lucy and Ricky Ricardo moving to Hollywood in the 1955 season, with Ricky to star in a film for MGM. Writer-producer Jess Oppenheimer conceived the idea in hopes of reviving stagnating ratings, and the show accordingly returned to the number one slot in April 1955. In addition to a plethora of MGM plugs, the move brought forth an impressive list of guest stars, including John Wayne, William Holden, Rock Hudson, and Richard Widmark.[31]

While it was common early on for filmed sitcoms and action series to shoot in Hollywood, a more significant change came when the New York–identified anthology programs began to make the move. The most significant relocation, at least in symbolic terms, came when the highly respected New York fixture *Studio One* (CBS, 1948–58) transferred production to CBS's Hollywood facilities in 1957. CBS vice president Harry Ommerle told *TV Guide*, "While there are darn good actors available here in New York, it's important that we get the top box-office names in significant numbers. We will not change the *Studio One* format; we just think we can get a bigger audience with this type of casting." *Variety* editor George Rosen joked in October 1957 that New York should be nicknamed "Studio None" because of these defections to Hollywood and commented that "all the media elements identified with big-time TV (producers, directors, writers, actors, etc.) are staking their future claims on the west coast."[32]

Another sign of television's burgeoning reliance on established film performers was the rise of the spectacular, a genre that was tailor-made for Hollywood film stars. NBC programming head Pat Weaver innovated this event programming, which featured famous stars, huge budgets, and color images. The spectaculars were usually live dramas and musicals modeled on Broadway shows or lavish variety revues, with 90-minute running times and budgets approaching $500,000. Given their potential to grab every audience segment, NBC publicized them to sponsors thusly:

> The Spectaculars will free television from the shackles of format and schedule. . . . Viewers will look forward to them with the anticipation of eagerly awaited special events. They will talk about them. And marvel at them. And watch them. For they are conceived with the idea of reaching the *total* television audience—not just a segment of it.

Variety cited the importance of the Hollywood star to this idea, noting that "[f]rom a standpoint of audience pull half the battle is won" with stars in leading roles. NBC began programming these shows during the 1954–55 season, in *TV Guide*'s words, "to forestall the possibility of viewers growing tired of standard TV fare." Accordingly, this upscale genre brought to the small screen the biggest Hollywood stars yet: Betty Hutton, Ginger Rogers, Gene Kelly, and Ann Miller were all paid handsomely—as much as $50,000—for single musical or dramatic performances that in return underscored their legendary status. If any television genre could be seen as measuring up to the reputation of the Hollywood star, it was the spectacular.[33]

On the opposite side of the cultural spectrum of the spectacular, yet curiously unveiling nearly the same caliber of star talent in guest roles, was the quiz show. Many panel shows featured Hollywood talent as guests, and there were even a number of programs whose premises were directly tied to the world of celebrity, from *Personality Puzzle* (ABC, 1953), which had contestants guess the identity of well-known guest stars based on evidence gleaned from personal possessions, to *Can Do* (NBC, 1956), where celebrity guests were challenged to perform odd stunts. The most successful of the celebrity-themed shows was *Masquerade Party* (NBC, CBS, ABC, 1952–60), in which panelists had to discern the identity of a heavily disguised celebrity guest based on clues contained within their costuming and makeup. Stars taking part as mystery guests included Lon Chaney, Jr., Ginger Rogers, the Three Stooges, and silent-era legend Mary Pickford.

The most beloved of the quiz shows were *What's My Line?* (CBS, 1950–67) and *I've Got a Secret* (CBS, 1952–76), in which panelists had to solve enigmas about guest contestants. These programs primarily focused on ordinary people, but each episode featured at least one celebrity guest. *I've Got a Secret* attracted many stars across the decade, including Boris Karloff (secret: "I'm afraid of mice") and Buster Keaton (secret: "I'm sitting on a pie"). The shows were easy and fun for stars to do, offering what game show historian Thomas DeLong describes as a "clublike" atmosphere. While the $500–$600 payment per appearance was probably just a minor incentive, DeLong proposes that the opportunity "to reaffirm the fact of their ongoing importance" lured many film stars. The chance to plug their feature film work was also an attraction, to the point where *New York Times* critic Jack Gould complained, "Every time a movie star appears the viewer must put up with dreary and continued interludes about his or her forthcoming picture." Similar circumstances surrounded *What's My Line?* which featured a celebrity mystery guest in each episode. Some of the biggest names in Hollywood appeared here, including Ava Gardner, Edward G. Robinson, Greer Garson, Lauren Bacall, Kirk Douglas, Dorothy Lamour, and Tyrone Power. All were treated like royalty, each had the chance to publicize his or her recent projects, and no appearance exceeded five minutes of breezy effort.[34]

Ginger Rogers revealed on Masquerade Party. CBS/Photofest.

Betty Hutton's June 1958 appearance on *What's My Line?* stands as an example of the benefits a game show appearance could provide to a star. Hutton was on the downside of her career by this point, yet her appearance opened and closed with affirmations of her stardom. Panelist Eamonn Andrews commented on the raucous reception she received upon coming onstage ("You sent the audience into raptures!"), and Arlene Francis prefaced her correct guess of Hutton's identity with the question, "Didn't Maurice Chevalier just make the statement that you're one of the finest performers he's ever seen?" Hutton then got the opportunity to plug her current Broadway show, leaving viewers with the thought that her entertainment career was not only still active, it was even thriving once again.

FILM STARS AND TELEVISION WORKING TOGETHER

By the mid-1950s and well on into the decade, then, average Hollywood film actors could be sighted on a variety of television programs alongside top-drawer stars making occasional appearances, which prompted an Associated Press journalist to comment in late 1953, "So many famous names in Hollywood are showing up on television that a

45

home viewer sometimes may wonder if he has been transported into a movie theater." There was a genre for every star's need: sitcoms and continuing-character dramas for character actors or aging film vets looking for career extensions, variety and game shows to afford exposure and publicity, anthology dramas for stars hoping to be recognized for their acting talents, and spectaculars for A-list stars looking for material and publicity that was as close to commensurate with their star power as television could muster. And all granted film actors the opportunity to make money, keep performing, or even just remind fans that they were still around. Somewhat hyperbolically, *Variety* indicated in a June 1956 article, "Pix Holdouts on TV—No More," that stars could no longer afford to ignore television: "It was a long time in coming, but the dawn has already come up on the era when even the best of them, be it films, legit or any branch of show biz, now realize that they can no longer bypass TV and keep pace with the shifting trends."[35]

Just as film actors came to rely on television, television leaned on film names in programming. In placing established film actors in hosting positions, featuring them in their own shows, and showcasing them in periodic appearances, program producers were depending on the same audience-luring tactics used by Hollywood since the establishment of the star system. *TV Guide* repeatedly addressed this issue in the mid-1950s, particularly in terms of what it meant for indigenous TV actors. In the March 1954 article "War of Two Worlds: TV and Movie Stars Battle for Dramatic Parts," the author discussed the increasing numbers of Hollywood stars on television and the resulting implications for television stars:

> As more and more Hollywood movie stars enter TV, the actors who established their reputations in TV itself are starting to worry about their jobs. [W]hen a TV sponsor has a choice between a Yvonne de Carlo or a Maria Riva, for example, he'll inevitably grab the movie star, even if he knows that the TV-trained star could deliver a better performance.

The article noted, "Hollywood beginnings are usually backed by a tremendous glamour build-up that TV players can only envy." Networks and sponsors fully exploited the publicity benefits of star attraction, and viewers quickly began to expect this, which helped to push *Studio One* and other programs westward.[36]

Hollywood stars also lent valued credibility to certain shows; *Gunsmoke* (CBS, 1955–75) received such a boost from John Wayne. Some claim that Wayne turned down the part of Marshall Dillon, but Charles Marquis Warren, one of the show's early producers, insists that no offer was ever made, largely because Wayne's stature would have precluded him from accepting in the first place. Wayne did, however, recommend James Arness, an actor under contract with his film production company, and, as a favor to help boost the show's prospects, Wayne agreed to introduce its premiere episode in September 1955. Low-grade B film Western heroes like the Lone Ranger and Hopalong Cassidy had roamed the television range since the late 1940s, but their shows were largely dismissed as kiddie fare. Thus, when the so-called adult Western emerged as a subgenre in the mid-1950s, its producers had to separate it definitively from previous incarnations of the TV Western in order to be taken seriously as legitimate entertainment and to attract affluent adult viewers and deep-pocketed sponsors. Wayne's introductory presence was an essential badge of legitimacy for *Gunsmoke,* as was his evolving image as a complex Western hero, which lent weight to his description of *Gunsmoke* as "the best thing of its kind to come along. . . . it's honest, it's adult, it's realistic."

Behind the scenes, the biggest impact of the willingness of stars to appear on television was the explosion in the influence of talent agencies, which substantially affected all entertainment industry operations. The power of the talent agency in relation to both broadcasting and Hollywood began in the radio era. In 1938, *Fortune* magazine observed:

> The commercial sponsor, adrift in the unfamiliar world of show business, demands concrete results. Rather than gamble on new ideas and new talent, he usually prefers to pay big money for established stars. The resultant competition for names has sent prices skyrocketing, and the talent agent with a stable of "name" entertainers has been placed in a very powerful bargaining position.

As Hollywood studio power declined across the 1950s, talent agencies were inversely strengthened. Frank Rose, author of a history of the William Morris Agency, describes the resulting situation:

> When the studios slashed production and freed their contract players to cut costs, they'd inadvertently handed the leverage to the stars—the stars and their agents. Independent producers were going

to banks to get financing, and bankers saw a proven box-office draw as good collateral. The asking price for top stars had shot up as a result, and the price for supporting players as well.

Given that television represented a brand-new labor market, agency and star leverage increased exponentially.[37]

The most substantial force in this regard was MCA and its telefilm company, Revue Productions, which packaged shows for the star clients it handled, including Jack Benny, Bob Cummings, and Ronald Reagan, and also created production partnerships with such stars as Jane Wyman. Frank Rose claims that more than a third of the biggest stars in Hollywood were MCA clients, considerably more than any single studio could claim in the 1950s. William Morris also had a number of key stars under contract, including Dick Powell, Teresa Wright, and Claudette Colbert, and the agency's packaged television shows included such prominent programs as *Four Star Playhouse*, *The Ann Sothern Show* (CBS, 1958–61), and *The Loretta Young Show* (NBC, 1953–61). By 1955, MCA and William Morris either represented talent or controlled the booking on forty-six of the top fifty-seven rated shows; in 1960, the two companies had a financial interest in more than 60 percent of the total prime-time lineup.[38]

With a complete stable of directors, writers, and actors under contract, these two agencies could use access to a particular star as a bargaining chip to force a network or producer into employing the others in a package. Their success then became self-perpetuating, as talent signed with those who could supply jobs, and William Morris and MCA were undeniably the most well connected to both film and television. This access to and oversight over performers drove up star salaries considerably: while networks were progressively gaining more programming control from ad agencies and sponsors, these changes helped to siphon some of that control over to stars and their agencies. As an anonymous talent buyer told *Sponsor*, "Whether we like it or not, the American public likes big names and the place to get them is at William Morris or MCA. You can't avoid dealing with them." Thus, the increasing willingness of film actors to appear on television greatly affected how television producers cast their programs and how talent agencies ran their operations. Especially in a period of film industry struggle, the considerable expansion of talent agencies in the 1950s would not have been possible were actors not willing and able to move between film and television.[39]

The power of talent agencies was also indicative of the level of freedom that stars had from film studio control. Though the studios initially tried to maintain their leverage over stars by threatening to blacklist them from features if they were tainted by television appearances, by the mid-1950s, the industry became too desperate, television became too serviceable, and talent agencies became too authoritative for them to follow through on their threats. As a result, stars were no longer resigned to being indentured servants of the major Hollywood studios. However, stars could also no longer rely on the studios' ongoing support owing to the industry's financial struggles. Plus, there was still a diffuse collection of masters to serve whether one appeared on television or not, from producers and agents to networks and sponsors. Negotiating all of these interests could be daunting. But the most motivated, shrewd, and adaptable stars successfully fought to survive and thrive in this new industrial landscape, whether television played a primary role in their performative careers or not.

Evidence of this survival is provided by the television activities of the film stars highlighted earlier in this chapter. Given the strength of his film career (and his bank account) in the 1950s, there was no compelling reason for James Stewart to turn to television. Yet Stewart was a regular presence on the small screen. Most of his appearances were tied to publicity for his feature films, including his June 1955 spot on the *Colgate Comedy Hour,* wherein a contrived "salute to the air age" served as the context for his appearance alongside clips from *Strategic Air Command* (1955). Stewart said of the value of similar work, such as his three guest spots on *Toast of the Town,* that "[a]n occasional appearance on television like this is a kind of teaser for my movies. It's like taking an ad out in 150 newspapers." Friendship was largely behind his eight stints on *The Jack Benny Show* between 1952 and 1964; Stewart and Benny were neighbors, and Stewart's wife Gloria, who was not an actress, joined him in comedy skits on seven of the episodes. Finally, Stewart's television work extended to dramatic acting, most notably in three episodes of *General Electric Theater.* These were arranged by his agent Lew Wasserman, also acting on the behalf of Revue Productions, the show's production company. Stewart agreed to make his dramatic debut on 1955's "The Windmill," in part because the show would allow him to plug *Strategic Air Command* yet again. 1957's "The Town With a Past" featured Stewart in a story to which he owned the rights, and "The Trail to Christmas" gave him the new opportunity to get behind the camera and direct. Thus, Stewart is a principal counterexample to the stereotype that film stars turned to television only in desperation.[40]

On the other hand, Robert Taylor's experience confirms that studios did restrict star appearances when they were able to contractually. Prior to 1959, MGM allowed Taylor only four appearances. As noted earlier, Taylor became MGM's first A-list star to appear on *Toast of the Town* in 1953, and he made a similar publicity appearance on Ed Sullivan's variety show in 1955, followed by a stint as the "mystery guest" on *What's My Line?* in 1956 and a 1958 cameo role in the MGM-produced *Thin Man* series (NBC, 1957–59). The fact that these few, primarily publicity-driven performances were his only guest roles on television while he was tied to MGM indicates that the major studios likely would have prevented extensive star appearances if they had held onto a greater number of contract stars in the 1950s. In that same vein, Celeste Holm's breakaway from Fox enabled her to return first to her roots on the stage and then to shift to anthology roles on shows like *Lux Video Theater* (CBS and NBC, 1950–57) and *Hollywood Opening Night* (CBS and NBC, 1951–53), where, she said in 1954 when asked why she would do television, "[one night] is better than ten years on Broadway. You reach so many more people." In fact, television subsequently became her primary acting outlet, from her short-lived 1954 sitcom on CBS, *Honestly, Celeste!*, to prolific anthology appearances in the 1950s and episodic series guest spots across the 1960s and 1970s.[41]

Returning to Taylor, he did opt for television in 1959 after negotiating a new nonexclusive and limited-film contract with MGM, starring in a crime series, *The Detectives* (ABC and NBC, 1959–62). Similar to Henry Fonda's arrangement for *The Deputy*, the show featured an episodic rotation of investigators, so Taylor was not the lead in most episodes. His contract specified that he would receive seven consecutive months off from the show, a time period that would leave him free for feature films or personal leisure. At the same time, he acknowledged to the press that he turned to series TV largely because of a slowdown in his theatrical career. He also told *TV Guide* in 1959 that money was his primary motivator in the endeavor: "I have no illusions whatever of contributing anything 'artistic' to the medium. Quite frankly, I am going into television largely because of the money involved. If this series is a success—and I'm certainly not kidding myself that it will be—I stand to come out of it nicely in a financial way." His reference here is to the component of his TV contract that offered 50 percent profit participation in the program

James Stewart and Beulah Bondi star in a February 1957 production of "The Town With a Past" for General Electric Theater. *CBS/Photofest.*

in addition to his $150,000 salary. After seeing so many freelancers like James Stewart profit substantially from production deals, he surely yearned to make up for what he had lost while locked in a studio contract. With his film career past the prime for such opportunities, he was still able to find them in television.[42]

Taylor's disparaging comments to publicity outlets about his television work could also be read as a smokescreen, a way to lessen the blow to one's image or to discount personal investment in case the show failed or the work was judged by others as beneath him. Mickey Rooney left a similar impression with his numerous claims that he was just in television for the money. In addition to quiz and variety show appearances, and after shooting two failed pilots, Rooney worked with William Morris to package a sitcom called *Hey Mulligan* (NBC, 1954–55), in which he played an NBC page hoping to break into film acting. Unfortunately, NBC scheduled it against the powerhouse *Jackie Gleason Show* (CBS, 1952–59), where it got blitzed by the number two program and lasted only a season. Of course it might not have done well against a test pattern, either; Rooney received scathing criticism for trying to play a character much younger than he really was. Critic Laurence Laurent wrote, "'Hey, Mulligan,' stop pining for Andy Hardy and act your age."[43]

The series misstep didn't prevent Rooney from continuing to pursue television, but he did appear to hedge his bets more fully in the press. Even after finding great success with an Emmy-nominated performance on *Playhouse 90* in 1957, Rooney professed to have few artistic illusions about the work. Asked by *TV Guide* if he had any qualms prior to the appearance, he responded, "The money was there." This highly acclaimed performance briefly made him a hot property again, but television also captured a low point for Rooney in December 1959, when he supposedly appeared drunk on *The Jack Paar Show* (NBC, 1957–62), acted belligerently toward Paar, and stormed off the stage. Paar ended the segment with the comment, "It's a shame. He was a great talent."[44]

Audiences could not help taking the same impression from many of the TV appearances of Errol Flynn. In fact, Flynn was the reference point for the 1982 feature film *My Favorite Year*, in which Peter O'Toole played a drunken, washed-up movie star who humiliates himself on a 1950s variety show. This film was not based on any specific incidents, and not all of Flynn's television work was entirely dismissible. Flynn biographer Thomas McNulty notes that while Flynn primarily did television to fill the financial gaps left by the decline of his film career, it likely "pleased and refreshed the artistic side of Flynn's nature to work in a new medium." During his time in England in 1954, Flynn shot twenty-six episodes of an anthology show—all as host, only six as star—that ran in U.S. syndication as *The Errol Flynn Show* in 1957. Most of the episodes he acted in allowed him to toy with his fading swashbuckler persona, such as "The 1,000th Night of Don Juan," which offered a winking portrayal of an aging, foolish Lothario and let Flynn openly acknowledge his transformed star image. His feature film work by the late 1950s largely consisted of self-referential roles, such as a knowing depiction of an alcoholic John Barrymore in *Too Much, Too Soon* (1958). Unfortunately, Flynn's life was heading down the same path as Barrymore's, defined by caricatured performances and substance abuse (the latter all too visible on the television screen). Steve Allen wrote of Flynn's appearance on Allen's eponymous show (NBC, 1956–60), "Errol performed creditably during rehearsal and was, as always, personally charming backstage, but by the time we were on the air—live—he was so spaced out on God-knows-what that he offered a very poor impression of himself." Flynn also barely appeared to be himself by the end of his life, as drug and alcohol abuse ravaged his formerly handsome features. *Variety* judged him to be "funny (if hard to recognize)" on a final variety show stint before his death in 1959.[45]

Though advancing age could be a visible problem for stars, it was not necessarily a handicap for character actors turning to television. The voluminous production needs of television were analogous to studio system–era demands for performers to fill a variety of supporting roles, and the anthology series in particular called for a wide range of portrayals from young to old. Furthermore, the fact that television was in desperate need of familiar names and faces to grab viewer attention even boosted some character actors into leading positions. Thomas Mitchell, for example, averaged seven anthology episodes a year from 1951 to 1958. These were not mere supporting performances: Mitchell won a Best Actor Emmy for his anthology efforts in 1953, thereby becoming the first star with both an Oscar and an Emmy statuette on his mantle. Indeed, Mitchell's name carried enough weight to land a series on the air. A televised version of the show *Mayor of the Town* featuring its radio star Lionel Barrymore was planned for 1954, but Barrymore fell ill and died later that year. The producers signed Mitchell as a replacement and were still able to sell the syndicated show to stations based on Mitchell's name recognition and track record as a popular character actor.[46]

As this case illustrates, character actors and lesser stars quickly became the workhorses of television programming, as the example of Mary Astor also confirms. After recovering from personal problems, Astor relocated to New York and was therefore in a prime position to capitalize on the heyday of live drama, starring in seemingly every anthology program on the air. In her autobiography, she wrote of how this experience revitalized her love of acting:

> It was experimental, crazy and wonderful. I was in them all. I played everything and had a ball. . . . You didn't have to give a damn whether you had a hit or not. You didn't have to sit up most of the night waiting for the reviews. And you didn't have to do the whole thing over again, tomorrow and tomorrow and tomorrow.

Upon following the flow of programming back to Hollywood in 1956, she found that the feature film community had largely forgotten about her but that her popularity with television audiences was still strong. Like Celeste Holm, she spent the rest of her career making guest acting appearances.[47]

These varied examples highlight the range of film star experiences within 1950s television and indicate the complex choices that actors faced as they weighed the value of small-screen work. Television could supply work that features weren't offering, keep one's acting slate and wallet full, or proffer valuable feature film publicity. Yet involvement with the new medium also held the potential to damage a star's reputation, sever a studio relationship, or present an unwelcome reminder that one's eminence was a thing of the past. And in television's early years, no one was certain exactly how valuable or problematic any of these denouements would ultimately be.

Nonetheless, there was one near certainty that television provided to film stars in contrast to their experiences with studio system film work: the freedom to make career judgments on their own. Having been controlled by Hollywood for so long, many stars yearned for their own creative control. Robert Taylor biographer Linda J. Alexander notes that Taylor was never one to buck the system (hence his record stay at MGM), but he did chafe under the studio's treatment of him as just a cog in their operations. Taylor valued the fact that "TV finally gave him an opportunity to use his intelligence and maneuver his own career rather than being told what to do." Taylor capitalized on his new-found autonomy with his role in *The Detectives*. This program was produced by Four Star Productions, an independent television company run by a group of established film stars that attempted to foster a new star-empowering production system in television.[48]

STARS BEHIND THE SCENES: FOUR STAR PRODUCTIONS

Stars like James Stewart and James Cagney were able to parlay the decline of studio contracts, the rise of independent film packaging, and new tax laws favoring self-incorporation into opportunities for creative control over their feature film careers. The concurrent growth of television supplied an additional outlet for such production, as stars formed television production companies and reaped considerable profits from program successes as a result. Most of these companies were small enterprises founded only to produce a single show that the star appeared in, but a handful of other stars used the developmental freedom of early television to become their own business moguls. Bing

Crosby Enterprises grew out of the singing star's radio work and became a highly diversified company, branching out into television production with anthology shows like *Fireside Theater* (NBC, 1949–58), *Rebound* (ABC and DuMont, 1952–53), and *Crown Theater with Gloria Swanson* (syndicated, 1954), as well as a handful of television specials starring Crosby. As accomplished as Crosby's television company was, however, it did not approach the output of Four Star Productions, which was owned and operated by three stars: Dick Powell, Charles Boyer, and David Niven. Overshadowed only by the popular prominence of Lucille Ball and Desi Arnaz's Desilu, Four Star developed into the most prolific and financially successful of the star-owned companies, and its achievements matched those of any television production company during the period. It also serves as a fitting example of what stars in the post–studio system era could accomplish with their freedom from the Hollywood studios.[49]

Four Star was the brainchild of Don Sharpe, a prolific radio packager and talent agent. One of the radio programs he developed was *Four Star Playhouse,* an anthology drama that aired on NBC in the summer of 1949 and presented Robert Cummings, Rosalind Russell, Fred MacMurray, and Loretta Young as its rotating stars. The program was intended as a response to CBS's shrewd moves across 1948 and 1949 to lure away NBC's most prominent radio stars, including Jack Benny, Red Skelton, and Burns and Allen. Reeling from these talent raids, NBC initially hoped that *Four Star* would be a building block for the construction of a renewed roster of star-laden programs. The show did not distinguish itself immediately, however, and it was given little time to find an audience, especially as NBC's concurrent moves into television meant that it had little patience for supporting a struggling radio program.

Sharpe himself moved into television packaging and producing in 1951, and one of his first ideas was to create a television version of *Four Star Playhouse.* He interested clients Dick Powell and Joel McCrea in the program and tried to convince Rosalind Russell to follow the show to television. McCrea reportedly shot an episode, and the program advertised his connection to the show in its early episodes, but he subsequently backed out of his commitment. Powell's biographer claims that upon seeing it, McCrea did not care for the quality of the episode he shot and, given that he was already well off financially and was more interested in lessening his workload than in increasing it, he declined to continue in television. For her part, Russell was not interested in series television at this point, nor was Barbara Stanwyck, another star that Sharpe and Powell encouraged to join. The two were finally able to persuade two freelance stars, Charles Boyer, a Sharpe client, and David Niven, a Powell friend, to join them.[50]

In mid-1952, Powell's lawyer, William Cruikshank, organized the company called Four Star Productions with Don Sharpe in place as president and profits split among Sharpe, Cruikshank, and the three stars. Production on *Four Star Playhouse* began shortly thereafter, with Singer Sewing Machines as its primary sponsor. After appearing biweekly during its first season, it became a weekly series for the remainder of its four-season run. The program's anthology episodes ran the gamut of genres, from thrillers to romances to comedies. Additionally, each star produced his featured episodes, primarily controlling story choice, script supervision, and casting. David Niven later told *TV Guide* of the stars' production autonomy in this manner: "We produced those shows and appeared in them, you know. We had complete script approval and we simply wouldn't do a script if it didn't intrigue us. And if a script was basically all right but not quite all there, we'd rewrite it ourselves. Furthermore, the sponsor had no script approval at all. We did exactly what we wanted to do." One should be suspicious of such declarations in a publicity source, yet all accounts of the program, including trade paper and secondary source accounts, do indicate that the actors had considerable control over the episodes in which they starred, especially in terms of story selection. Even if this material is merely calculated publicity, one is struck by the repeated insistence on how pivotal this production control was to the quality of the program. A *TV-Radio Life* article in particular stresses that the show's success was rooted in the production autonomy it gave to its stars, as they were the best possible judges of how their images should be showcased within the program's narratives. Here again, we see the rhetorical argument that this star-laden program was an unalloyed projection of the stars' own individualities and sincere artistic aspirations, not just a vehicle for making money, resurrecting a fading career, or marketing sewing machines.[51]

At this point, *Four Star Playhouse* still had only three stars on board. Initially, the solution was to rotate in a different actor each month to act as the titular fourth star, and Ronald Colman, Joan Fontaine, Merle Oberon, and Teresa Wright repeatedly filled this role. After making similar occasional appearances, Ida Lupino was permanently installed

The star-owners of Four Star Productions:
Charles Boyer, Dick Powell, and David Niven.
CBS/Photofest.

as the fourth star in spring 1954, though she never had the ownership stake in the company that the other three original stars did.

Being tied to television for a weekly show was frequently cited as a deterrent to film actor appearances, and *Four Star Playhouse*'s creative periodic format greatly helped to offset this drawback. It required only a single appearance a month by any of its stars, a practice already well established within the variety show genre to forestall performer exhaustion and overexposure. The fact that the show was shot on film and not live was also was an attraction for the movie-trained actors. David Niven, for one, professed to hate live TV; writing in his autobiography, he volunteered a vivid opinion of live television: "Without exception, the most ghastly torture ever invented for people in my profession, it incorporated the worst features of films, radio and the legitimate theater."[52]

The production method of rotating filmed episodes also granted Four Star's headline stars a measure of career freedom, and the production schedule of *Four Star Playhouse* reflected the ongoing big-screen pursuits of its cast. The primary stars' busiest year in terms of outside work was 1955, when Dick Powell appeared in a remake of *It Happened One Night,* David Niven starred in *Around the World in 80 Days,* and Charles Boyer filmed *Lucky to Be a Woman* in Paris. Four Star planned for these interruptions by filming as many as four episodes featuring each star before the season started, as well as using guest stars (primarily Ida Lupino) to fill in the remainder of the season. Thus, *Four Star Playhouse*'s programming structure and production planning enabled its principal stars to maintain their film careers while still enjoying the diverse benefits of a television series.[53]

At this point, Four Star was a typical star-owned production company, with a single show responsible for the company's prosperity. Business savvy and ambition on the part of the star-producers, especially leader Dick Powell, made much more possible. The relatively modest popularity of *Four Star Playhouse*—it never cracked the top twenty in weekly ratings—was not equal to the immense prosperity of a show like *I Love Lucy,* but the measurable profits and critical respect that the program earned, including numerous Emmy nominations and Screen Writers Guild and Screen Directors Guild Awards, did constitute a foundation upon which to build. Such expansion began with two anthology programs that were similar in spirit to *Four Star Playhouse.* First was *Stage 7,* which ran on CBS from 1954 to 1955 and featured a rotation of Frank Lovejoy, Pat O'Brien, Dennis Morgan, and George Brent, among others. This program was succeeded by *Star and the Story,* syndicated in 1955 and hosted by Henry Fonda. Profits from these programs were then funneled back into more production.

Wisely, these profits were spent on popular genres and prominent stars. As the industry began to shift from anthology drama to filmed Westerns, adventure series, and domestic sitcoms, Four Star followed. To bridge this transition, Dick Powell cleverly launched a Western anthology program in 1956, *Dick Powell's Zane Grey Theater* (CBS, 1956–62). The company followed with a sitcom for CBS called *Hey, Jeannie,* which ran from 1956 to 1960, and an ABC adventure show, *Wire Service* (1956–59). The latter program drew its stars by once again borrowing from *Four Star Playhouse*'s shrewd scheduling practices, presenting a rotating cast featuring film actors Dane Clark, George Brent, and Mercedes McCambridge. Four Star began to develop a reputation among film stars as a safe place to try out series television; television critic John Crosby praised the company for being "a bellwether in leading top movie names to embrace television." In fact, the notion that Powell could cast anyone he wanted with just a phone call became a standard item in publicity on the star-producer. Robert Taylor claimed that his friend Powell sold him on the Four Star–produced *Detectives*, and Hal Humphrey wrote, "The success of *Zane Grey Theater* may in large part be due to Dick's ability to snag the cream of the guest stars. He can call Joan Crawford direct and say, 'Honey, how about it?'"[54]

While such casual casting may have indeed existed in some measure, formal ties between Four Star and William Morris certainly enhanced the roster of performers. William Morris struggled to compete with larger counterpart MCA, especially because MCA had received a special Screen Actors Guild waiver—allegedly pushed through by SAG president and MCA client Ronald Reagan—that allowed it to operate both as a talent representative and a production company, despite the conflict of interest evident in such a configuration. This arrangement enabled MCA to create shows for its own talent and thereby dominate the television schedule, whereas William Morris and other agencies remained barred from this dual option and had to find more inventive means to get their talent on the air. One solution for William Morris was to partner with Four Star Productions. By the late 1950s, most of Four Star Production's featured stars were William Morris clients, Dick Powell associates, or both, including established film actors like Tom Ewell (*The Tom Ewell Show*, CBS, 1960–61), and June Allyson (*The June Allyson Show*, CBS, 1959–61), who not coincidentally was also married to Dick Powell. Conversely, William Morris used Four Star to develop new talent. For instance, the agency arranged a guest star spot for client Steve McQueen on Four Star's *Trackdown* (CBS, 1957–59) in March 1958 and then packaged a new show for Four Star to produce for McQueen, *Wanted: Dead or Alive* (CBS, 1958–61). This relationship with William Morris surely increased Four Star's institutional credibility and its ability to attract stars both old and new.[55]

Four Star Productions also enhanced the careers of its star-owners, and for Niven and Powell especially, it illustrated how beneficial TV could be for stars who had previously fought against the restrictive supremacy of the Hollywood studios. Dick Powell had gained fame in a 1930s cycle of musicals for Warner Bros. and then left the studio when he could not break out of the crooner mold. A brief stay at Paramount granted little else, and when the studio passed him over for the lead in the 1944 noir thriller *Double Indemnity* (it went to Fred MacMurray), he exited. Subsequently, RKO offered Powell the part of detective Phillip Marlowe in *Murder, My Sweet* (1944), and his career was renewed. In his new persona as a tough guy, Powell subsequently starred in *Cornered* (1945), *Johnny O'Clock* (1947), and *Pitfall* (1948). His career on radio also echoed these changes, as he performed in such 1940s radio dramas as *Rogue's Gallery* (Mutual, 1945–46) and *Richard Diamond, Private Detective* (NBC, ABC, 1949–1952), which actually incorporated Powell's singing background. While Powell appreciated these opportunities to complicate his crooner image, he also feared that he was simply trading one typecast persona for another and that his film career was not progressing.[56]

Even so, Powell was initially hesitant about making the move to television. He told critic Hal Humphrey in November 1951 that he was not interested in the new medium: "TV is too much of a mishmash now, and I don't want to run the risk of getting caught up in one of these stinkers that I see on my own TV set." These sound like the words of a star who would avoid television for a number of years; yet Powell appeared on *Four Star Playhouse* less than a year later. Nonetheless, he would continue to disparage television throughout the remainder of his career. In 1953, Powell reiterated the notions that only movie actors who were unemployed would do television and that a series should be avoided at all costs: "If you're seen in any medium too often the public tires of your face. I wouldn't accept 39 consecutive weeks of TV unless they gave me a five-year guarantee with it." *Four Star Playhouse*'s rotating anthology mode resolved Powell's concern about overexposure, but his ongoing battles with the networks and industry trends that marginalized independent production companies like Four Star frustrated him. In a 1962 *TV Guide* interview, Powell criticized just about everything in contemporary television, to the extent that interviewer Bill Davidson penned, "In our breakfast conversation Powell bespoke so many other heresies that were it not for the opulence of our surroundings I would have thought I was attending a TV revolutionists' meeting presided over by FCC Chairman Newton Minow with David Susskind as the sergeant-at-arms." Perhaps because of his concerns about his place in network-dominated television production, Powell strove to keep a viable film career across the 1950s, albeit one exclusively behind the camera. At work on the ill-fated RKO film *The Conqueror* (1956),

Powell told *Variety* that he would leave television and devote his career to the production of motion pictures with RKO if the film were a success. Unfortunately, it was a box office flop. Powell did subsequently begin a seven-picture contract in 1956 to direct for Fox but only completed *The Enemy Below* (1957) and *The Hunters* (1958).[57]

Despite his frustration with the challenges of independent television production in an age of increasing network authority, Powell's television career achieved heights of success that his film production endeavors never approached. Former Four Star executive Burt Rosen has lamented that few at the time recognized, or have since recognized, Powell's level of business insight: "In television, Dick was king, but he never got that kind of credit. . . . [He] turned out to be the epitome of what a television executive, a studio executive, was, should be and will ever be." Historian Mark Alvey even comments that Powell "was a more successful producer of motion pictures—for the small screen—than any of the old-line Hollywood studios. One wonders what Jack Warner must have thought."[58]

Like Powell, David Niven suffered from repetitive roles during the studio era and then a late 1940s career lull, primarily due to his advancing age limiting his ability to convincingly continue in his specialty: the roguish playboy lead in romantic comedies. Niven also yearned for the production control that Four Star Productions afforded. Biographer Sheridan Morley claimed that Niven had always envied the actor who was in a position to produce his own work, if only because it "meant that he had somewhere to work whenever he chose to do so." This belief in production control as a career safety net likely grew out of his frustrations with the exclusivity of the studio system. The *Los Angeles Times* quoted his reaction to Louis B. Mayer's threat that by doing television, Niven could expect never to work at MGM again: "Didn't seem terribly important at the time because nobody was offering me any work in his studio." With *Four Star Playhouse,* Niven himself would dictate when, where, and on what projects he would work.[59]

In the latter regard, producer status meant that Niven now had the autonomy to try to break away from his entrenched film persona. While this persona largely remained attached to him both before and after his television appearances, Niven appreciated *Four Star Playhouse*'s modular format and the freedom to choose his own scripts, which at least opened up the possibility for a wider range of portrayals. He told the *Los Angeles Times* in 1955 that the anthology program

*Dick Powell oversees production on
the set of* Four Star Playhouse *in 1953.
Wife June Allyson is seated behind him.
CBS/Photofest.*

provided him with "[g]ood juicy parts an actor can get his teeth into. None of these stereotyped boy-meets-girl parts. An actor in the movies or on the stage is lucky if he gets a good role every few years. I've played more than a dozen this year."[60]

In fact, Niven believed that television truly saved his acting career by granting him opportunities that he never could have gotten from Hollywood in the early 1950s. In an article purportedly written by Niven in 1956, the actor pinpointed with great passion what *Four Star Playhouse* did for him as an actor. It is worth quoting at length:

> About four years ago I took a good look at [my career] and was exceedingly depressed by what I saw—a performer in what is tactfully described as 'the middle thirties' still wandering vaguely about the screen with a cup of tea in one hand and a duchess in the other. . . . I was fast approaching that "no-man's-land" through which all actors

A Four Star publicity still highlights the diversity of David Niven's portrayals on Four Star Playhouse. *Niven earned an Emmy nomination for "The Answer," pictured on the bottom left.* CBS/Photofest.

must some day pass when they feel down the back of their necks the hot sticky breath of leading men in their early twenties, and from where they see a solid phalanx of well-established character actors blocking their path in front. Believe me, that is no place to hang around very long in company with a cup of fast cooling tea and an aging duchess. To coin a phrase and further mix the metaphors— *Television has saved my bacon.* When Charles Boyer, Dick Powell and I formed the Four Star Playhouse four years ago, filmed television was very much in its infancy and the noises directed at us by many big shots in the movie industry were chilling in the extreme; it was mentioned quite casually but much too often for comfort that we could expect to see very little of the inside of the film studios from now on if we were intent on deserting to the enemy. I don't know why Powell and Boyer pressed on so bravely in the face of all this, but I know only too well why Niven did—he was caught in the middle of "no-man's-land" with his bank balance down and had to make an agonizing re-appraisal with the greatest possible dispatch. 63

It is impossible to discern if Niven truly wrote these words or if a publicist or agent created them, but the sentiments expressed echo those written in his autobiography and declared in interviews. Regardless of their origin, these remarks are a testament to the calculated impression propagated repeatedly by Four Star publicity: this television company granted a film star total freedom to express himself, and such autonomy was well worth any repercussions of petty vengeance that might reverberate from Hollywood.[61]

Niven's rhetoric regarding the diverse parts supplied by *Four Star Playhouse*, however, seems hyperbolic: when one studies most of the episodes he appeared in, the majority merely replicated parts similar to his romantic comedy film roles. Even so, a number of episodes did allow Niven to stretch beyond the confines of his persona and display his acting range. Niven earned an Emmy nomination for the December 1954 episode "The Answer," in which he played a drunken vagrant who enters a bar, ranting that he has written a great play that could save humanity, if only people would listen. Such performances in turn regained the attention of Hollywood, and he subsequently experienced the biggest success of his career with the MGM-distributed *Separate Tables* (1958), which earned him an Academy Award for Best Actor.

This was an important personal achievement for Niven, and it also led to a milestone for television after Niven returned to the medium to host another Four Star anthology program, *The David Niven Show* (ABC, 1959). As the *Los Angeles Times* announced:

> When David Niven last Monday night accepted the Oscar for the best motion picture performance by an actor in 1958 and on the next night bowed in on TV's little screen as the host of a new series of half-hour dramas, there was a sort of double-barreled symbolism involved that might well make a footnote to the changing history of Hollywood.[62]

The scenario of a film actor walking off the Academy Award stage and onto a television series would have been unthinkable only a few years earlier. Clearly, the film industry did not blackball Niven for appearing on television and, conversely, Niven did not shun television once he regained a foothold in the film industry. He may have been a unique case; as actress Lauren Bacall put it: "he remains the only leading actor I have ever known whose career was totally revived and turned around as a result of television." Still, the trajectory of his career suggests that, contrary

64

to what many have assumed, by the late 1950s, stars could indeed move with relative freedom between film and television. To paraphrase Mark Alvey, one wonders what Louis B. Mayer must have thought.[63]

Actually, Jack Warner and Louis B. Mayer would have had to be impressed at the success of Four Star Productions, which had assets valued at $25 million by 1960 and was recognized by *Variety* in that year as one of the "Big 4" prime-time telefilm suppliers, along with Warner Bros., Revue Productions, and Screen Gems. The future of the company also seemed bright; Four Star went public with a stock sale in August 1960, planned to venture into feature filmmaking in the early 1960s, and expanded its syndication catalogue by buying up Marterto Productions in 1961.[64]

With so preeminent a position in the early 1960s, it is curious that only a few years later Four Star was nearing insolvency, with only a few first-run shows on television and virtually all of its contract talent gone. Although one might assume that Four Star was marginalized by the continued growth of network control over prime-time programming and syndication, Mark Alvey has shown that many independent companies still thrived in the 1960s and 1970s. Instead, it is likely that the death of Dick Powell from cancer in 1963 dealt the heaviest blow to the company's fortunes; he had been both the public face of the company and its strongest leader. June Allyson claimed that she lobbied for one of the company's standout creative talents—Aaron Spelling—to take over; given how Spelling's television career later turned out, such a move likely would have saved the company. But former ad agency executive Thomas J. McDermott took the helm instead and, according to Burt Rosen, ran the company into the ground. Rosen said of the period immediately after Powell's death, "People started leaving, shows started getting cancelled." And Charles Boyer noted in 1972, "Unfortunately, when Dick Powell died, it was no longer the same—he was adored by the sponsors and the networks." With Powell no longer at the helm, Four Star withered.[65]

But the prosperity of Four Star Productions across the 1950s illustrates how a group of well-known film actors with a measure of business acumen could forge new careers for themselves on television in the 1950s. By accommodating star talent with such benefits as production control, flexible scheduling, and profit participation, Four Star attained a status that attracted even more talent. The creative freedom facilitated by *Four Star Playhouse*'s production setup also enabled its stars to benefit heavily from publicity that constantly emphasized the power and prestige represented by their positions in the company. The rhetorical power of the latter indicates one of the substantial benefits of a relationship to television for 1950s film actors: the image of a career on the downturn could be counteracted by the image of a career on the upturn owing to increased authorial responsibility and substantial production control behind the camera. And by perceptively exploiting the economics of the industry, anticipating industry trends, and establishing relationships with other production companies and a major talent agency, the former film star–members of Four Star Productions made a considerable mark in television. With an estate worth more than one million dollars upon his death, Dick Powell was without question one of the most successful established film stars on 1950s television. The fact that his achievements were more the result of his actions behind the camera than in front of it indicates that the impact of film stars on 1950s television was not always directly visible on the screen.[66]

The crossover trends described in this chapter not only affected television programming and film star employment; they also had the potential to alter the structural mechanisms of the star system and even the fundamental mythologies of stardom that the film industry had systematically cultivated for decades. Character actors like Alan Mowbray and Eve Arden, who had always been supporting players in movies, were now placed center stage in sitcoms, overturning long-established hierarchies of stardom. Stars like Ronald Colman and Betty Hutton, who had developed larger-than-life personae on the big screen, now carried those images into similar roles on sitcoms but portrayed them on small, grainy, black-and-white boxes in America's living rooms in between— and sometimes even during—commercials. Stars with carefully constructed, cohesive star identities, like Humphrey Bogart and Ginger Rogers, went on *The Jack Benny Show* and acted in skits that mocked those identities, drawing attention to their contrived simplicity. Figures like Charles Boyer and Bette Davis, whose stardom had been defined by their distance and eminence, were now made to appear accessible and ordinary in cameo appearances on sitcoms like *I Love Lucy* or on talk shows like *This is Your Life* (NBC, 1952–61), where both film stars and everyday citizens were given virtually the same treatment.

Moreover, the career extensions that television enabled meant that the graying of classical film's matinee idols, which the film industry worked to keep offscreen, was brought to the forefront by TV. As scholar Susan Hayward has described, the aging of stars, especially of actresses, destroys the mirage of deific perfection built up by star publicity; she writes, "ageing is too real—not the 'real' we want to see."[67] And after the major studios released their pre-1948 film libraries to television in the mid-1950s, that deviant reality was constantly juxtaposed on TV schedules against the illusion of transcendence that these stars had embodied in their classical heydays. No viewer could watch Bette Davis in her 1958 appearance on *General Electric Theater* and in a televised airing of 1942's *Now Voyager* without recognizing the genuine fallibility of even the most exalted of movie stars.

These circumstances meant that while a television viewer in the 1950s could find many Hollywood film actors on television, she still would not often see the highest tier of stars in her living room. The stigma lingered that television work simply was not appropriate for an elite film star. Said an MCA representative about Ingrid Bergman and Marilyn Monroe, "[T]hese stars shouldn't appear on television. They are too big and important. Such exposure would only dilute [their public image]." And an unnamed producer warned *TV Guide* about Bette Davis's intention to move to television: "Bette's too high-voltage for TV. . . . Who can match her scene for scene? Put her in a two-shot and you can't see anybody else on the screen." Similarly, early fan magazines persistently circulated the notion that television required natural performers and that the excessive glamour of film stars was in fact too superficial and artificial for the intimate and domestic medium of television. An anonymous author in the fan magazine *Radio Stars and Television* speculated in 1949 on the potential television success of certain Hollywood actresses, theorizing that "Rita [Hayworth]'s super-glamour will not click with a home audience that demands more than mere beauty. However, Eve Arden, who has been movie-typed as a warhorse, is a television natural, as she combines beauty with natural charm and wit."[68]

Significantly, this article defines film stardom in a negative vein: Hayworth apparently had nothing but "mere beauty" to offer to television audiences, while Eve Arden's television stardom was counterposed as a positive, genuine representation unfettered by contrived "super-glamour." This distinction has great relevance for the next chapter, which includes an in-depth look at Faye Emerson, a former Warner Bros. actress frequently lauded for the glamour she brought to television. How exactly was Emerson's glamour appropriate for television in a way that Rita Hayworth's supposedly was not? And how did the fundamental differences between film and television as they were developing across the 1950s come to affect which stars were likely to succeed and which were not? Did faces, voices, and personalities "read" differently on the small screen versus the big screen? The answers may well lie in the genres that were responsible for fostering the first indigenous broadcast stars: the presentational modes of the talk show, the game show, and the variety show.

CHAPTER 2
FAYE EMERSON
AND THE EARLY
TELEVISION
PERSONALITY

When one thinks of the definitive stars of 1950s television, names like Milton Berle, Jack Benny, Dinah Shore, Arthur Godfrey, Arlene Francis, Sid Caesar, and Ed Sullivan come to mind. All of these figures were beloved by Americans during the 1950s, yet none of them found any traction on the big screen. The ineffability of media stardom and the unpredictability of entertainment success make it impractical to isolate a singular reason why these stars were successful minimally in cinema yet substantially so in broadcasting. It can be acknowledged, however, that despite their disparate personalities and styles, each of these artists excelled at presentational modes of performance in hosting programs within early television's unique genres of variety-comedy and talk. These performance methods were imperative for television stardom in the medium's earliest days.

In *Hitch Your Antenna To the Stars,* an exceptional analysis of broadcast stardom, Susan Murray outlines some of the fundamental qualities that defined early commercial broadcasting stardom, particularly in the omnipresent "vaudeo" arena of the televised variety show. She argues that while the concept of personal authenticity was central to both film and TV stardom of this period, it was more overtly mobilized in screen performances on television than in feature films, where the paramount qualities of spectacularity and inaccessibility onscreen drove audiences to theaters and magazine racks to consume star images on a regular basis. In contrast, the domestic and commercial base of television, and the direct-address mode of the variety show specifically, required its featured entertainers to exhibit connotations of naturalness and sincerity during performances—especially in order for hosts to engender the trust necessary to pitch products to audiences in their living rooms. In turn, TV capitalized on medium-specific associations of authenticity to engender performative sincerity. Murray writes:

> [W]ithin the context of the discourses that constructed television's aesthetic, television viewers were encouraged to believe that they could actually locate the true personality of a television star somewhere within his or her performance. In fact, this belief might have been stimulated by the popular rhetoric on television's intrinsic aesthetics and the "naturalness" from its spontaneity that television performers displayed. In other words, because television was said to produce intimacy, immediacy and spontaneity, it also generated authentic identities.

This is not to say that intimacy and immediacy were essentialist, inevitable qualities of the technology of live television, but that these features could be readily evoked and exploited to the new medium's advantage, especially with regard to performers and their impression of presence.

Because special qualities were called for to command viewer attention, television stars still shared with film stars a certain combination of the ordinary and extraordinary. But, more so than for film stars, ordinariness was fundamental to screen performance for early television stars. Murray quotes an advertising agency study's conclusions from 1954 that TV's ideal personalities for delivering commercial messages, the bottom-line function of hosting, "are those who present themselves as human and fallible, who by their identification with consumers induce the consumer to identify himself with them. . . . Such personality is reassuringly like you or me, or like our husbands or wives. And the product becomes more believably identified with real human needs." This is an overstatement; one doubts that any viewer's spouse was quite like Milton Berle. But the key point is that the performative skills of television's nascent talent were directed toward fostering in the audience a sense of an intimate, personal connection with star power and the entertainment world. Television analyst Leo Bogart described this sense aptly in 1956: "[T]he quality of direct and intimate contact . . . is carefully nurtured by skillful performers. This very illusion of personal communication with a glamorous, famous personality gives the broadcast media much of their appeal."[1]

This personality ideal was not created by simply placing dynamic entertainers in front of a camera and having them act as they would naturally. A convincing expression of unpretentiousness essentially qualified within early television as a systematic mode of performance, yet it still required the calculated construction of a star image in order to resonate with audiences. These dual demands emerge strikingly in Murray's analysis of Arthur Godfrey, whose popularity declined after a scandal complicated the mythology of warmth and genuineness that had been built into his persona. Murray argues that the popular talk and variety show host had previously "*appeared* untainted by the machinations of celebrity, wealth, and (ironically) the commercial trappings of the broadcast industry" through a humble, down-to-earth manner and a consummate ability to affably mock the contrivances of product pitching while still lending credibility to the featured products. But an awkward on-air dismissal of a performer in 1953 was followed by numerous press exposés claiming that Godfrey was in reality an egotistical tyrant who perpetrated a simulated act of congeniality onstage whilst berating his associates behind the scenes. Those who subsequently shunned Godfrey were said to be outraged more by his evident insincerity toward audiences than his sour disposition.[2]

Murray's characterization of early television stardom in presentational genres prompts intriguing questions regarding film actors who forged careers in television. If ordinariness was quintessential for television talent, how might a crossover film star's prior elevated status be recuperated by the upstart medium? What qualities of stars' images would transfer from their film to television work, and what qualities would be either downplayed or accentuated? Were certain film actors more suited to television's presentational and representational practices than others? How did these patterns vary across different genres and develop as early television matured into a standardized mass medium? While these questions will be attended to across the entirety of the book, I shall begin this chapter by specifically addressing the role of the presentational host in non-narrative genres during the initial years of commercial television, where qualities of the ordinary and the authentic were most foundational. I shall then focus on Faye Emerson, a former Warner Bros. contract player who became the paradigmatic "personality" of early television.

"HOLLYWOOD'S ANSWER TO THE HOME ECONOMICS TEACHER"

Despite the markedly different styles of performers like Milton Berle and Jack Benny, these stars were unified by their personas of affable accessibility and their skillful employment of both verbal and visual comedy. Early live television's reliance on visuality and spontaneity favored this style of performance and its roots in vaudeville-based entertainment. It is ironic, however, that a medium basing itself on visuality generally showcased male stars who looked older, less handsome, and less virile than their film counterparts. Apparently central to their functions as living room–entertainers and product spokesmen was the need for these figures to appear "human and fallible" to viewers while artfully displaying their proficiencies at live performance and improvisation. These qualities were not necessarily called for in film work; accordingly, there was not an abundance of variety show hosts drawn from the film industry. Those who were, including *Colgate Comedy Hour* hosts Donald O'Connor and Bud Abbott and Lou Costello, as well as Jack Carson (*All Star Revue*, NBC, 1950–52) and Don Ameche (*Don Ameche's Musical Playhouse*, ABC, 1951), had ample backgrounds in vaudeville entertainment and musical theater. Similarly, Bob Hope, who never had a series but hosted numerous variety specials across the 1950s, started in vaudeville and had mastered a self-conscious, quip-heavy, mugging style of comedy in his films that was easily adaptable to broadcasting's presentational standards.[3]

Although they had some presence in variety-comedy hosting, male film stars more commonly helmed quiz and panel shows, which typically featured an emcee and a handful of panelists who all displayed their wit in answering questions, discussing topics, or interrogating guests. The quasi-intellectual milieu of such shows drew from the higher cultural status of film stars, especially those with accomplished oral skills, such as hosts Basil Rathbone (*Your Lucky Clue*, CBS, 1952) and Conrad Nagel (*Celebrity Time*, ABC and CBS, 1949–52), and panelist Sir Cedric Hardwicke (*Who Pays*, CBS, 1959). Here the point was not to fill the television frame with visual antics but to enchant the audience with verbal dexterity and creative wordplay.

Few were more masterly at this than Groucho Marx. Radio producer John Guedel, impressed by Marx's ad-libbing during an appearance on *The Pepsodent Radio Show Starring Bob Hope*, developed *You Bet Your Life* in 1947 specifically for the comedian, whose film career had sputtered. The show was a popular and critical hit, netting Marx a prestigious Peabody Award for comedy performance in 1948; after a bidding

*You Bet Your Life's
Groucho Marx
and the secret
word "duck."
NBC/Photofest.*

war won by NBC, it moved to television in 1950, where it remained on Thursday nights until 1961. More a comedic showcase than a true quiz program, *You Bet Your Life* presented Marx interrogating guests, responding to their answers with his customary trenchant wit, and then proceeding to ask trivia questions for modest prizes. The show also melded production techniques; an hourlong rough cut was assembled from a multicamera film shoot before a live studio audience, and then that material was edited down to a half-hour program for broadcast. This process ensured that only the best material would air; it also gave Marx free rein to let interviews meander down intriguing, sometimes even risqué paths, knowing that inappropriate or unfunny material could be pared out later.

As such, *You Bet Your Life* capitalized upon both the deliberate oversight enabled by film production and the energy and spontaneity of live production. This combination was a perfect vehicle for Marx's comedy skills, as he expertly guided the guest and audience interplay and wowed audiences with his seemingly instantaneous witticisms. While some of this material was written out beforehand, Marx could deliver a scripted line as convincingly as an ad lib, a talent ideally suited to the show and to early television's fusion of simulated and real spontaneity.

Many of Marx's performative affectations for the show were anchored in his film persona, from his trademark cigar and moustache to his good-natured putdowns and leering at female guests. Nonetheless, even though his asides to the camera recalled his direct-address tendencies from features, Marx adopted a more nuanced performance style for the show that contrasted with his frenetic work in features. Rather than playing the instigating clown as he had among his brothers, here he acted as the bemused moderator. *Time* magazine provided an eloquent description of his more subdued gestural posturing for television in 1951: "the perfectly timed twitch of the brows; the play of the luminous brown eyes—now rolling with naughty thoughts, now staring through the spectacles with only half-amused contempt; the acidulous, faint smile; the touch of fuming disgust in the voice; above all, the effrontery." Such visual subtleties came across solidly in the medium close-ups of Marx that dominated the otherwise static multicamera show, and they likely led the audience at home to feel a comfortable rapport with Marx. The end result of these performative elements was enormous popularity for Marx across the 1950s; as biographer Stefan Kanfer writes, "At an age when many men were collecting Social Security payments, Groucho found himself more celebrated than he had been as a movie star."[4]

Female stars, whether from the film world or indigenous to broadcasting, were not so pervasive as men were in hosting positions on variety and game shows. Dismissive patriarchal attitudes toward female intellect and authority mitigated against their headlining presence in the latter genre, while cultural discomfort with women in exhibitionist comedic performances limited their hosting of vaudeo shows. In both cases, the boundaries for what qualities would be considered acceptably authentic, ordinary, and extraordinary for female performers were heavily constrained by the cultural and commercial demands of television (including the fact that networks and sponsors heavily targeted the lucrative middle-class female audience). Lynn Spigel's *Make Room for TV,* about the introduction of television culture into the American home, offers just such a characterization in its analyses of daytime magazine shows. Spigel shows how producers appealed to the middle-class housewife through the "mixing of upper-class fantasy with tropes of averageness," with the hostess addressing the viewer on her own level while encouraging consumer behavior. She quotes one producer from the period:

Those who give an impression of superiority or "talking down" to the audience, who treasure the manner of speaking over naturalness and meaningful communication . . . or who are overly formal in attire and manners, do not survive in the broadcast industry. . . . The personality should fit right into your living room.

Spigel concludes that producers preferred the average-looking woman: "[T]he ideal hostess was decidedly not a glamour girl, but rather a pleasingly attractive, middle-aged woman—Hollywood's answer to the home economics teacher."[5]

As this quote implies, glamorous Hollywood actresses were thought to be incompatible with the demands of commercial television, and such publicity emphasized a rhetorical difference between the contrived, constructed, excessive image of the Hollywood actress and the genuine, sincere, natural image of the television performer. In a 1949 *Radio Stars and Television* article entitled "Glamour is the bunk!" author Harry Conover described the success of an actress whose "natural personality came over the screen with that wonderful wholesome charm that is a 'must' for tomorrow's Miss Television." According to Conover and others, this element was expected to limit the prospects for the Hollywood star on television. For instance, an article in the fan magazine *Radio Stars and Television* asked the question, "Is Hollywood Doomed?" Written by an anonymous "prominent Hollywood figure," the 1949 article quoted a "veteran radio producer":

Lana [Turner] will be practically helpless in television. I'll tell you why. The carefully nurtured and artificial dramatic quality of a girl like Lana doesn't click with average viewers sitting at home. Televiewers look for a more intimate, natural, homey kind of performance. Glamour alone won't click. Remember that television comes right into the home and sort of joins the family . . . the gentle, personal pathos of Cass [Daley] is eminently more suited to televiewers than Lana Turner's glamour.

In a similar vein, Conover observed in *Variety* in 1950 that the "zooming television industry is beckoning to its screens a whole new roster of girls who can register zestful, natural vivacity rather than static beauty."[6]

Such qualities marked the preeminent female stars of presentational genres, the so-called femcees of early television who hosted daytime and prime-time variety and talk shows. *Newsweek* described the femcee figure in 1954 as television's "one original contribution. . . . She is, or at least tries to be, calm, witty, incisive, reassuring, personable, and more-or-less sexy. Above all, she is a girl who can smile at that bright red light on the TV camera and keep talking (and smiling, if possible) as long as it shines." These women had to be attractive but not overwhelmingly so, they had to be self-effacing yet still authoritative, and they had to align themselves with the middle-class audience, not the distant world of glamour and celebrity.[7]

Dinah Shore was an archetypal femcee. In her study of Shore, Lola Clare Bratten observes that prior to hosting her first series (*The Dinah Shore Show*, NBC, 1951–57), the singer tried out for the lead role in the 1951 MGM musical *Show Boat* but was passed over in favor of Ava Gardner. While Shore had the better singing voice by far, Brattan writes, Shore's "natural girl-next-door looks could not withstand the competition from more beautiful stars as the film screen's room-sized close-ups showed." Film technology enabled the dubbing of Gardner's voice, but it could not lend Shore a larger cinematic presence. On the other hand, it was live television technology that enabled Shore's small-screen magnetism. As Brattan argues: "Her suitability as a television star was not only the result of her talent but, just as importantly, her ability to appear natural and relaxed on the small screen of 1950s television and within the confines of its cumbersome technology."[8]

A *TV Guide* feature on Shore similarly stressed that it was Shore's inimitable ability to be herself on camera that was responsible for her success. In this piece, Bob Banner, executive producer for *The Dinah Shore Chevy Show* (NBC, 1956–63), said, "You never have to invent a character for Dinah because on television, intimate medium that it is, what you *are* comes through." And director Bill Asher in the same feature asserted, "With Dinah, it's not just a performance; it's especially for you. And that's a quality you just can't manufacture." Of course, as noted earlier, these qualities most certainly could be and were manufactured, and they had to be especially carefully negotiated for female hosts, given their potentially transgressive positions of power. Shore put forth a careful capitulation of her authority to the *Saturday Evening Post* in 1957: "I know one thing: nobody, man or woman, likes a domineering female. I select guest stars for my show who are so strongly masculine that I can't possibly overshadow them. I think it very important for me not to sacrifice any femininity that I may have on TV. To

76

me, there's nothing more unattractive than a woman who's lost sight of the fact that first of all she's a woman." Unquestionably, any woman acting as herself on television could not afford to lose sight of this fact.[9]

The unfeigned personability that Shore evinced often extended to her film star guests. As a case in point, a May 1958 episode of *The Dinah Shore Chevy Show* presented guest stars Ginger Rogers and Ida Lupino mocking both star pretension and publicity attempts to make stars seem both ordinary and extraordinary. The featured skit involved fellow guest stars Elaine May and Mike Nichols posing as fan magazine reporters doing a piece on Shore, Lupino, and Rogers for the "Women's Touch" section of *Widescreen Magazine.* May and Nichols intend to profile the stars' domestic talents—Ginger supposedly makes her own clothes, Ida is a whiz at housekeeping, and Dinah is a great cook— stressing that the three stars can perform these fundamentally ordinary tasks in spectacular fashion. In trying to come up with a title for the piece, Nichols suggests "Just Plain Folks," but May reminds him that they already used that title for a piece on Zsa Zsa Gabor. Extending this theme of the laughable falsities of publicity, we see that none of the stars have any skill at their supposed talents. Shore puts a cake into the washing machine, Rogers merely tosses fabrics around, and Lupino rests in fine jewelry and furs without a clue of how to clean the house, though she points out that she does have her garbage gift-wrapped: "In Beverly Hills, they won't pick it up any other way." Similarly, after Shore contorts herself into a uncomfortable glamour-girl pose for the photographer, May absurdly responds, "That's what we want, the real Dinah Shore."

In such a manner, episodes like this projected Shore and her film star guests as unassuming folk more at home with mocking their publicity images than embodying them. Similarly, television was by extension showcased as a place for the stars to escape the pompous aura of the film world, thereby allowing audiences to feel as if they were part of an insider culture. Of course, these portrayals were themselves contrived constructions that drew from the same well of image manipulation that film publicity did. Even so, they served a distinct purpose in allowing television to pose itself as a unique medium in comparison to film and in granting stars the opportunity to foster intimate connections with television viewers.

While Dinah Shore's appeal was based on her low-key, all-American personality, her equally successful colleague Arlene Francis was more identified with the urbane sophistication and elegance of a New York socialite. As such, Francis blurred the line between the television everywoman and the star who was supposedly too grandiloquent for the medium. Francis was everywhere in the mid-1950s: on television at least six hours every week via the daily daytime *Home* show (NBC, 1954–57), the prime-time *Talent Patrol* (ABC, 1953–55) and the quiz show *What's My Line?* and on the covers of *TV Guide, Look,* and *Newsweek.* Her television persona was shaped most strongly by her panelist duties on *What's My Line?* where she joined columnist Dorothy Kilgallen and humorist and publisher Bennett Cerf as a panelist nearly every Sunday night from the show's inception in 1950 until its end in 1967. From the witty repartee of its panelists to their formal wear, *What's My Line?* carried an air of New York refinement. Rather than serving to alienate audiences as television spread across the nation in the 1950s, these qualities were complemented by an informal cordiality among its participants that acted as middle America's personal invitation to this social world. Francis's own steadfast charm played a key role here. In addition to her "cultivated high polish," television scholars Marsha Cassidy and Mimi White argue, Francis was popular because of her "ad-lib wordplay, her reputation for down-to-earth charm, and her easy sense of humor," and she "excelled on television precisely because she did not come across as a snob." She also was not glamorous in either her looks or her comportment. *Newsweek's* 1954 profile of Francis framed this in terms of the typical medium-specific division: "She is not beautiful, a fact that kept her from making a splash in Hollywood."[10]

It was this intriguing collection of personal qualities that led NBC's Pat Weaver to greenlight Francis as a host for *Home,* the midday companion to *Today* (1952–present) and *Tonight* (1953–present). Weaver had high aspirations for this magazine program, which he envisioned as an upper-middlebrow alternative to typical daytime fare as part of his wider attempts to bring cultured fare to the masses through television. Francis had the attributes of accessible sophistication suited to such purposes. What resulted, however, was an awkward mix of homemaking tips and product demonstrations with reports on public affairs and interviews with civic leaders, and transitory allusions to female empowerment tangled with the constant linkage of womanhood to consumerism. These conflicting elements reverberated in Arlene Francis's star persona, as well. Even prior to her work on *Home,* Francis was publicized contradictorily as both a devoted wife and mother and a politically astute career woman. The intellect and verbal acuity that she displayed on *What's My Line?* further marked her as a potentially disruptive person. These factors stood out even more awkwardly in the daytime world of *Home,* and such dissonance in both show and star would help to explain *Home's* short life relative to its long-running siblings.[11]

Nonetheless, Francis continued to carefully calibrate her image such that she was able to maintain her active career on television after *Home's* demise. The nightclub atmosphere of *What's My Line?* accommodated her distinctive identity, but NBC even gave her a second chance at daytime with the chatty *Arlene Francis Show* (NBC, 1957–58). She was able to sustain her career despite a potentially transgressive image largely because of her overall resignation to the period's primary standards of femininity, from her elegantly simple attire to the suppression of her political viewpoints. Francis closed her memoirs with a regretful acknowledgment of the latter, in the wake of interpreting a recurrent dream about being unable to find a telephone with a mouthpiece: "In a flash of understanding, I realized how deeply my inability to express myself without becoming apprehensive about what 'they' might think had affected me. In short, my 'don't make waves' philosophy had inhibited my life to an incalculable extent, for in my desire to keep things peaceful all the time, I had forgotten that a few waves are necessary to keep the water from becoming stagnant."[12]

These thoughts, as well as the general descriptions above of the qualities of presentational stardom on early television, point the way toward the career of talk show host and quiz show panelist Faye Emerson. Named *Variety's* Top TV Star of 1950, Emerson was described by television host Garry Moore in that same year as "next to Milton Berle, the big name in television." She never approached Berle's heights of popularity and viewer devotion, but Emerson was among the most prolific and popular of early stars on television. Her TV career began in 1948 with a hosting role on a local New York program, *Paris Cavalcade of Fashions,* and she subsequently achieved national fame in the early 1950s with *The Faye Emerson Show* (CBS, ABC, NBC, 1950–51), a fifteen-minute interview program, and *Faye Emerson's Wonderful Town* (CBS, 1951–52), a half-hour variety show. Following those programs, she became a regular quiz show panelist on *I've Got a Secret* and *What's in a Word* (CBS, 1954) and a discussion moderator on such shows as *Author Meets the Critics* (NBC, ABC, DUM, 1948–54). The latter programs indicate Emerson's more cerebral attributes, but her mind was not her most publicized asset: her cleavage was. Indeed, the low-cut evening gowns she wore when hosting programs brought her national fame, as well as ample critical attention. Her son William later claimed, "When a cartoon showed a small TV screen containing only a V neckline, the reader knew who was being talked about."[13]

This considerable fame was bracketed by periods of comparable failure for Emerson. Her substantial, nearly overnight success on television followed a pedestrian four-year film career in Hollywood, in which Emerson floundered in a series of undistinguished roles. Correspondingly, despite her early 1950s fame, Emerson disappeared from the entertainment landscape just a decade later in large part due to transgressive elements of her image. Why was Emerson a failure in 1940s Hollywood but a blazing success as a femcee on early 1950s television? How, like Arlene Francis, did she successfully conform her intellectual and socialite status to medium and audience demands but, unlike Francis, fail to sustain that success? How does the overall trajectory of her television career, from the pinnacle of television stardom in 1951 to limited visibility in 1961, reflect developments in early television's history, as well as changing opportunities for film performers on television's presentational genres? The answers to these question will highlight both the industrial conditions that made possible such pioneering moves to television by film actors and the standards of performance that television was beginning to formulate in its earliest years.

FOUR YEARS AT WARNER BROS.: "IMPOSSIBLE TO TYPE!"

Faye Emerson signed a standard option contract with Warner Bros. in 1941 and inaugurated her acting career with a string of bit parts in pictures like *Bad Men of Missouri, Manpower,* and *Nine Lives are Not Enough,* all released in 1941. Her first substantial role came in *Born for Trouble,* a 1942 film costarring Van Johnson and seemingly modeled on *His Girl Friday* (1940), with Johnson and Emerson playing a romantically entwined crusading pair of newspaper reporters. Like Rosalind Russell's Hildy Johnson, Emerson's Gladys Wayne is a feisty reporter battling both for a story and for the attention of a man. This role may have portended a future persona of the tough, resourceful heroine, but her next significant role, in the B film *Lady Gangster* (1942), transformed this toughness into an element of turpitude:

Emerson played a manipulative gangster's moll who, in the end, tries to go straight for the love of a good man. She does succeed and thus is largely a positive character despite her shady past. This redemption notwithstanding, Emerson subsequently moved to a string of one-dimensional roles as a villain, portraying a Nazi spy in *Secret Enemies* (1942) and a manipulative con artist in *Find the Blackmailer* (1943).

At this point, it appeared Emerson was heading toward a career as a shady siren. Publicity materials underscored this, with pressbook articles entitled "Faye Emerson, Film Vixen, First Acted in Church" and "[Emerson] Plays Role of Screen Heavy and Loves It" predicting her future success. Nonetheless, her next set of roles was marked only by an inconsistency in personae: she played a Moroccan rebel in the action film *Desert Song* (1943), a saucy showgirl in *Between Two Worlds* (1944), a jilted lover in *The Mask of Dimitrios* (1944), a mousy secretary turned savvy investigator in *Danger Signal* (1945), and a patriotic factory worker and soldier's love interest in *The Very Thought of You* (1945).[14]

Throughout this period, studio pressbook articles accordingly stressed her versatility and range of portrayals. One article, headlined "Faye Emerson Perfect Type for No 'Typing,'" contained a separate photo caption which described her as a "woman defying every rule for type-casting." Another article joked, "It rather looks like the casting department has thrown the book at her." Such publicity carried over into fan magazine articles. One touted her as "Impossible to type!" Another featured her in an article entitled "Here's How to Be a Spy: In Five Not-So-Easy Lessons" and heralded, "If her studio needs someone to fill a spy role in a hurry, Warner Bros. actress [Faye Emerson] has proof of her 'femme fatale' versatility." The rest of the article featured pictures of Emerson made up in various guises: a grandma, a tough guy, a maid, a schoolmarm, and a "Mata Hari." Interestingly, this piece was a component of the advertising for *Destination Tokyo* (1943), in which Emerson played a minor role as the dutiful wife of a submarine commander, not a spy role, or even a role involving any sort disguise. This ad thus indicates the extent to which Emerson was publicized as an actress who could embody any role in any film. Fittingly, in 1945 the *Los Angeles Times* noted her "chameleon-like adaptability" and defined her as a "star noted for film versatility."[15]

While the above accounts praised Emerson's wide range of roles, a consideration of the previous chapter's discussion of the classical

Hollywood star system would indicate that a "chameleon-like adaptability" might be problematic for Emerson, as Warner Bros. was unable to establish a consistent persona for the actress. One could argue that her versatility became her persona, much in the way of an actor like Paul Muni. Muni's versatility, however, was embodied not just in publicity, but in the very nature of the roles he took, with his own identity shrouded behind the masks of biographical personages. Whereas Muni's extensive use of makeup and masks thus perpetuated an esteemed persona of changeability and acting range, Emerson had no such iconography to draw upon in her more pedestrian roles as contemporary females.

In fact, close analysis of Warner Bros. publicity stills of Emerson suggests that, rather than featuring her in a wide range of roles in order to establish a persona of performative variety, the studio was simply systematically searching for a persona match by running her through a variety of "looks." In particular, it appears that Warner Bros. repeatedly tested her out in the personae of other, already established stars of the period, including Joan Crawford, Katharine Hepburn, Dorothy Lamour, Greer Garson, and Lana Turner. She is almost unrecognizable from one publicity photo to the next: her hair color changes from platinum blonde to brunette to stark black, her hair length shifts from lengthy to shorter styles. Even her facial features seem to transform across the different images.

Warner Bros. was thus never able to tie Emerson to a persona consistent with the industrial model of Hollywood film stardom. After testing her out in a variety of portrayals, all that resulted was an actress praised for versatility but still fourth- and fifth-billed in most films. Without a consistent screen persona, it was difficult to match Emerson up with productive leading roles. The studio publicity that touted her range actually masked a problematic industry status for Emerson. Therefore, after five years in Hollywood, Emerson's film career was still undistinguished.

TELEVISION STARDOM IN NEW YORK

Faye Emerson's career and personal life took a turn in 1943 when she met Elliott Roosevelt, the son of the president, at a party hosted by Howard Hughes. They quickly became involved and married in December 1944. Shortly thereafter Emerson and Warner Bros. mutually agreed to end her contract, and she retired from the screen. Emerson's

The many faces of
Faye Emerson at
Warner Bros.
WISCONSIN CENTER
FOR FILM AND THEATER
RESEARCH.

marriage to Roosevelt took her to New York, where she soon became ensconced in the Manhattan social scene. After a few years spent socializing among the city's upper crust, she desired a return to acting and appeared on Broadway in *The Play's the Thing* (1948) with Louis Calhern. Reviews for the play and her performances were positive; the *New York Times* wrote that she brought "high spirit and versatility" to her role, and the play ran for nine months.[16]

As Emerson was becoming more enmeshed in New York life, both socially and professionally, television too was increasing its presence. TV was already well established in New York by 1948. Because of her local celebrity, Emerson was in a prime position to first establish a career on local television and then advance as the new medium did. In fact, her very lack of Hollywood employment in the late 1940s was crucial for her television career. As *Daily News* columnist Earl Wilson deftly described in 1949, "With no movie ties forbidding TV, Faye's in on the ground floor, ahead of most glamourpusses." Unlike those "glamourpusses," Emerson also had no investment in a high-profile Hollywood image that would be tarnished by association with the new commercialized medium, and she had no potential studio backlash with which to contend.[17]

Emerson made her television debut on May 11, 1948, when she performed in an adaptation of "The Play's the Thing" for the program *Tonight on Broadway* (CBS, 1948–49). She received her first series work from August to December 1948 as narrator of a local fifteen-minute fashion program called *Paris Cavalcade of Fashions* (NBC, 1948–49). The show that subsequently sparked her rise to national stardom reportedly came about by accident in October 1949. Actress Diana Barrymore was scheduled to host a fifteen-minute interview program on CBS but had to cancel because of illness. Emerson, scheduled to appear as a guest, filled in as host. The audience response to her performance was overwhelmingly positive, and this literal overnight success led the network to develop a program for her. Emerson began with a local interview show, then in March 1950 was granted a national late-night slot on the CBS network. She also appeared in a similar program for NBC, the first instance of one actor having shows on two different networks simultaneously. These shows were each seen just once a week, but in September 1950, Emerson dropped the NBC version and put all her energies into hosting a thrice-weekly evening show for CBS.

84

Sponsored by Pepsi-Cola, *The Faye Emerson Show* was a fifteen-minute interview program appearing on Tuesday, Thursday, and Saturday at 7:45 P.M. EST. Not necessarily admiringly, *Time* magazine referred to the program's content as the "kind of chitchat that used to be heard only in beauty shops and over tea tables." Viewer letters provided the topics for most of the shows. Emerson opened each show by reading a viewer letter, indicating a desire to take up an issue raised by the letter, and then presented either the letter writer or a person connected with the relevant issue as the evening's primary guests. For example, an episode aired on September 8, 1950, featured a letter from Bill Green, a New York cabdriver who listed a variety of complaints about riders who used the city's cabs in improper ways. Emerson then brought Green out, and along with a special guest star, film actor Zachary Scott, the three discussed proper taxi-riding etiquette.[18]

Every episode was similarly oriented around a single theme: wigs, fencing, baseball, butlers, ghosts, fashion, horoscopes, and so forth. Most of the guests were either ordinary citizens like Green or experts on an episode's topic, such as Mel Allen discussing baseball announcing or IBM employee C. C. Hurd explaining the wonders of a room-sized computer that could calculate complex math problems in mere minutes. A few episodes touted more famous celebrity guests: one show featured Frank Sinatra, an episode on boxing brought forth Rocky Marciano and Jake LaMotta, and a program focusing on a Frank Lloyd Wright–designed theater presented the architect himself and playwright Tennessee Williams.

In addition to the focus on a singular topic, every episode followed a regularized format. After a brief moment of Emerson introducing herself and a subsequent animated Pepsi jingle, Emerson read part of a viewer letter or simply asserted the episode's theme. She then introduced the various guest stars and began chatting. At some point in the conversation, she would indicate a desire to drink a Pepsi-Cola and either wait for an assistant to serve her or walk over to a bar on the set and serve her guests. As she served, Emerson delivered her pitch for Pepsi, including praise for Pepsi's "wake-up tang," its "friendly, zestful" flavor, and its "more bounce to the ounce." After the product pitch and after all guests took a sip of their Pepsi, Emerson completed the interview and led a final jingle presentation.

As was common with many of the single-sponsorship variety and talk shows of the period, the product pitch was deftly integrated with the show's content. For instance, during an episode on baseball, Emerson segued into her advertisement by noting, "Baseball is the great American game; Pepsi is the great American drink." A show focusing on home aquariums brought Emerson's observation that there's "nothing fishy about Pepsi," and a program on the development of Silly Putty granted a golden opportunity to cite a Pepsi slogan, as Emerson noted that the playful material had "more bounce to the ounce." Further, the product pitches were often selectively presented so as not to degrade the cultural status of any of the more notable guest stars. When Frank Lloyd Wright and Tennessee Williams appeared, Emerson did not bring the drink over—she drank alone—nor did she reference any of the Pepsi slogans. On an episode guest-starring Hollywood film star Douglas Fairbanks, Jr., and a group of aspiring young actors, Emerson took only the unknown performers with her to drink Pepsi and listen to her pitch, leaving Fairbanks offscreen for the commercialized moment.

In addition to such deft negotiation of the taint of crass commercialism, Emerson's ability to present the canned slogans in a natural and exuberant manner brought them across all the more effectively. In fact, her manner of presentation throughout the entirety of each episode matched those elements Pepsi wanted to highlight about their product. One newspaper reviewer echoed this with the comment that Emerson had "more bounce to the ounce than most TV ladies," and the other key sloganeering words, such as "friendly" and "zestful," captured her television persona appropriately. She was noted for her boundless energy and vivacious manner, which came through forcefully both in the guest interviews and in her Pepsi pitches. This fit between personality and product ostensibly naturalized the potentially fragmentary commercial ruptures and made the obligatory commercial pitch less obtrusive.[19]

In fact, many elements of *The Faye Emerson Show* embodied this ideal of a natural, unpretentious program. Production materials indicate that the general framework for each episode was scripted: it was previously established where Emerson would stand, how she would justify moving to a different part of the set, and how she would make a transition into the Pepsi advertisements. But the actual interviews were largely improvised, with only brief phrases and questions scripted out beforehand. Emerson's subsequent ability to converse naturally with each guest helped to gloss over the repeated advertising slogans and legitimate the presented content. Authenticity also frequently emerged simply because of the circumstances of live recording, with the kind of

Faye Emerson entertains Douglas Fairbanks, Jr., and a pair of NYU fencers.
CBS/Photofest.

mistakes now mythicized in accounts of "Golden Age" programming. In each of these cases, Emerson always very casually dismissed the mistake, thereby matching the spontaneity expressed in her interviews. Emerson and her guests also frequently called mocking attention to the conventional aspects of her show, much like variety hosts such as Jack Benny did. In one episode Emerson called her assistant to bring a Pepsi and commented, "See, that's how we work in our commercials." In another case, during a murder mystery episode with TV detective William Gargan as guest star, an important prop turned up missing, and Gargan joked that perhaps someone absconded with it in rehearsal.

Further, Emerson explicitly tried to foster familiarity with the viewer, particularly in references to viewers as her personal friends. On *The Faye Emerson Show*'s premiere, Emerson indicated that Pepsi asked her to introduce the drink to some friends, and she used this reasoning to justify her hosting of the show, telling the audience, "As far as I'm concerned, all you people out there are my friends." These references to audience members as friends and as part of a direct relationship were quite common. At times, Emerson even meshed these allusions with her product pitches, pouring her guest a Pepsi, then turning to the camera to ask the audience to join her for one, as if they were sharing a living room. In this manner, Emerson once again naturalized the product advertisement, here by situating it within the viewer's own world.

Reviews of the program frequently alluded to this element of closeness and to the importance of the ingenuous television host to this period of television. Hal Humphrey, television critic for the *LA Mirror,* sketched the talk-show television personality thusly: "[T]he Godfreys and Emersons approach TV and the viewer as if they were paying you a personal visit. They are not 'on stage' in the sense that they were doing a show. This 'we're-just-your-neighbors' type of thing has made for some awful nauseating TV viewing, but it also has produced a flock of video shows which are becoming solid clicks under the stewardship of performers who have found that they have that TV personality." Fan magazine writer Joan King Flynn described viewer response to Emerson in a similar vein: "Many a neighbor said to another, 'Last night Faye told me about a wonderful new show' or 'a marvelous party' or a 'darling hair-do. . . . ' As one friend to another, they sought her advice." Additionally, Val Adams of the *New York Times* spoke of Emerson's "art of playing 'professional personality.' . . . She just sits and oozes personality." *Cosmopolitan* described her show as displaying a "casual air of intimacy, as though she were trading chit chat across a tea table."[20]

THE NATURAL GLAMOUR OF FAYE EMERSON

In the ways described above, Emerson embodied the early television personality, the prototypical star figure being fostered by the new medium. Her manner of address perfectly matched the genres that ruled television in the early 1950s, which were based on a presentational style of informal discussion in which Emerson excelled. Further, the personable appeal of her program and its surrounding publicity and criticism fit neatly within the paradigm of television stardom described earlier, where both the nature of the talk show that she hosted and the manner with which she hosted helped to create a notion of the "real" Faye Emerson appearing on television screens, speaking personally to the average viewer at home.

And yet, the focus put on Emerson's beauty and glamour in publicity might seem to contradict the impression that television needed to fully tone down the usual extravagances that were associated with film stars.

Indeed, her prior connections with the glamour of Hollywood and her current status as a sophisticated New York socialite were frequent topics in publicity profiles of her life. Further, she was repeatedly referred to as a "glamour girl" and a "blonde bombshell" and endlessly described in press materials as a strikingly attractive woman. Publicity articles on Emerson contained such headings as "Faye Emerson's Got Glamor" and "Glamour Girl of the Television Screen," and *Look* magazine noted that Emerson's audience was "made up of tired housewives who crave 'glamour after a dull day.'"[21]

Not surprisingly, while Faye Emerson's public persona was perpetually tied to a glamorous appeal, this glamour was most frequently framed as wholly natural and even attainable for viewers at home. In a presumably ghostwritten fan magazine article entitled "Just Be Natural," Emerson described firsthand her simple hairdo and makeup, appropriate for anyone at home: "The trick is that everything is keyed down to highlight mouth and eyes . . . a technique I use on stage, screen and TV. Fine for everyday too." Such characterizations of her natural beauty and charisma were consistent; one article described the "easy, friendly manner that is Miss Emerson's special charm." Another touted that "[s]he's often unself-conscious as a puppy," and *Cosmopolitan* praised her "sophisticated simplicity." An extensive profile in *Radio Best* mentioned her "uncluttered" home and pointed out that her favorite foods were simple dishes, she wore simple suits, and she bought "good basic things" when shopping. A *TV Show* article even attempted to justify her glamour in relation to television's demands: "She's completely natural and unselfconscious, and makes no secret that she tints her brown hair gold because blondes show up better on TV." The best encapsulation of her "natural glamour" came from the *Washington Post:* she had "denim overall virtues" but with "occasional sequin glints."[22]

Thus, though beauty and glamour were constant features in press coverage of Faye Emerson, this emphasis was almost always recouped within a description of her natural characteristics. Certainly the fact that she hosted a talk show, thereby acting as "herself" and addressing the audience directly, lent her televisual persona a considerable level of intimacy and authenticity. Extratextual material on Emerson then constructed the same notion of personality that viewers gathered from her television program. While Warner Bros. publicists had struggled to find a promotional strategy for Emerson that could make her a film star, on television she was able to craft an appropriate televisual star image that capitalized on the medium's unique traits and contextualized her beauty within markers of authenticity. No longer forced to play other actresses' and characters' images as in her Hollywood career, Emerson could take advantage of the distinctiveness of this new medium by constructing a singular televisual image defined as an embodiment of her own personality.

One aspect of Emerson's "natural" image would prove to be more challenging to negotiate, however. Emerson's dresses often featured low-cut necklines baring varying degrees of cleavage. Considerable controversy resulted, as women in particular were said to fear the dangers of allowing such a display of sexuality to appear in the nation's living rooms. Critics took considerable delight in creatively referring to Emerson's bust. *New York Herald Tribune* columnist John Crosby wrote, "Miss Emerson, I'd be the first to admit, fills a ten-inch screen very adequately. Very adequately." He noted, "*The Faye Emerson Show*, I assume, is aimed primarily at women, but I know men, including this one, who are helplessly fascinated by it for reasons which never occurred to CBS." Likewise, critic Earl Wilson mocked an Emerson radio appearance with the following: "Faye Emerson on the radio just doesn't seem right. Such a waste of . . . er . . . visual talent."[23]

Emerson addressed the cleavage concern on *The Faye Emerson Show* a number of times, such as when she read a letter from a local woman's group that accused her of tastelessness in her costuming and touted a pledge signed by each of the group's thousand members agreeing never to watch her show again. She defended her choice of dress in the face of such criticism by resorting to naturalism. "I wear on TV just what I'd ordinarily wear at that hour of the night," she told *Time* magazine. Emerson also claimed that the vast majority of viewers voiced their support for her dresses through letters to her.[24]

The neckline controversy, added to concerns about off-color jokes and suggestive gestures on variety shows and the violence displayed on crime dramas, led the FCC and Congress to take up the issue of television censorship in a series of debates throughout 1952. The National Association of Radio and Television Broadcasters, the industry's self-regulatory trade organization, responded, in hopes of staving off outside intervention, by instituting a Television Code in March 1952. This move proved detrimental to the bawdier variety programs, and it also likely affected the way Emerson was allowed to dress. The guideline involving

Faye Emerson's controversial cleavage. CBS/Photofest.

necklines was relatively nonspecific—"The costuming of all performers shall be within the bounds of propriety and shall avoid exposure or such emphasis on anatomical detail as would embarrass or offend home viewers"—but such vagueness could prove quite restrictive, given that a network or sponsor would want to avoid embarrassment or offense in any measure. Ultimately, the controversy over her neckline surely brought her positive publicity and perhaps more viewers; nevertheless, Emerson regretted being placed in the center of a public debate over morality.[25]

But because Emerson was able to mix her sexuality, an obvious attraction to male viewers, with her wit and an authoritative ability to discuss virtually any topic with any guest—often confronting issues of interest to female viewers—she enjoyed broad popularity. Indeed, it seems that in television Emerson was finally able to exploit a singular persona, one she matched to the demands and requirements of a new medium quickly building on the notions of intimacy and spontaneity. While this presentational, naturalistic persona may not have been conducive to the construction of a character-based persona in Hollywood film, it was well suited to early 1950s television and one of its most popular genres. Mixing equal parts of glamour and naturalism, sexuality and intelligence, sophistication and intimacy, and consistency and spontaneity, Faye Emerson successfully exploited and even helped to shape the developing performative standards of early television.

BACK TO HOLLYWOOD? BACK TO TELEVISION

By 1951, because of her popularity and her suitability for many forms of early television programming, Emerson was on television constantly. Critic John Crosby quipped in a later interview, "There must easily be half a dozen Faye Emersons because she seemed to be everywhere." In addition to hosting her own show, she appeared periodically in the early 1950s on panel shows like *Who Said That* (NBC and ABC, 1948–55) and *Life Begins at Eighty* (NBC, ABC, DUM, 1950–56), variety and talk shows such as *The Garry Moore Show* (CBS, 1950–51), and dramatic anthologies including *Silver Theater* (CBS, 1949–50) and *Chesterfield Presents* (NBC, 1952). Such onscreen ubiquity reflected her offscreen popularity. She was named *Look*'s Most Appealing Female Personality of 1950 and *Variety*'s Top TV Star of 1950; she placed first in *TV Forecast*'s 1951 Popularity Poll; and she was honored as one of twenty-five "American Women of Achievement" by the Boston Chamber of Commerce, a list that also included businesswomen, doctors, entertainers, and artists. Columnist Harriet Van Horne noted, "You couldn't pick up a newspaper and not see her picture. You couldn't go to an event of any consequence and not see her. She was everywhere." Emerson's second husband Skitch Henderson described life in New York with her thusly: "It was like walking down the street with the Pope."[26]

In light of Henderson's reference to New York City, however, one must bear in mind that this was a period with limited national set and station distribution. Only 9 percent of homes owned a television in 1950, only 24 percent in 1951, and no more than 34 percent in 1952. Additionally, television signals were primarily available only in urban areas, with expansion into rural localities beginning in earnest in 1952. Thus, Emerson's popularity, albeit substantial, was based largely in urban domains, especially in New York City. Film critic Rex Reed described his childhood impression of Emerson in this manner: "You sat in your living room at home in Podunk, Illinois, and you thought, that's what New York is. That's why I want to go to New York and not stay in Podunk, because there are people like Faye Emerson there." Additionally, many of the topics covered on *The Faye Emerson Show* related to the cultural attractions and employment opportunities offered within the New York area, like the Dodgers-Yankees World Series, a Broadway musical, how to get into show business in New York, the NYU fencing team, and the New York High School for the Performing Arts.[27]

Emerson did have measurable nationwide fame, however. Featured in the pages of *Look* and *Cosmopolitan,* she particularly influenced national fashion. She was even credited with launching a hairstyle fad in 1952. Previously famed for her "chignon look," which consisted of her hair completely pulled back and bound at the nape of her neck with an attached bun, Emerson began wearing a so-called poodle cut, basically an addition of bangs to the chignon style. The poodle cut swept the nation, and the American Hair Design Institute released a statement concluding that TV must have more influence than films on the women of America. They noted that even though a number of film actresses, including Ingrid Bergman and Judy Holliday, had worn the poodle cut in their films, only when Emerson wore it on television did it become a national trend: "It was Faye and TV that supplied the spark needed to light the conflagration under the poodle cut." Thus, while Emerson's popularity was at least initially an urban phenomenon, her emergence in national fashion pages indicated the level of her fame and influence across the country.[28]

This popularity convinced Hollywood to try and draw Emerson back into films. A November 1950 publicity article claimed, "Faye Emerson, hotter than a firecracker, is wanted by nearly every major studio in town for a picture," and a January 1951 article pointed out that her television fame upped her asking price for movies to five times what she made in the 1940s. Nonetheless, she repeatedly turned down movie offers, including Bing Crosby's *Here Comes the Groom* (1951) and *Deadline, U.S.A.* (1952) with Humphrey Bogart, reportedly leaving her agent "groaning." Emerson did star in one independent film in this period, *Guilty Bystander* (1950) with frequent Warner Bros. costar Zachary Scott, but the fact that she demanded in her contract that the film be made in New York or its immediate vicinity serves as an indication of why a resurrection of her Hollywood career would not take place: she was simply too attached to New York. Skitch Henderson confirmed this, noting that Emerson was a "devotee of New York nightlife" and felt that Hollywood was an empty place to which she had no interest in returning.[29]

Further, she frequently claimed that she never really cared for the process of making movies, telling one paper that it was a "tedious task." Friend Cleveland Amory also felt that television was a more appropriate medium for her desires to express herself: "I think she kind of looked down on [movies as] just being show business. But with television, there was a combination of show business and getting a voice out there. That wasn't true in movies." In a related vein, she even reportedly preferred the more improvised performances in her talk shows and quiz programs to dramatic anthologies. The *New York Times*'s Val Adams noted: "in front of the camera [Emerson] prefers to create her own act rather than the prepared assignment of others."[30]

This publicity may have just been empty rhetoric, but Emerson did indeed continue her life in New York as a television personality rather than use her popularity as a ticket back to Hollywood. In addition to taking occasional roles in Broadway plays, Emerson began hosting a new show in June 1951, *Faye Emerson's Wonderful Town,* airing every Saturday at 8 P.M. EST on CBS. *Wonderful Town* brought a new format for Emerson. Each episode focused on a U.S. city and tried to provide viewers with a general impression of that city. Though it was framed as a cultural experience, *Wonderful Town*'s explorations of various cities were really just contrived frameworks for variety performances. Emerson acted as emcee, introducing various singers and dancers, and as an interviewer of guests. The majority of the guests were well-known entertainers or artists, and all were connected to the featured town in some way, usually as a birthplace. Towns covered on the show included Brooklyn, Baltimore, Philadelphia, Boston, and New Orleans. Occasionally, fictional towns based on a theme, such as College Town, Music Town, and Fashion Town, served as an episode topic.

Despite purporting to reveal the true essence of each city, the shows were filmed at a studio in Manhattan, not in the actual cities. As a result, the majority of the program's guests were entertainers based in New York, not true residents of a certain metropolis. Because *Wonderful Town* attempted to represent each city, including famous landmarks and cultural centers, it utilized elaborate sets and was filmed in a large studio at Grand Central Station to accommodate the sizable stage sets. Accordingly, whereas *The Faye Emerson Show* cost about $5,000 per episode, *Wonderful Town* had an average budget of $15,000.[31]

The June 23, 1951, episode of *Wonderful Town* depicted Chicago, and it followed a typical format for the program. The episode opened with a performance by Benny Goodman on an orchestral stage, followed by a brief conversation between Goodman and Emerson. Emerson then moved along to a set approximating Marshall Field's on Michigan Avenue and stopped to chat with television star Dave Garroway. Singer Kay Armen next appeared for a song, and actress Cornelia Otis Skinner performed a brief playlet about Chicago. After another song from Armen, Emerson interviewed a cow (in puppet form) who revealed the true story behind the Chicago fire; it was Mrs. O'Leary's fault for placing the lantern behind the cow. At the end of the show, Emerson and all of the guests gathered in a living room set for a goodbye to the audience.

Despite such vivid skits, *Wonderful Town* was not nearly the success that *The Faye Emerson Show* was for a variety of reasons. First, a number of critics felt that the shows served up superficial views of each city. Commented Fred Rayfield:

> What "Wonderful Town" turns out to be is another variety program with a gimmick. The gimmick—of wrapping everything around one town—might be rewarding and interesting if we really got a look below the surface of the town. What we're evidently going to get are Chamber of Commerce handouts and all the beaten-to-death stereotypes about each particular city.

Similarly, *Chicago Herald American* reviewer Janet Kern called the show "as dull as dishwater" for its lack of insight into each town.[32]

While the content was problematic, its execution helped to limit the show's appeal, as well. Because the episodes were not filmed in the actual cities and instead were represented through sets, a sense of artificiality predominated. The expressionistic sets were surely eye-catching, but Emerson and her guests frequently pretended that they were actually in the city when interacting on the sets, lending an awkward feel to the exchanges. As a case in point, in the July 1951 episode featuring Minneapolis, Emerson and guest Cedric Adams stood on a modernist, abstract set depicting the roof of a building. Emerson told the audience that she and her guest were standing on top of the Foshay Tower, the tallest building in the city at the time. They used the supposed height of their perch to look out upon Minneapolis and point out such landmarks as Lake Minnetonka, the University of Minnesota, and the city of Saint Paul. Of course, audiences both in the studio and at home saw none of this, only Emerson and Adams gazing just left of the camera as they pretended to have dynamic attractions in their sights. This lent a sense of falseness and incompleteness to the show quite different from the spontaneity and authenticity of Emerson's previous interview program. Cost-cutting moves, such as sparse and reused sets, also cut into the credibility of the show's depiction of Minneapolis and other cities. The most colorful reaction to these deficiencies came from *Saturday Review*'s Robert Lewis Shayon, who called his viewing of the Minneapolis episode "the most unsatisfactory experience I have had in a long time."[33]

Emerson's image as host was also different for this program. Rather than her previous spirited, vivacious personality, she came across as much more staid and composed in trying to convey a sense of respect for each city. Additionally, her dresses were considerably more conservative, described by one author in an article entitled "What Happened to the V?" as "prim, modestly clad regalia." Some reviewers, especially those who felt she had lost the natural effusiveness that had made her a success in *The Faye Emerson Show*, met these changes in her image with disdain. The author who had previously defined Emerson as a mix of the denim and the sequin explained the disappointment of *Wonderful Town* in this manner: "she ceased using her more solid virtues and had to play the sequin side for all it was worth. The results were OK but it was like the waste of a great natural resource." *Chicago Herald American*'s Janet Kern claimed that this image change meant that Emerson "lost much of her prestige and standing in the TV field."[34]

A final problematic aspect for *Wonderful Town* was scheduling. It aired every Saturday night on CBS against NBC's *Your Show of Shows* (1950–54), starring Sid Caesar and Imogene Coca. This ninety-minute program of live comedy sketches and musical routines penned by such writers as Mel Brooks, Neil Simon, and Woody Allen was hugely popular with audiences, often drawing half of the time slot's audience. *Wonderful Town,* in comparison, averaged only a 16 percent share of the audience and sometimes dropped as low as 8 percent. CBS quickly became dissatisfied and decided to cancel *Wonderful Town* and replace it with a glitzier program that might better match up to *Your Show of Shows.*[35]

Emerson reportedly responded by battling with the networks and the sponsor over the format for the show, though there are contradictory versions of this in the press. According to the *Washington Post,*

Emerson had hoped to transform the show into a more informal documentary tour of actual cities, but the producers felt that a sleek variety show with celebrity guests was a more appropriate format to compete with the Caesar-Coca show. On the other hand, *Variety* claimed that Emerson fought to keep the variety format and that sponsor Pepsi was the one battling for a change. Whichever version is true, it seems clear that the disagreements over potential changes for the show circulated around whether the show should appear spontaneous and low-key or deliberate and lavish. Given Emerson's talents and her previous success with *The Faye Emerson Show*, the former approach would have been ideal. Yet it was never pursued.[36]

CHANGING INDUSTRY, CHANGING IMAGE

Faye Emerson's Wonderful Town ended its run in April 1952, and it would be the last national program that Emerson would host regularly. She did continue frequent guest appearances on quiz shows and variety shows, but both viewers and critics noticed that she was no longer a regular weekly presence on television. One fan magazine called her the "former queen of the TV lanes" in only March 1953, and a letter to the *Cincinnati Enquirer* in July 1953 asked, "What happened to Faye Emerson? Why doesn't someone give her a regular job?" The trade press did report rumors that she was a candidate for host of a filmed anthology drama for Pepsi in May 1953, but these accounts once again conflict as to why she did not receive the job. Some claimed that Pepsi simply preferred actress Arlene Dahl over Emerson. Others alleged that Emerson would not agree to participate in national tours of bottlers' factories, a publicity requirement of the Pepsi contract. Whatever the reason, she was passed over for the hosting task, as well as many others for which she was being considered, including replacing Jack Paar in his variety show in 1955, hosting her own variety show in January 1956, and co-hosting *Tonight* with Steve Allen in January 1957.[37]

The primary reasons why Emerson never again hosted a national program on a regular basis hinge on programming developments in television across the 1950s and changes in Emerson's own personal life. On the personal level, Skitch Henderson claims that Emerson's difficulties in controlling her temper and her consumption of alcohol doomed her career. Despite her cheery on-air persona, she had a very combative personality and frequently battled with Pepsi executives over all facets of her show. Pepsi got fed up with her obstinate disposition and finally canceled her contract in 1954. Because of this furor with Pepsi, Henderson claims that no other sponsors were willing to approach her for a long-term contract.[38]

While those troubles were behind-the-scenes, Emerson's public image also became problematic owing to the ascension of her neckline and the expansion of her waistline. In relation to the former, some cynical critics felt the Television Code doomed certain actresses, with Emerson frequently used as evidence. Additionally, Emerson had fought her weight throughout her career, and by the mid-1950s, she seemed less concerned about controlling it, to the point where critics began making disparaging comments. New York's *Gotham Guide* asked in February 1955, "Why is pretty Faye Emerson allowing herself to get so fat?" and a writer for *TV Star Parade* penned, "somebody should call a meeting about her figure—the lady is really getting to be a plump dumpling." In a medium that asked a great deal of a woman's image, but most especially for a performer whose popularity and publicity had always been tied to her body image, such weight gain was highly problematic. It conflicted with her image as the elegant sophisticate, and it signified unruliness—most problematic for a femcee who was supposed to be "reassuring" and "more-or-less sexy," according to cultural standards. Close friend Doris Lilly said, "When she put on all that weight, she knew it was a problem."[39]

Beyond these surface changes to Emerson herself, general programming shifts across the 1950s were also responsible for narrowing the opportunities for a performer of her type and gender. First, the increasing amount of filmed programming by the late 1950s was seen as a hindrance to Emerson's talents, chiefly her spontaneous energy. A *Long Island Press* commentator came to this conclusion: "[Emerson] might have stayed indefinitely on the crest had she not turned to film. Since Faye's drama and impact depend so much on a 'live' presentation, this was a serious mistake and, as it developed, the beginning of the end." This notion is similar to the reasons behind the demise of *Wonderful Town*. It indicates that as live programming disappeared, the attributes that had made Emerson famous were increasingly less central to the medium.[40]

In a related evolution, Emerson's greatest success had come within a genre that was on the decline as the decade progressed. The interview–talk show format decreased precipitously from a total of ninety-four hours of programming across all three networks in 1954 to only

twenty-three in 1959. With the simultaneous growth of the representational formats of situation comedy, action-adventure, and drama programming, the number of presentational-format shows that could best
display Emerson's skills were few by the late 1950s, a development that
affected many female personalities. The role of prime-time talk show
host had been filled by numerous women on early television, including
Wendy Barrie (*The Wendy Barrie Show*, DUM, ABC, NBC, 1949–50)
and Maggi McNellis (*Maggi's Private Wire*, NBC, 1949). The presence
of such performers declined as the decade wore on, however. Jay Nelson Tuck of the *New York Post* asked in 1957, "Where are the dames of
yesteryear? . . . They've mostly been replaced by either old feature
movies or syndicated film shows, many of them second, third, or fourth
reruns." More accurately, they were replaced by male-dominated programming. Any female hosts who wanted to maintain their careers had
to do so in the daytime. This left host-personalities like Faye Emerson
with little space to continue their prime-time hosting careers, and it
prevented the rise of other female-centered programs and genres.[41]

Emerson expressed her frustration with this confining situation for
women on television in a newspaper article that was part of a syndicated column, "Faye Emerson on Radio and TV," which ran from 1953
to 1958. Most of the articles she penned for this series were fairly
undistinguished and generic, consisting of behind-the-scenes entertainment gossip, blurbs from press releases, and critical reviews of TV
shows and plays. Political issues seldom emerged in her column; on
those rare occasions, however, articles were most apt to lament how
women were treated within the television industry. In one article,
Emerson complained about the paucity of female news commentators:
"it would seem to me that there is room for a few ladies on television
talking about something besides cooking and fashion. I claim women
have minds too!"[42]

The consternation expressed here would be another reason for
Emerson's decline: she refused to contain her opinions to cooking and
fashion and instead spoke out more and more on controversial political
and cultural issues such as the anti-Communist fervor and the burgeoning feminist movement. Emerson's intelligence and political acumen were met with derision across the decade. Such was the experience for many female television performers. C. Robert Jennings
addressed this very issue in a 1958 *New York Times Magazine* article,
"Quiz Shows: The Woman Question," in which he tried to discern why

so few women appeared as contestants on quiz programs. One of the article's sources, Dr. Ernest Dichter, a New York motivational researcher, explained one reason: "The woman who knows a lot of data is somehow queer. She wants to affirm herself in other ways because she is suspect if society knows this is all she has collected." The article also presented interviews with three female former quiz show winners; all three denied a characterization of themselves as "feminist champions striking a blow for equality."[43]

Both industry publicity and comments attributed to Emerson reveal similar attempts to soften her image as an intellectual early in her career so she would not be perceived in an emasculating way—a striking parallel to the ways in which the force of her glamour was toned down. A 1950 profile by Val Adams stressed that Emerson's mental sharpness and political insight were never overwhelming to audiences at home: "Although she has definite ideas and positive opinions, she expresses them in a nice easy way rather than the 'now get this!' manner of an army sergeant, a common failing of many career girls who try to sell their intelligence." And a 1950 *Cosmopolitan* article emphasized that Emerson herself believed that her level of intellect was "good, but not unusual" and had more to do with "a probing interest in almost everything that takes place anywhere" than true "intellectual prowess."[44]

Outward expression of any such prowess could be problematic for Emerson, as evidenced by a complaint letter she read on a May 1951 episode of *The Faye Emerson Show*. Emerson had expressed concern in an earlier episode that the Korean conflict would escalate further, and the letter writer felt that this position revealed Emerson's ignorance of the U.S. government's view of the war, particularly its claim that the conflict would be over shortly. The letter included the admonition, "Better stick to the plunging necklines, Faye; politics is not for little girls." Emerson responded thusly: "Politics is everybody's business, and I'm certainly not a little girl. [I will keep broaching political topics on the show], but I will try not to jam my opinions down your throat." Emerson often distanced herself from pronouncements of her intelligence in this manner; she deflected praise about her intellect in the *Cosmopolitan* profile by saying, "The thing with me is that I have a mind cluttered up with a lot of trivia that doesn't amount to a damn." Clearly, like Arlene Francis, Emerson and her publicists were well aware that she had to qualify displays of her intelligence in order to maintain her broader popularity, much as she had to contain her sexuality within acceptable parameters.[45]

Nonetheless, Emerson departed from Francis's approach as the 1950s continued, becoming less willing to express her opinions in a "nice easy way." She let her political orientation guide her actions both on and off television screens, thereby going well beyond the publicity image of a mere "TV quiz show brain" who collects reams of innocuous facts. She campaigned fervently for Democratic presidential candidate Adlai Stevenson in the mid-1950s, and she became involved in industry politics through the television performers' union, AFTRA, where she openly battled the anti-Communist faction called Aware, Inc. Emerson's son William said that she realized expressing strident opinions and challenging the union heads would cost her jobs and money, but her frustrating experiences within AFTRA in particular compelled her to begin openly airing her opinions.[46]

For example, she appeared on a number of talk shows in the mid- to late-1950s, frequently debating such conservative figures as William F. Buckley. In one appearance on *Tonight*, Emerson and television critic John Crosby debated Aware founder Vince Hartnett and president Godfrey P. Schmidt about blacklisting issues. Hartnett reportedly became so infuriated with Emerson's positions that he physically confronted her backstage after taping the program. Emerson also generated controversy in 1957 when she was hosting a brief segment on a local New York show with Mike Wallace called *Newsbeat*. Wallace read the news for the bulk of each episode, and Emerson filled the final five minutes with a segment called "The Woman's Touch," which consisted of musings on women's issues and current events. On one segment, she argued that the United States should open up a dialogue with China; for this, both newspapers and the ordinary public heavily criticized her. One letter to the editor snidely commented, "surely a session of Congress will have to be called to weigh the remarks of such a learned and distinguished stateswoman who I am sure will go down in history."[47]

Emerson also began to speak out on feminist issues in the latter half of the 1950s, including her desire to see more women employed in the television industry. In 1957, she lamented the fact that only men had covered the previous two political conventions. She referred to this as "a deplorable situation." She also briefly hosted a New York program in 1956 called *Women Want to Know* and stirred up controversy with the premiere episode's topic: sex education. Charles S. Aaronson authored an editorial in *Motion Picture Daily* blasting Emerson and the show for the topic, "which has no conceivable place in such a mass medium of wide dissemination as television." He also cynically noted that having the "glamorous Faye Emerson" moderate the discussion was "little less than the height of folly."[48]

No critics at the time cited Emerson's increasing political outspokenness as a reason for the decline in her career. It seems likely, however, that the frequent references to her breasts and her changing physical image were a way to mask these viewpoints. Just as Charles S. Aaronson could dismiss Emerson's ability to address a serious political issue because of her beauty, other pundits could simply reduce her to just her breasts and body image, thereby dismissing her political positions without even raising them. Quiz show host Garry Moore, a close friend of Emerson's, specifically identified Jack O'Brien as a reviewer who repeatedly commented negatively on Emerson's displays of cleavage. In Moore's mind, the staunchly conservative O'Brien did this because in his capacity as a television reviewer he was not in a position to criticize her politics; he could, however, chastise her for the physical image she presented on television.[49]

As such, Emerson's identity as a sexual object ended up defining her television persona and her representation of femininity. Even though she was a politically minded intellectual and was eager to display this side of her personality by the late 1950s, she was ultimately reduced to a sexual object and a glamour queen. Fittingly, *TV Guide* responded to Senator Margaret Chase Smith's serious suggestion that Faye Emerson was "the type of woman needed in the nation's capital" with a comical projection of the results. They predicted that she would campaign on the "Plunging Neckline Platform" and give an inaugural address presenting "a hard-hitting attack against those Paris designers who were plotting to bring back the high neckline."[50]

Such dismissive depictions frustrated Emerson throughout her television career. Friend Dennis Patrick said, "if I ever saw a woman who would like to take two tits and throw them out a window somewhere, Faye Emerson would have done it." A fascinating article that Emerson penned for the men's magazine *Esquire* indicates as much. In "Eggheads Make the Best Lovers," Emerson explained that she found men with brains much sexier than men with brawn, particularly because they treat women with so much more respect:

We women have an inferiority complex about our minds, built in from the time we were in our rompers. We've all been told that although we were adorable and curly-haired and dimpled and the future-mothers-in-law of men (note: not of daughters!), we were mentally inferior to the male of the species. And when we grow up and meet a man who treats us with respect, he instantly captures our attention. The odds are high that he will be an egghead because only eggheads are smart enough to have figured out that women are people and not just amorous props.

One could imagine that she felt the same about television as she did about brawny men.[51]

For the latter half of her career, Emerson continued her mix of local programs and periodic appearances on network shows, including a regular role as a quiz show panelist on *I've Got a Secret.* Her contract with that program ended in 1958, however, and it was not renewed. Producer Gil Cates claimed that her request for a $50-a-week raise was rejected by the network; because of her increasingly controversial image, producers were not willing to entertain any demands on her part. Emerson appeared on television only twice in 1961 and but once the following year. She maintained her political activities, though, most notably traveling on her own to Washington, D.C., for the August 1963 civil rights march. In a move that surprised many, even her closest friends, Emerson left the United States only six weeks later, ostensibly to travel around Europe. Tired of the requirements of her celebrity and the demands it placed on her image, she insisted that she would happily rid herself of her televisual image, including letting her weight grow naturally. She told the *New York Post:* "the first thing I'll definitely do is cut off my hair, let it grow to its true color, whatever that is! I think there'll be a little silver in it. This, now, is the way people expect me to look, but it isn't really me." Instead of just playing the image of "the natural Faye Emerson" on television, she now truly strove for it in a way that she could not when she was still attached to the medium.[52]

After traveling throughout Europe for the next year, Emerson settled in Majorca, Spain, where she lived for the next twenty years. She returned to the United States only twice, the second time in 1976. During that final trip, she was recognized in a restaurant and took this as a signal that it was still too early for her to return to America. Her popularity in the early 1950s had been so extensive that even twenty-five years after her last appearance on American television screens, she was still recognized. But for all of her visibility in the early 1950s, the length of her television career was brief, and her decision to leave the country speaks volumes about her collective experience with the medium.[53]

While Hollywood had been unable to devise a star-character persona for Faye Emerson in film, she succeeded as a representation of "herself" on television. This televisual image as a "personality" resonated with prominent early television genres and allowed Emerson to carve out a niche in the medium and gain nationwide fame. Emerson enjoyed additional advantages because she lived in New York in the late 1940s and she was no longer contracted to a major film studio. Both of these factors put her in a unique position to benefit from the new medium before other established film actors were either able or willing to make the career shift. But when the genres in which she excelled faded away, the medium moved toward different modes of programming and production, and her own real personality became considerably more complex and more difficult to package neatly for mainstream consumption, television no longer had a space for Emerson.

Thus, Faye Emerson's initial success epitomizes the fluidity of early television, just as her later failure illustrates what was lost once the networks consolidated their power over the medium. But although Emerson herself was left behind, the traits she established as essential to the success of the television personality lingered for decades to come. Emerson succeeded only briefly as a packaged personality; the fact that she could not truly be herself on 1950s television underscores the constructed nature of this representation that was of such consequence to early television and the talk show format. Cleveland Amory claimed, "Faye Emerson was the first television star created by television," and it is quite revealing that Amory chose to use the word "created."[54] Indeed, the "television personality" was a collection of constructed allusions to authenticity that grew out of the new medium's industrial, cultural, and aesthetic bases. This was not a difficult character to invent in Emerson's case, as she had a minimal star image before beginning her television career. In subsequent chapters, however, we shall see that even more substantial star images could be manipulated to serve analogous demands for televisual expression.

CHAPTER 3
THE STAR AND
THE STORY
ANTHOLOGY
DRAMA HOSTS

All my career I've been playing different kinds of
characters, then suddenly they tell me I'm playing
a guy named Joseph Cotten. Joseph Cotten? What
does he act like? I couldn't find anything in the script
that would give me a clue.—Joseph Cotten, host of
The 20th Century–Fox Hour

Joseph Cotten's uncertainty[1] was shared by many stars who hosted anthology programs. As with variety and talk show hosting, this task involved the stars acting as themselves and directly addressing the home audience via studio cameras. Rather than the informal and extemporaneous manner called for in presentational genres, however, a heightened sense of decorum was necessary for those who helmed the anthology drama. These hosts were not preparing audiences for a nightclub or living room affair; what had to be transmitted here was the feel of an evening at the theater or the sensation of passing from a living room into an exceptional world of fiction. Nonetheless, a sense of intimacy was still called for to make audiences feel personally invited to the experience (as well as to contextualize commercial pitches). Such a variegated persona could not have been easy to adopt, especially for actors accustomed to performance in Hollywood film. A star image born of fictional performances onscreen and partly fictional publicity offscreen had to be adapted for a presentational guise within a theatrical genre. Despite the inherent difficulties, many film stars successfully did so in the 1950s, as anthology hosting became a commonplace position for Hollywood talent. A look at how these personas and programs were combined captures the appeal and utility—as well as the occasional futility—of this crossover relationship.

The great majority of early live anthologies from New York functioned without hosts. In 1951, only seven of the twenty-five network-aired anthology dramas had someone appear regularly to introduce the evening's stories. Not coincidentally, however, as the number of filmed anthologies increased, so did the presence of hosts. In the 1955–56 season, there were twenty-nine anthologies running over the network airwaves, and fourteen of them were helmed, mostly by established Hollywood talent. Almost all of the hosted shows were shot on film and had half-hour running times; almost none of the exclusively live, hourlong anthologies, such as *Kraft Television Theater* and *Goodyear Playhouse,* featured recurring figures other than sponsor announcers, like Ed Herlihy for Kraft, and product demonstrators, like Betty Furness for Westinghouse's *Studio One.*

Filmed shows lacked the prestige and high-culture connotations of the live shows, and entertainment emanating from Hollywood was usually critically derided in comparison to New York fare. The critical establishment that judged television in its early years put great stock in the unique artistic value of live production and believed that filming a prestigious genre like the anthology drama violated an essentialist principle of the medium, limiting its potential to match or supersede the status of the movies. Prominent critics trumpeted the cultural value of material associated with New York–based productions, while dismissing Hollywood-originated work. Foremost among them in this belief was the legendary *New York Times* critic Jack Gould. In a 1952 article lamenting what he called the "colossal boner of the year," referring to the conversion of numerous programs from live to film, Gould wrote: "Take away the actuality of television and there is lost the heart of TV. To regard television merely as a variation on the neighborhood motion picture house is to misunderstand the medium." His dismissal of the revamped *Schlitz Playhouse of Stars,* which in 1952 shifted from an hour to a half hour, increased the number of filmed episodes, and added film star Irene Dunne as hostess, is also characteristic. He complained that these changes transformed a once-promising show into a completely pedestrian program, and he condemned the role of the celebrity host as empty commercialism: "What Miss Dunne was supposed to be doing is completely beyond this corner's comprehension, but presumably her presence did provide the added touch of Hollywood glamour which helps sell beer."[2]

But though critical accolades were important to a new medium trying to carve out a credible niche within the entertainment world, most vital to commercial television's long-term survival was sponsorship and viewership, and here the filmed anthologies delivered. The ambitious live shows did bring journalistic praise, and thus served their purpose for sponsors like U.S. Steel who were looking to burnish their corporate images. But it was the more mundane filmed shows that steadily climbed in the ratings and satisfied consumer products sponsors like Proctor & Gamble and Lever Brothers. The 1955–56 season ended with six anthology programs ranking among the top thirty in the Nielsen ratings: all were shot on the West Coast, only one was live, and four had hosts with roots in Hollywood film. Jack Gould may not have liked it, but the "added touch of Hollywood glamour" was embraced by audiences and, in turn, sponsors and networks. This need for glamour also explains why many of the anthology programs that were distributed via syndication (and thus at a competitive disadvantage to network fare for reasons detailed later in this chapter) carried the names of their star-hosts in their titles. Examples included *Crown Theater With Gloria Swanson* (1953), *Ethel Barrymore Theater* (1953), *Edward Arnold Theater* (1954), *Ida Lupino Theater* (1956) and *Douglas Fairbanks, Jr. Presents* (1953–57). This badge of celebrity was vital for shows fighting to maintain visibility on station schedules.

Additionally, star-hosts could be used to deflect the negative connotations associated with filmed programs, especially the overt commercial content as compared to the more subtle institutional advertising common in the live anthologies. A 1955 *Time* magazine article noted the rise in hosts and the value of their ability to "ease the way into the sales message" and "make commercials as painless as possible for viewers." As intermediaries between the program material and the commercials, star-hosts served to separate the specter of crass commercialism from the implied prestige and quality of the dramatic material. Michele Hilmes has addressed this issue using the example of Cecil B. De Mille's role in introducing and closing episodes of *Lux Radio Theater* (NBC and CBS, 1934–55), an anthology program that featured topline Hollywood stars in movie adaptations. De Mille's fame not only served as a lure for radio audiences; more revealingly, Hilmes argues that *Lux* explicitly drew on De Mille's mythic persona as a showman and filmmaking genius to signify the program's cultural legitimacy, a factor that belied his minimal production involvement behind the scenes. In such cases, a notable figurehead could pose as a creative contributor and thereby subtly negotiate the commercial underpinnings of the show and circumvent obvious markings of sponsor control. Joseph Cotten echoed this rhetorical elision in describing his function as host of *On Trial* (NBC and CBS, 1956–59): "I'm a sort of format. No sponsor in his right mind wants to come right on and say 'I'm the sponsor and here's what I'm selling.' It would scare people. He needs a middle man to make the audience feel at home with him." Because Hollywood representatives appeared to be separate from the economic inner workings of television, their very presence as hosts served as artistic endorsement of the show's supposed altruistic intentions.[3]

In truth, of course, some of the stars were present just to draw a paycheck for the minimal work of a few minutes spent talking to the camera, or they were using the limited commitment merely to test out television. Otto Kruger, host of *Lux Video Theater* during its 1955–56 season, spoke of the ease of his task and the resulting laurels: "All I do is come up and tell the people who I am and what we're up to. I don't have a single thing to do with producing, directing or casting the show. Yet I get letters every week complimenting me on my production, my directing, my casting, even my script adaptations." In fact, Hal Humphrey cited such hosting roles as "maybe the best way to handle the problem of TV-or-not-TV" for hesitant stars, because they could try out the medium in a position of prestige without committing to a full-fledged acting role.

Such was the motivation for Irene Dunne to helm *Schlitz Playhouse*. After her triumphant, Oscar-nominated role in *I Remember Mama* (1948), Dunne struggled to find another part to equal it and retired from the big screen, largely due to lack of interest, in 1952. She viewed television as a possible option, however, and signed on with *Schlitz* for twenty-six episodes. Reflecting her desire to ease slowly into television, she chose not to act in any of the plays, though her hosting duties initially consisted of a brief playlet performance prior to the episode in order to set forth the theme for the evening. Jack Gould was not the only critic to deride these segments. *Variety* complained that they were distracting, and when the playlets were subsequently replaced by Dunne simply previewing the episode in the usual manner, *Variety* observed that she now "had little to do . . . indicating that the producers hope to capitalize on her name alone." Dunne herself must have perceived this as inadequate, and she left the show when her contract expired. Though she would make a handful of subsequent acting appearances on anthology and variety shows, Dunne saw television as little more than a diversion and chose to put most of her time toward philanthropic efforts.[4]

James Mason had an even less successful experience with his hosting stint. CBS brought the *Lux* anthology to television in 1950, but its early years were undistinguished, and the network did not balk when competitor NBC lured *Lux Video Theater* away. In adding the previously hostless half-hour show to its schedule in 1954, NBC expanded it to an hour and hired Mason in hopes that his image of British refinement would replicate DeMille's authorial presence and bring a sheen of prestige to the show. Unfortunately, Mason struggled mightily with the live production methods used by *Lux*. He was visibly nervous in his introductions and epilogue interviews with stars, and he reportedly was struck completely silent during a lengthy stretch of one episode when a teleprompter failed. *Variety* wrote that during his premiere episode, Mason seemed "both ill at ease and expressionless"; two months into his duties, the trade paper commented that he was "as erratic as ever and he just doesn't seem to get the idea."[5]

In addition to his problems with live delivery, Mason told the *LA Times* after *Lux* cut him loose in May 1955 that, like Joseph Cotten, he had struggled with the concept of playing himself in the presentational setting: "They told me to act myself. But I was not acting myself at all; I am a quiet, retiring sort of individual, and I would not think of getting up before a bunch of people and showing off about a product." The "self" he adopted for the show did not come across well; critic Laurence Laurent complained, "Mr. Mason appears to be a snob, ill at ease and condescending. . . . If this guy wants to get back into my home, he'll have to acquire manners." Henry Fonda professed to feel similar discomfort with the role of host, which he performed for Rheingold Beer's *The Star and the Story*. He told *TV-Radio Life* that it simply felt awkward to speak directly into the camera. These examples affirm the argument presented in the previous chapter: acting as oneself constituted a skillful performative mode that had to be adapted precisely to television's unique demands. Incidentally, Fonda also could not have enjoyed the critical drubbing he took for performing in the brewmaker's ads.

Especially harsh was John Crosby, who shared both profession and a perspective on filmed television with Jack Gould:

> This series adds Henry Fonda to the rapidly growing list of stars who are picking up an easy buck playing host. A host is a guy who says: "Well, we have a very interesting story tonight set in a mining town in Wales. But first. . . ." And then he drinks some beer. And then at the end he says, "Next week, we have a very interesting story set in a mining town in Pennsylvania." And drinks some more beer. That's virtually all he does. He doesn't even have to carry the checks home. They mail them. It's nice work if you can get it.

Fonda, who had taken a break from Hollywood between 1949 and 1955 to perform in theater, later said he regretted having accepted that work, telling the *LA Times* in 1959: "They showered me with gold. I should've turned them down—but I didn't."[6]

On the opposite side of the spectrum from Fonda and Mason were stars like Robert Montgomery and Loretta Young, who were deeply involved in producing their anthology shows and who received critical and public accolades for their genuine contributions to the development of 1950s television. Montgomery was a television pioneer, becoming one of the first established film stars to commit to series television and the very first to launch a celebrity-produced anthology show, *Robert Montgomery Presents.* Montgomery had been an iconoclast throughout his Hollywood career, helping to form and presiding over the Screen Actors Guild, battling MGM for more varied parts during his contract years, and striving to experiment with cinematic expression—most notably with his directorial efforts on *Lady in the Lake* (1947), which is shot from a first-person subjective perspective. A similar spirit of creative ambition led Montgomery to relocate to New York and jump into live television in 1950.

The show Montgomery created was not innovative initially; in fact, it essentially began as another televised version of *Lux Radio Theater,* focusing on adaptations of Hollywood films. *Variety* even referred to Montgomery's hosting job as "De Mille-ing" the show. Unlike De Mille, though, Montgomery did play a central role in the production of his program, and his creative guidance was essential to the show's success, especially once it ceased using Hollywood texts because of copyright limitations. Montgomery ferreted out new properties for the show to adapt and worked with writers to develop original stories. He

A publicity still alluding to the host's creative control over Robert Montgomery Presents. *NBC/Photofest.*

personally recruited appearances from stars like Helen Hayes, Jane Wyatt, and James Cagney. In order to keep the show on the air year-round, Montgomery developed a special "summer stock" version of the program featuring a repertory company of regular actors, including his daughter Elizabeth (later the star of *Bewitched*). Such creative innovation helped to keep *Robert Montgomery Presents* on the air until 1957, and it made Montgomery one of the highest paid and most respected star-producers on 1950s television. His influence even reached as high as the presidency: the White House hired Montgomery as a consultant to coach Dwight D. Eisenhower for his television appearances.[7]

While Montgomery's work gained him considerable critical respect, Loretta Young became beloved by audiences, especially women. Like Montgomery, Young had evinced an independent spirit during her film career, going freelance within the studio system in 1939 and playing an active role in designing her own career and star image. Young carefully constructed a multilayered, even contradictory star image as a glamorous fashion plate offscreen, an accomplished actress onscreen, and a morally pious woman in both arenas. The high point of her film career came in the late 1940s with a series of successful romantic comedies and moralistic dramas, culminating in a Best Actress Oscar win for *The Farmer's Daughter* (1947) and a nomination for *Come to the Stable* (1949). Young's film career declined quickly thereafter, though, because she was approaching forty in an industry that coveted youth and because the films she most preferred to make, dramas with high-minded themes that also allowed her to display nuanced acting skills, were becoming limited in number. Thus, Young watched with great interest as colleagues like Robert Montgomery and Lucille Ball forged new and varied careers in television. She also heard warnings from her William Morris agents and studio executive Louis B. Mayer that if she went to television, she would never work in the movies again, but when weighing the burgeoning opportunities for older actresses in television against those threats, she decided to play the odds.

Many of her female colleagues chose to follow the path that Ball had forged and turned to continuing-character series. Young chose instead to follow Montgomery's example; in 1953, she formed her own production company and created an anthology program. This was a rare choice for an actress; prior to 1953, only Irene Dunne had helmed a prime-time anthology. But only an anthology could fulfill Young's desire to both maintain her image of fashionable glamour and to act in diverse roles; the screwball nature of the post-*Lucy* sitcoms that many stars were appearing in would minimize those possibilities. Meanwhile, NBC was looking for a distinctive show to add to its Thursday schedule. CBS was increasingly settling for a regularized schedule of standard sitcoms and dramas, but NBC under Pat Weaver's leadership thought that more ambitious, original programming was still needed to keep audiences tuning in. Young's program meshed with this orientation.

Initially titled *Letter to Loretta*, the filmed show's introductory sequences were shot on a living room set, touted as a replica of the actress's own. Drawing on her established Hollywood image as a fashion maven, each episode began with Young swirling through a doorway wearing a glamorous evening gown or cocktail dress. She then would read a purportedly real fan letter asking for Young's advice about a moral issue and subsequently star in a half-hour teleplay dramatizing an ethical lesson to be learned from the letter's queries. *Letter to*

Loretta was unique in two primary regards: it drew upon religious material—Young often closed episodes with biblical citations—and it was
heavily weighted toward feminine sensibilities in everything from the
letter format, which connoted women's magazine advice columns, to
the ostentatious display of fashion in the program introductions. The
latter elements were quickly deemed problematic by the show's sponsor, Procter & Gamble, because they perceived that not enough male
viewers would tune in; only a half-season after its premiere, the show
was renamed *The Loretta Young Show,* and the introductions were
shortened. After the second season, the letter device was also eliminated. The fashion component, however, remained, as did the show's
moral tenor and the emphasis on female-centered stories. While Young
continued to act in many of the show's episodes, and hosted all of them
(except for a half-season period in 1955 when she was off the screen
due to illness), the heavy workload led her to step aside more frequently
in later seasons.[8]

Two factors demand analysis in regard to *The Loretta Young Show:*
the glamorous presentation of its star-host and the pronounced gendered emphasis of the show. Beginning with the former, Young's famous entrances illustrate that a film star's glamorous aura did not have
to be entirely downplayed to find a space on 1950s television; it did,
however, have to be molded to generic specifications. Whereas Faye
Emerson adapted her performance of self to the talk show, where ad-
libbing and informality were most valued, the theatrical flair of the anthology show encouraged Loretta Young to maintain a more formal
presence that favored allusions to the decorum of Hollywood glamour.
Nonetheless, as the negative reaction to James Mason's perceived snob-
bery would indicate, even an anthology host had to perpetuate the illusion of an intimate, relatively commensurate relationship with the audience. Young successfully lessened the potential distance between her
glamorous image and the middle-class viewer being targeted by the
show through her gracious introductory interactions with the implied
audience and through her teleplay performances. The letter device particularly allowed Young to appear to personally respond to her audience, and the fact that she would act out the part of the letter writer in
episodes connected her directly to her fan's lives. Even once the show
turned away from the letter device, the relationship between Young's
hosting and acting performances on the show was still essential. Historian Madelyn Ritrosky-Winslow writes:

*Loretta Young in
her evening finery.
NBC/Photofest.*

According to Young, her image of enduring beauty and glamour *and* the opportunity to play a variety of characters (including unglamorous roles) were important to her. Indeed, she felt more comfortable playing unglamorous roles knowing the audience also got to see her as glamorous Loretta Young. Since Loretta Young, host, appeared to be the "real" Loretta Young, she could embody two contradictory yet marketable representations. Young the glamorous movie star was also Young the informal TV personality and confidante.

Perhaps this also explains why Irene Dunne was unsuccessful in her hosting stint. *Variety* found Dunne's presence to be distracting and too extravagant, because she was merely glamorous window-dressing and lacked an associative connection to the show she purported to represent, as well as to the audience. Loretta Young's presence and star image, on the other hand, was tightly woven into all aspects of the show, with her persona fueling both the hosting segments and the moral dramas that followed. Such a fusion enabled her glamorous displays of fashion and allowed her to develop into a celebrity beloved by female viewers in particular.[9]

The latter factor raised the specter of culturally derided soap opera, however, a genre at odds with the cultural prestige associated with legitimate anthology drama. Not surprisingly, the majority of anthology hosts were male, and while a broad cultural bias toward men as more authoritative figures than women would explain this gap, we can also consider the association of female broadcast performers with the soap opera, a form scorned for its superficiality and commercialism. By the late 1930s, radio had cemented a rhetorical split between the differing complexions of prime-time and daytime programming, with the latter culturally codified as a feminized form of melodrama for housewives and the former embodying masculine-identified genres of drama. Many of these assumptions carried over to television, but with the medium still trying to find its way in the early 1950s and daytime television relatively undeveloped, female-centered drama did find a space in prime time, as *The Loretta Young Show* would indicate. The show was nonetheless frequently scorned for this female-centeredness. In fact, *Variety*'s reviewers appeared to be competing to see who could come up with the cleverest gender-based mockery of the show. A sampling of potential winners:

- "Any male watching this was either trapped or lost the race to the tuning knob."
- "Many of the male viewers must have stepped out to the kitchen for a sandwich and something to drink while the femme contingent happily clutched damp hankies to streaming eyes."
- "It's strictly a hen party for the soap trade and any male trapped by it must have been paying off for a football game he caught earlier in the day ('You had the Rams, now let me have Loretta')."

This lopsided appeal may have been problematic for the cultural stature of the program—Jack Gould's lone review of the show across its eight seasons dismissed its premiere as "nothing but a trite farce"—but for sponsor Proctor & Gamble and its featured products of Tide laundry soap and Lilt home permanent, the scorned "femme contingent" was exactly what was desired. *Variety* acknowledged this with more witticisms: "There's little attempt in this series to disguise the fact that the audience aim is the consumer, in this case the shopper who wheels her basket up to the soap shelf. Let others cavil at such dramatic pattern, the sponsor shrugs off the soap opera connotation and happily scans the re-sults, good enough to bring repeated renewals." A confluence of high-class glamour and low-class soap opera, *The Loretta Young Show* embodied the complex paradoxes of early television's fluidity.[10]

There were surprisingly few attempts to replicate Young's success, and none of them prospered for long. Proctor & Gamble turned to Jane Wyman in the fall of 1955 to bolster the sagging ratings for its long-running *Fireside Theater* (NBC, 1949–58). Wyman seemed an ideal choice for the half-hour filmed show, which had a legacy of presenting human-interest stories in the vein of popular women's fiction of the time. Wyman certainly had an appropriate star image for this, having recently appeared in two family melodramas for Universal, *Magnificent Obsession* (1954), for which she received an Oscar nomination, and *All That Heaven Allows* (1955). With Wyman's cinematic successes in mind, many questioned why she would choose to turn to television. The reasons she gave at the time revolved around her preference for the variety, challenge, and security offered by an anthology series. She later claimed, if only in hindsight, that her film career actually was on the wane at that point because of her age and a decline in her preferred roles. No matter the reason, Wyman did concentrate on television in the years to come. In addition to hosting *Fireside Theater,* Wyman acted in nearly half of the show's plays, and she had considerable production control over the program, which was retitled *The Jane Wyman Show* in 1956. Wyman's star power did not provide the ratings boost Proctor & Gamble was hoping for, however, and the show was retired in 1958.[11]

The late 1950s were a time of struggle for all anthology programs, and two more Young-inspired shows would join Wyman's as participants in that decline. *The Barbara Stanwyck Show* (NBC, 1960–61) was problematic because it tried to insert a star who was not like Loretta Young into a show much like hers, complete with the glamorous entrance and female-centered tales. Reviewers dismissed Stanwyck as an inferior Loretta Young imitation and wrote the show off as soap opera pap. "[T]here was nothing to attract anybody but the dames who have survived afternoon TV with a desire for more glycerine," said one reviewer. *The DuPont Show with June Allyson* survived for two seasons, from 1959 to 1961 on CBS, as a high-budget show striving for respectability, but it too was largely dismissed by critics, accused of "reaching down to the level of women's mag fiction." Allyson complained about such automatic dismissals, telling the *LA Examiner*, "[A]ny show that stars a woman just naturally seems to be called a soap opera, whether it is or not." Especially at a time when evening television was becoming the province of general audience fare and male-oriented genres, female-identified shows were quickly being marginalized.[12]

Shirley Temple was one of the few female anthology hosts to avoid the soap opera stigma, mainly because the show she helmed was chiefly directed toward children. Temple emerged from a near-decade retirement to host *Shirley Temple's Storybook* on NBC, a show specifically tailored for her, which first ran periodically in 1958, then every third Monday night in 1959, and the similar *Shirley Temple Show*, airing on ABC every week during the 1960–61 season. Temple was lured from her entertainment exodus by the prospect of easy work that her own children could watch. She had little production input on the show, which presented dramatizations of beloved children's stories, and acted in just a few episodes, while her hosting duties required only a few days' commitment each month in exchange for a salary and profit participation. She also shrewdly capitalized on the merchandising possibilities of the show with the rerelease of a set of Shirley Temple dolls, as well as the publication of a series of tie-in children's books. In turn, Temple's timeless child star image was ideally suited to the show's fairytale orientation and had the potential to draw in audiences young and old. Children would tune in for the stories and Temple's tender delivery, and adult audiences were enticed by the image of the grown-up, now raven-haired "curly top" and the complexly alluring, lingering connotations of the child star within the womanly hostess. *Time* magazine wrote of the premiere episode, "Shirley Temple, now a full-bodied 29, had bridged a whole generation without losing so much as a dimple." Temple declined to carry on after two seasons of her show, and after a handful of other minor television appearances, she returned to maintaining a domestic career and later pursued political and diplomatic opportunities.[13]

Though Temple's television work presumably had little impact on her future civic endeavors, Ronald Reagan's relationship with *General Electric Theater* unquestionably did. Reagan's film career had nearly dried up by the early 1950s, but he was initially reluctant to turn to television. He was especially wary of attaching himself to a continuing-character series, because he feared overexposure and the perceived career limitation of being associated with a single character. He also realized, however, that he soon wouldn't have a viable acting career to limit. Earl Dunkel, a General Electric employee who helped conceive *General Electric Theater,* stated, "As far as actors go, he was really hard up at that time. He didn't have much of an income." Thus, Reagan decided to test out television via the anthology drama, with guest appearances on *Ford Theater* (CBS, NBC and ABC, 1949–57), *Lux Video Theater,* and *Schlitz Playhouse of Stars.* He also tried hosting by periodically helming the musical variety show *The Orchid Award* (ABC, 1953–54). Success in these ventures convinced him that hosting an anthology drama could be the key to his career resurrection, and he advanced his commitment to television by signing on with *General Electric Theater* as both host and occasional star. He did request that he act in no more than six shows a year, and that in hosting shows, he appear only in the opening and closing moments in order to avoid the dreaded overexposure.[14]

Another key factor in Reagan's decision to sign on as host was his desire to start laying the groundwork for a possible future political career by projecting a self-assured image. *General Electric Theater* gave him an appropriate outlet for this aim by situating him as an authority on a popular yet respected program within a prestigious genre. General Electric and Reagan also agreed that he would not have to do on-air advertisements for the corporation. Dunkel declared, "We very carefully wouldn't let him do that because it would cheapen his role overall for him to get right down to the product nitty-gritty." This discriminating connection to *General Electric Theater* would cement Reagan's image in the public consciousness more so than his films ever could. *TV Guide* characterized Reagan in November 1958 as a "living TV symbol as vividly distinct in viewer's minds as the flowing script of the sponsor's initials on its products."[15]

For their part, General Electric favored Reagan because of his established star identity. The first season of the show had aired without a host, and producers felt that a host was needed for its sophomore outing in order to tie together better the disparate properties the program presented and to put forward the company's image more strongly. In addition to public awareness of his onscreen image, fostered most memorably by his performance as George Gipp in *Knute Rockne, All American* (1940), audiences might have been familiar with Reagan's offscreen activities, such as his former presidency of the Screen Actors Guild; his work for the Motion Picture Industry

Ronald Reagan representing General Electric Theater. CBS/Photofest.

Council, a public relations organization started by Hollywood producers to improve the industry's image; and his staunch yet tempered anti-Communist stance. Dunkel characterized what producers and General Electric executives were looking for in a host: "Good moral character, intelligent. Not the kind with the reputation for social ramble. . . . When Ron was suggested, it went through almost immediately."[16]

Reagan's involvement with General Electric went beyond the television show. The company asked Reagan if he would go on factory tours for them to represent the company to the labor force and to involve General Electric in positive community relations. Reagan enthusiastically agreed, viewing this as an opportunity to hone his public relations skills. He told *TV Guide*, "I want to meet and shake hands personally with each of the employees of General Electric." Reagan later acknowledged his fondness for these tours and the public speaking experience they gave him, and his talks were received very positively, as plant managers and local Chambers of Commerce repeatedly asked for more Reagan appearances. Dunckel revealingly describes Reagan's public speaking success: "The fact that he was a movie star gave him the entree so people would listen. Then what he had to say was so compelling that people were, for the most part, convinced and supportive." One could say the same for his role as host on the television show and, later, his role as a politician. *General Electric Theater* had granted Reagan an essential platform for launching his legendary political career, and the public goodwill that he fostered as the national face of both a popular, prestigious show and a major corporation provided an immeasurable boost to his visibility and credibility.[17]

These examples illustrate that successful hosts established a symbiotic relationship between the show and their star identities. The handful of failed experiments largely stemmed from a measure of dissonance between star image and program orientation. With this in mind, the case of Adolphe Menjou and *Favorite Story* comes to the fore, as both the star and the program presented substantial challenges. *Favorite Story* was a syndicated anthology program, and syndicated fare was industrially and critically marginalized, dismissed as largely irrelevant by television's ambassadors of taste. Lacking the cultural credibility and financial resources, as well as the immediate status, of live network programming, the syndicated television film had special challenges in competing with network programming and attracting name talent. One of the first relevant stars to commit to syndication was Adolphe Menjou, when he agreed in 1952 to host *Favorite Story* for one of the premiere syndication producers of the period, Frederic W. Ziv. An active performer since the silent film era, Menjou saw his career wane by the 1950s, and he was even a potentially controversial figure owing to his vehement anti-Communist posturing. As we shall see, syndicated fare was a vital alternative for Menjou given the status of his career at that point. *Favorite Story* is also an intriguing example because of its uniqueness within syndicated programming itself. Most syndicated telefilms were akin to Hollywood B movies, mainly low-budget Westerns and action-adventure series. *Favorite Story,* on the other hand, was an anthology drama, a genre that carried more highbrow connotations than typical syndicated programming. How could a producer create and sell a show of syndicated stature, with a tightly controlled budget and limited resources, but with a network nature (meaning prestigious programming with highbrow connotations)? And how could the presence of a flawed star like Adolphe Menjou be utilized to negotiate this combination?

Adolphe Jean Menjou was born in Pittsburgh, Pennsylvania, but his Francophone name and Continental manner conjured up a sense of foreign nobility that became key to his film persona. In his autobiography, Menjou noted how his waxed mustache particularly led him into villain roles in the silent era: "[W]hen they cooked up a story with a real, low-down nasty, he was always a foreign nobleman, with hemophilia, three discarded mistresses, and a yen to marry an innocent and beautiful heiress. That was where I shone. Casting directors thought I looked the part." The role that catapulted him to stardom was in Charlie Chaplin's *A Woman of Paris* (1923). Here, Menjou portrayed Pierre Ravel, a wealthy French playboy. In his opening appearance in a restaurant, much of the iconography that would come to define Menjou's persona is evident: Ravel is impeccably dressed in dinner clothes, he gazes and smiles smugly at other patrons, and he casually flicks a cigarette toward the floor. In only one brief scene is he not in dinner clothes, and throughout the film he carries props of the upper class: a top hat, gloves, a pocket watch. Throughout the film, his character is ironic and unsentimental, especially to his despairing love interest. To her angry retort, "You'll never see me again," he replies, "Very well, phone me sometime." In this role lay the seeds of what would become the Menjou persona: a refined, immaculately outfitted and urbane lover who was often playfully amoral and suavely controlling. Menjou's studio through much of the 1920s, Paramount, then worked toward building that persona through publicity and promotion. He described in his autobiography, "In thousands of photographs, cartoons, and caricatures printed in newspapers I saw myself depicted as a sort of supersophisticate." In what would become his most familiar distinguishing trait, Paramount emphasized his wardrobe, publishing descriptions of his garments and his annual clothes budget and penning articles that characterized him as a clotheshorse and a fashion trendsetter.[18]

Menjou survived the transition to sound and built upon his silent film persona in such films as 1930's *Morocco*. Here Menjou played Monsieur Le Bessier, a wealthy playboy and a "citizen of the world," according to a character who introduces him in a nightclub. In this early scene, Menjou's character strolls about the room, greeting numerous foreigners as if to illustrate his introduction. Once seated in the club, he coolly appraises the crowd, urbanely smoking, and later casually flirting with nightclub performer Amy Joly (played by Marlene Dietrich). Throughout the film, this impression of social command is enhanced further, as Le Bessier confidently works his way into a relationship with Joly, scheming to remove a rival from the scenario. Although he is depicted as manipulative, Le Bessier is also somewhat sympathetic: he truly loves Joly, but she chooses his rival, played by Gary Cooper. This combination of debonair flair with calculating control was in evidence throughout his 1930s performances, including such films as *The Front Page* (1931), *A Farewell to Arms* (1932), and *Convention City* (1933). Studio promotion of this period particularly focused on his status as a clotheshorse, an intellectual, an art collector, and a man of the world.[19]

Of all his supposed "real-life" traits, fashion received the most attention. Pressbooks were filled with articles about his status as one of the world's best-dressed men, and one suggested that local newspapers run a local best-dressed man contest to exploit the arrival of the latest Menjou picture. Menjou's image as a worldly intellectual with knowledge of multiple languages was also heavily publicized. Claimed one pressbook article, "He keeps his familiarity with four languages besides English—French, German, Italian, and Spanish—oiled and primed so that he can use them at a moment's notice." Further, Menjou's "ethnic" background, chiefly his connection to French and Irish culture, was often cited. While acknowledging his American nationality, one publicity article lent greater credence to the fact that Menjou's father was French-born and his mother was Irish: "He can be as sophisticated as only a Frenchman knows how to be—and as sentimental as an Irishman." Also rating frequent mentions were his various art and antique collections, such as an assortment of exquisite Chinese eggs, and his collections of extravagant clothing, including spats, dressing gowns, and cravats.[20]

Though this publicity touting Menjou as a leading fashion plate, cultural aficionado, and intellectual certainly was a screen and publicity construction, Menjou claimed in his autobiography that he naturally fit some of these characteristics and at times consciously conformed to them, especially his reputation as a fashion maven. Further, he truly did have a large collection of various antiques, partly for financial investments. To support the notion that audiences might have been aware of this aspect of his life, we can look to a 1952 print advertisement in which Menjou appeared for Rheingold Lager. For the ad's picture, Menjou held his stamp collection folder up to the camera for display. The caption read: "'Once you've been introduced to collecting, you

A typical Menjou look from the 1930s.
WISCONSIN CENTER FOR FILM AND THEATER RESEARCH.

never get over it,' advises actor Adolphe Menjou. 'I not only collect stamps, but paintings and Oriental ivory pieces.'" Additionally, the "News from the World of Stamps" section of the *New York Times* contained several articles in the late 1940s and 1950s following the auction of portions of Menjou's stamp collection.[21]

In all likelihood, Menjou had to trade in his antique collection to achieve financial stability once he reached his fifties, a point at which leading man roles as a debonair playboy would be hard to find. Further, shifts in Hollywood star images diminished his leading role opportunities; the "European type" may have prevailed in the 1920s, but the rise of the American hero embodied by John Wayne, Gary Cooper, and Henry Fonda and the cultural milieu of the 1940s sounded the death knell for starring roles of this sort. Primarily relegated to character actor status in the wartime and postwar era, Menjou most often played the role of the gruff elder, while still maintaining aspects of worldliness and intellect. In essence, he began playing an aging "Menjou type," more caricature than fleshed-out character, in such films as *You Were*

123

Never Lovelier (1942), *State of the Union* (1948), and *To Please a Lady* (1950). Across these films, Menjou played authoritarians either comically or sternly exhibiting impatience toward the leading actors' actions. One of the few instances of off-casting for Menjou in this period came in *Across the Wide Missouri* (1951), although the role still exhibits key elements of the Menjou persona. In this frontier adventure film, Menjou played Pierre, a scruffy, destitute yet cheerful French trapper. On his head, Pierre wears a beret, an earring, and a thick beard, and his clothes consist of dirty blue jeans and a torn baggy coat—clearly counter to Menjou's image. Even so, Pierre acts as translator for the various Native American tribespeople traveling with his hunting group, and he frequently dispenses romantic advice to the lead character (played by Clark Gable), thereby exhibiting his familiar characteristic of worldly knowledge. Pierre is still a comic personality throughout, though, exhibited by his constant propensity to nap and his frequent drunkenness. In this vein, the typical Menjou character was now a blustery father figure, often used for comic relief, rather than a suave man of the world.

FREDERIC ZIV AND THE STATUS OF SYNDICATION

By the early 1950s, Menjou's film career consisted almost solely of such character roles. A new opportunity, however, presented itself in 1952 when noted syndication producer Frederic W. Ziv asked Menjou to host *Favorite Story*, a half-hour filmed anthology drama. Historian Hal Erickson argues, "When Ziv came up with *Favorite Story*, Adolphe Menjou frankly needed the work." For his part, Ziv has claimed that Menjou was rich by this point due to shrewd investing and thus did not need the salary Ziv was offering, but because he wished to sustain his acting career, which had indeed waned, he agreed to host *Favorite Story*. Ziv started the company that bore his name in 1937, and he set out to produce syndicated programming for radio stations, including such shows as *Boston Blackie* (1945–49), *Philo Vance* (1948–50), and *The Cisco Kid* (1947–56). Ziv entered television production in 1948 by producing fifteen-minute compilation programs, including *Yesterday's Newsreels* (1948–50). There were numerous holes in the daily schedule in this early period, so stations gladly put his shows on the air, and Ziv gained a strong foothold in the non-network television programming market. In 1950, Ziv moved his facilities to Hollywood and began to produce filmed programs, beginning with *The Cisco Kid* (1950–56).[22]

Before delving into *Favorite Story* and Menjou's role on the program, it is necessary to consider the industrial circumstances of syndicated programming in order to establish exactly what position the show was in and how Ziv operated within these circumstances. To understand the broad function and image of first-run syndication in broadcast history, we must begin in the radio era and make the key distinction between the local and the national. Local stations, producers, and sponsors simply could not afford the programming and advertising costs that national networks, producers, and sponsors could. Frederic Ziv spoke of this in an interview: "The thought occurred to me that all the national advertisers at that time had their choice of expensive radio programs, the local and regional advertisers did not. So I determined to create and transcribe radio programs—expensive radio programs—in terms of the local and regional sponsor." Thus, Ziv mainly produced programs sold directly to local entities. This method necessitated a distribution system wherein programs were recorded on discs and mailed to stations or sponsors. In contrast, networks usually fed live broadcasts directly to their affiliates.[23]

Two interrelated factors resulted from the disparity between regional and national programming: (1) a lowbrow cultural image attached to syndicated programming and (2) monopolistic network control over the broadcasting system. First, the transcriptions used in syndicated programming helped lead to a cultural and critical bias against transcriptions. The quality of the recorded discs could be poor, and even a quality recording could be garbled by inadequate station playback equipment. Granted, the quality of recordings had vastly increased by the mid-1940s, yet syndicated programming still carried a label of inferiority—explicitly so because of an FCC rule requiring that stations announce when programming was transcribed, which stemmed from an earlier judgment that live broadcasting provided a valuable public service. Thus, because of the very nature of the productions, syndicated programming could easily be judged as culturally inferior. Of course, the potential competition brought by syndicators meant that the networks had a great interest in perpetuating this negative image attached to recorded programs. Because of monopolistic control over land lines and transmission cable, only the networks could supply live broadcasts. Therefore, they needed to make stations dependent on live programming to prevent transcription producers from gaining substantial airtime. Networks had a vested interest in showcasing live programming as vital and in portraying themselves as operating in the public interest with culturally superior live shows.

The notion that recorded syndication programming was inferior in content quality to what the networks could render live was partly true, especially because of the distinct financial advantages held by network-related producers. Networks could force affiliates to run network programming at prescribed times and thereby dominate the more lucrative prime-time hours, where larger audiences meant higher advertising revenue. This left syndicators with only so-called fringe time, the late afternoon and late evening slots. Fringe-time slotting assuredly marginalized the status of the programming, and smaller audiences also meant less advertising revenue. Add to this the expenses of distributing these recorded programs across the country, and it is clear why syndicators simply could not match network production budgets, let alone their cultural status.

As with many of radio's industrial structures, the syndication-network relationship largely carried over into television. Syndicators maintained both their image of inferiority as well as their very real insufficiencies in production budgets and programming slots. The more expensive medium of television only exacerbated these conditions, especially in the early 1950s before substantial set and station saturation—and thus higher advertising revenue—took hold. Further, early stations were mainly concentrated in larger cities, where network control was the strongest, meaning profits simply were not so abundant for syndicators. The networks gladly perpetuated their preeminent image and the critical establishment supported it as well. As a result, syndicated programming remained largely marginalized.[24]

Selling programs to stations and advertisers thus required innovation in both programming and promotion, and few syndicators were as adept in these areas as Frederic W. Ziv. Jeff Kisselhoff, author of an oral history on television, says with affection, "Nobody gave it to 'em like Ziv." Ziv said of his company's work: "No one else created the kind of sales and promotion helps that we did. Let's say a bakery in Indianapolis bought one of our programs. He would receive posters, window displays, store displays, newspaper ads, and newspaper stories to feed to the editors." Such gimmicks are reminiscent of the schemes devised by the publicity departments of the classical Hollywood film studios, and they attest to Ziv's business acumen. From the company slogan, "Your Outstanding Source of Dependable Programming," to innovative techniques to attract star names (such as percent-of-profit deals), Ziv battled ardently against syndication's inferior position.[25]

As noted above, though, early television's industrial circumstances brought substantial challenges, especially financial ones. As Ziv admitted in a 1975 interview: "In the early days of television, we had to produce these things cheap. There's just no question about it, and cheap is the word. Not inexpensive, cheap." Nonetheless, Ziv felt strongly that his shows matched up in quality to the networks. Leon Benson, a Ziv producer, director, and story editor explained: "There was nothing deficient in [Ziv's] productions. The same crews, the same people were used except there was a great cost consciousness." This meant exploiting low-budget telefilm genres akin to B movies: action-adventure, mystery, and Western programs. While costs may have dictated this choice, Ziv claimed these genres were specifically chosen to draw in audiences, as well:

> It was obvious to all of us who had our fingers on the pulse of the American public that they wanted escapist entertainment. Now what is escapist entertainment? The western has always been dependable escapist entertainment. . . . We did not do highbrow material. We did material that would appeal to the broadest segment of the public. And they became the big purchasers of television sets. And as they bought television sets, the beer sponsors began to go on television. And the beer sponsors, for the most part, wanted to reach the truck and taxi driver, the average man and woman. They were not interested in that small segment that wanted opera, ballet, and symphony. The western is an almost foolproof entertainment vehicle.[26]

The *Favorite Story* program on which Menjou appeared, then, is a curious example because it was a telefilm anthology program, not a Western or similar fare. Though he objected to their domineering tactics, Ziv could not argue with the success of network programs and formats. Because the precarious financial situation of the syndicator dictated a low-risk approach, Ziv thus tried programming formats already proven successful by the networks. The anthology drama genre was proven by the early 1950s, and *Favorite Story* accordingly became one of Ziv's handful of attempts at such drama on television. More important, especially from businessman Ziv's view, *Favorite Story* had been one of Ziv's most successful and popular radio shows. With its established fan base and proven potential for success, *Favorite Story* was a logical choice for television development.

Favorite Story began on radio in 1946 with film star Ronald Colman as host. On each episode, a celebrity guest chose a famous story from classic literature—his or her supposed favorite—for a half-hour radio adaptation. The show presented adaptations of such works as *Pride and Prejudice, Great Expectations,* and *Cyrano de Bergerac,* and guest selectors included some of the most noted celebrities of the time: screen stars Gregory Peck, Shirley Temple, and Cary Grant; film directors Alfred Hitchcock and Frank Capra; radio stars Burns and Allen and Jack Benny; bandleaders Artie Shaw and Kay Kyser; poet Robert Frost and writer Sinclair Lewis; athletes Rogers Hornsby and Jack Dempsey; and scientists Lee De Forest and Albert Einstein. The guest celebrities, however, never actually appeared on the program (they only lent their names) and the choosing of stories was in effect just a publicity hook. Production documents indicate that celebrities were asked for their favorite stories, but they had to select from a predetermined list and were not always matched up with a story they selected. The name value of the selectors was especially crucial in terms of the financial benefits: because the selectors never appeared on the show, Ziv did not have to pay them any salary. In contrast, the popular, and expensive, network radio anthology *Lux Radio Theater* paid its headlining guest stars, such as Clark Gable, Bette Davis, and Ginger Rogers, $5,000 per appearance. Ziv could utilize the lure of similar names but without any expense beyond plugging a star's upcoming movie or a writer's book.

The notion to produce *Favorite Story* as a telefilm came as early as 1948. The program's writers, Jerome Lawrence and Robert Lee (who would become Broadway playwrights), hoped to produce the episodes for first-run exhibition in theaters, as part of double features, then to present subsequent runs on television. A letter written in June 1948 by Lawrence and Lee proposed the following:

> [A] series of moderate-budget motion pictures embodying an extension of the [*Favorite Story*] formula. Each picture will be the Favorite Story of a different top-flight star, who appears at the start of the film and narrates portions of it. . . . The films will be of brief feature-length . . . so that they will fit into an hour television-broadcast unit; provision will made for possible "act breaks" in which the television commercials may be subsequently inserted. . . . We anticipate no reluctance on

the part of advertisers to buy for television what has previously shown in theaters; in fact, the radio drama which commands the largest audiences today is based on adaptations of motion pictures.

Though the latter part of the letter was prescient, the theater-to-television format was never explored by Ziv. Instead, *Favorite Story* was brought solely to television in 1953 as a half-hour anthology drama. The stories would still be adaptations of works by prestigious authors, but Lawrence and Lee mainly shifted to adapting short stories in order to better accommodate the restrictive half-hour running time.[27]

Favorite Story's adaptation of classic short stories by such authors as Balzac, Dumas, and Hawthorne was strategic for several reasons. First, this choice could be viewed in financial terms: many of these stories were in the public domain and could be adapted without a significant monetary charge for the rights. Second, relying on a proven property could further minimize risks, or in the words of a 1953 *Variety* review of the program, "Adapting the classics is about as neat a means of insuring story value as can be found." Finally, the use of prestigious literature could also potentially help to battle the lowbrow image of syndication. This last point, though, appears to challenge Frederic Ziv's comment, "We did not do highbrow material." After all, adaptations of tales by Tolstoy, Dostoevsky, and other authors in the canon of great literature surely carried a high-culture status. When questioned about this apparent contradiction, Ziv responded that the focus was not on the highbrow quality of the literature; these were just good stories. In this sense (and remembering that these adaptations lasted no longer than twenty-eight minutes), Ziv could boil these tales down to their core action and present them in an attractive package for the "truck and taxi driver" that sponsors wanted to reach.[28]

One element the masses wanted was stars, and it was here that Ziv was willing to spend the most. Accordingly, the radio version of *Favorite Story* featured film star Ronald Colman as host at an exorbitant salary. Said Ziv of the importance of having an established star: "[We] tended to pick a name that needed no additional words to describe. If you said 'I have a show with Ronald Colman,' you didn't have to add any words. Stations were receptive, networks were receptive, sponsors were receptive, audiences were receptive." Colman declined to host the television version of the program, though, presumably because he was already involved with development of his own network television sitcom, *The*

Halls of Ivy. As it turned out, Ziv eliminated the celebrity-selector format for the television version of the show. Production files do not indicate the reason for this, but it is likely that the producers felt it would be necessary for the celebrities to appear on television if their names were being referenced, which would have added a prohibitive expense. Plus, given the early low status of television, especially syndicated programming, celebrities of the caliber utilized on the radio version would not have wanted even just their names attached to the show.

Nonetheless, it was essential that Ziv retain a celebrity-host. Because each episode would present a different story, a host was needed for program continuity and identity. Further, the shows were quite ambitious in condensing the sometimes complicated stories into a half-hour format, and a narrator could help to elide narrative gaps efficiently. Finally, having a noted Hollywood star, even only a former one, would provide publicity for the show and potentially raise its status higher than that of a typical syndicated show. Thus, in place of both Colman and the celebrity-selector format of the radio version came just one figure: Adolphe Menjou.[29]

Before moving to an analysis of his role, I must note that writers Lawrence and Lee initially did not want to hire Menjou. Bob Lee in fact wrote a three-page letter to Lawrence explaining in great detail why he felt Menjou would not be an appropriate host for *Favorite Story*, focusing on two main concerns: Menjou's image within the Hollywood political community and the potential incongruity of his current persona with the show. First, Menjou's steadfast right-wing beliefs were problematic. One of the most fervent anti-Communists in Hollywood, Menjou fully cooperated when asked to testify as a friendly witness at the 1947 HUAC hearings. Throughout the 1950s, Menjou railed against Communist infiltration of both the U.S. government and Hollywood. He told the *Los Angeles Times* in 1952, "Believe me, this country is in trouble! . . . If there is not a change in government there will not be a United States as we know it within the next two years." In 1959, just as the blacklist was losing its force, Menjou decried the hiring of Hollywood Ten member Dalton Trumbo to write the screenplay for *Spartacus* (1960), insisting that the Communist threat had not yet passed. In his autobiography, producer/director Stanley Kramer described Menjou's fervent politics:

> Very sophisticated, extremely aware, he was almost psychopathi-
> cally defending the money and property he had acquired over the

years of a successful film career. To him, there *was* a "commie" behind every tree, and anyone to the left of Hamilton Fish was a "pinko." He was a reincarnation of a witch hunter of the Middle Ages.[30]

These issues were very much in circulation when *Favorite Story* was casting in mid-1952, and Bob Lee approached others in Hollywood about the idea of Menjou as host for *Favorite Story*. Writing Lawrence of the reactions he received, Lee reported:

> We had no idea the violent feelings against this man from all quarters of the motion picture industry. . . . He is not disliked for his politics. He is disliked for his irresponsible and half-cocked blathering. Intelligent persons of every political complexion in Hollywood (where he lives, his neighbors) are resentful of his blanket indictments of the industry which has supported him quite nobly for several decades. Of a half a hundred people whom we have queried about Menjou in the past few days, I have not heard one good word for him. The opinions range from a shrug to vitriol.

Echoing the above discussions, Menjou himself acknowledged that his beliefs were an employment obstacle; not surprisingly, however, he attributed these difficulties to Communist infiltration of Hollywood. In the February 1952 *Variety* article "Menjou Says Anti-Reds Can't Get Jobs in Pix," Menjou claimed, "If you open your mouth against Communism you're dead. You can't get work." Correspondingly, according to a personal letter he wrote in July 1956 to FBI director J. Edgar Hoover, Menjou planned to tone down his public anti-Communist rhetoric for the sake of his career but was no less concerned privately:

> I am absolutely horrified and appalled at what is and has been going on in Washington. A lifetime Republican I am seriously considering not voting this year. . . . I am convinced that most of the leaders have not the vaguest idea of the evils of Communism! I no longer have any desire to be labeled "controversial." It is economically unsound in my business. So I just sit and fume.[31]

Given these assumptions, Menjou might have been interested to read the rest of Bob Lee's memo. Lee wrote that "in the effort to be a true liberal," he wanted to consider Menjou's potential as host independent from political or personal feelings: "[A]ny judgment that we wish to make regarding Mr. Menjou must, in absolute fairness, be based on his professional ability and stature, and on his commercial ability to sell goods." Thus, Lee professed that his biggest concern was with Menjou's appropriateness for the role, not his politics (of course, he believed that Menjou did not measure up here either). Lee subsequently conveyed a revealing impression of the actor's film persona at that time:

> In our proposed undertaking, the viewer will be offered entertainment of unquestioned importance and literary stature. Is Menjou a star who is associated in the public mind with such works? He is not a star. He is a successful featured player. . . . In pictures he has played, expertly, secondary roles of a comedy nature, for the most part. Comedy is surely his forte. . . . Compare him with the man he is intended to replace. . . . Colman was the symbol of the stories we offered in the *Favorite Story* series: prestige, entertainment, charm, wit. . . . Menjou represents almost the antithesis of these symbols.

Arguing that "*prestige* is of the essence," both Lee and Jerome Lawrence composed an April 1952 memo to Ziv executive vice president John Sinn, who was in charge of packaging the talent for *Favorite Story.* Lawrence and Lee wrote: "The *Favorite Story* properties—important, rich with prestige, often costume pieces—are not a *natural* avenue for the most profitable display of Menjou's talents."[32]

Presumably, Menjou's post-1940 work as a character actor and caricature of his earlier persona led the writers to believe that Menjou would not be appropriate for the hosting role, especially as he apparently no longer carried the connotations of high culture that Ronald Colman supposedly did. Actors who Lawrence and Lee felt were more suited to the task included Claude Rains, Joseph Cotten, Cedric Hardwicke, David Niven, and Laurence Olivier. It appears, however, these men were never seriously pursued. In an exasperated response to Sinn's preference for Menjou, Lee penned, "To [Sinn's] question 'Who if not Menjou?'—tell him 'Anybody except Lassie and Buddy Ebsen!'"[33]

This dissension logically raises the question, why *did* Ziv ultimately hire Menjou as host of *Favorite Story*? First, John Sinn heavily endorsed Menjou, who, along with his (Menjou's) wife Verree Teasdale, had worked with Sinn on a fifteen-minute radio chat program called *Meet the Menjous* (1949–50). Through this association, Sinn found Menjou to be an agreeable host. As Bob Lee described it: "I think John has been charmed by Menjou. John knows him. John has worked with him, and sold him successfully." Ultimately, then, perhaps Lawrence and Lee were overruled by Sinn. As for Menjou's political image hindering his employment, Frederic Ziv claimed in a personal interview that the blacklist controversies did not matter to him. While this may have been contemporary pride speaking, Ziv did indeed employ other actors involved on both sides of the Red Scare, including Lloyd Bridges, whose name was still on the blacklist when Ziv hired him for *Sea Hunt* (1957–61). As to Menjou's specific reputation, Ziv claimed, "I didn't give a damn."[34]

In this vein, we must consider again the constraints Ziv faced in his productions. Ziv felt strongly about the value of the Hollywood star name, but because of the status of syndicated programming in this early era, few notable stars were willing to appear on filmed television programs. Particularly in 1952, with television still literally and figuratively striving to sell itself, this unwillingness was a major challenge for syndicators. Bob Lee had written in his lengthy letter to Lawrence about Ziv's impressive stable of stars under contract, "Why take second-raters, when the Bogarts, the MacMurrays, the Dunnes, the Colmans want to work with you?" But these stars were working on Ziv radio programs, not television shows. Also, despite the fact that A-list Hollywood stars had long been a staple on radio dramas, such was not yet the case with television. Not until 1954, with Eddie Cantor signing on to do a Ziv variety show, did a star of significant profile associate himself with one of Ziv's programs A *Billboard* article in fact presented this contract as a "crucial test for syndicated programming":

> The major sponsors of syndicated shows have continually demanded network-type shows with name stars, to put them in a competitive position with the national advertisers. Recognizing this, the top distributors have been shooting for the stars in an effort to keep the cash register ringing. The question is whether the syndicated market can actually pay the price of such properties.

In 1952, syndicators could not yet even think of paying such a price. Thus, if Ziv wanted a recognizable Hollywood name to helm *Favorite Story*, it would have to be one who fit the current situation: one whose film career had declined, whose personal reputation and age prevented the offer of frequent acting jobs, and who would accept a limited salary. In short, it would be Adolphe Menjou.[35]

Even if Menjou were an appropriate choice from these perspectives, the show's creators still had to mold his host persona as Ronald Colman's replacement, in order to satisfy Lawrence and Lee. Given the writers' favored choices—Olivier, Niven, Hardwicke—it is clear that they were hoping for the rhetorical benefit of a European actor representing high culture and quality. While Menjou was not European, his Continental accent and appearance at least echoed the prestige of Britishness. Even so, his foppish, caricatured post-1940 roles—plus, doubtless, his political outspokenness—hindered his status as a representative of dignified high culture. Thus, the producers and writers of *Favorite Story* had to match Menjou to the intended prestige of the dramas, which meant emphasizing or even resurrecting those elements of Menjou's persona that did represent prestige and sophistication. Especially needed were those aspects of his "real" persona, in terms of his constructed biography, that fit these requirements, that would elevate his image, as well as the program's.

This image burnishing began with strategically positioning the show as a special cultural experience with Menjou as the ideal guide. In place of the radio program's focus on stories chosen by celebrities, the television version shifted to a theme of taking the viewer around the world to witness the enactment of distinguished stories. Because many of the stories were based on works by famous, often European, authors, and thus utilized what were supposedly overseas locales, this thematic shift was most appropriate. The script for an early commercial for the show indicated as much and set forth Menjou's basic role. The teaser opens in a map room and has Menjou flipping through various maps, introducing himself, and pointing out, "I've just been looking over the maps of some of [the] strange and faraway places we'll be visiting on my new television series!" He then lists various exotic story settings for future shows, hoping that the show would go "wherever we can find a story that *may* be your favorite." The explicit dialogue and the geographical mise-en-scène created an atmosphere of exotic adventure, and Menjou's persona as a worldly, traveled, and cultured man gave him a certain air of authority in asking viewers to come along with him—also evident in the frequently used closing lines for each episode: "Will you meet me here in the map room next week at this time? Of course you never need a passport or visa when you travel with me and I promise you a trip of thousands of miles from your own living room."[36]

Adolphe Menjou introduces Favorite Story.
WISCONSIN CENTER FOR FILM AND THEATER RESEARCH.

Menjou's actions and dialogue in the introductory and closing frames of each episode echoed these elements. Each took place in a map room, with the camera initially panning across various maps along the wall of a room, then stopping and tracking in on a large globe situated in front of a world map. In these openings, Menjou usually sat on or stood near a desk placed by the globe and either approached a wall map or opened up a smaller map to point out the setting for the upcoming episode. For example, the script for the episode "Strange Journey" describes Menjou's actions during the prologue, as he handles a map of the British Isles: "Expertly, he measures the distance by sea from the Post of London to Land's End, flipping the compass over and over in a 'walking motion' to tote the distance."

Thus, the openings implied not just Menjou's knowledge of these foreign lands but also his basic knowledge of travel and exploration. In addition to his interactions with the maps, Menjou often dealt with other props connected to a worldly persona and specifically appropriate to Menjou. He was usually dressed in his standard fine attire, a double-breasted suit with lapel carnation. Before exiting from the map

135

room at the beginning of the story, he at times would put on his trademark homburg hat and carry a cane and gloves. As will be elaborated upon shortly, in his role as host Menjou entered into the program itself, and for numerous episodes, he would begin to put on a costume appropriate to the period of the story. The script for "The Crime of Sylvestre Bonnard," a tale set in the nineteenth century, describes the host's introductory costuming ("Menjou looks at his own reflection in the glass; he cuts a dapper figure, in his fin de siècle elegance") and details Menjou's subsequent dialogue ("Thought I ought to slip into something more appropriate to the period"). Thus, the text contains allusions to his famous fashion sense and his supposed well-developed knowledge of history.

Worldly knowledge was generally evident in Menjou's introductions to the episodic stories. For "Work of Art," Menjou explained a bit of the history of Switzerland, the setting for the story, as well as the geographical qualities of the terrain over which the story would travel. His knowledge of languages was marked in the ending sequence of the same episode, as he exclaimed: "Well, gute Nacht Switzerland! Au revoir, candlestick! And arrivederci to another *Favorite Story!*" He went on to note that these three languages were all spoken in Switzerland. Similarly, in the opening to "The Gambler," Menjou noted that the evening's story was "by that author with the unpronounceable name, Fyodor Mikhailovich Dostoyevsky." Of course, Menjou pronounced it effortlessly, emphasizing his ease with both language and high culture.

Beyond a general evocation of Menjou's encyclopedic knowledge, certain episodes also explicitly addressed those activities for which Menjou might have been known. One example, "The Postmistress," involved post office embezzlement. This plot element was a somewhat minor aspect of the story, which focused on the maturation of a spoiled young woman, but the opening used the post office setting to draw another page of Menjou's biography. The script reads: "[Pan] to Menjou, who is seated at the desk, which is comfortably littered by the paraphernalia of a working philatelist . . . tweezers, reading glass, albums, catalogues, etc. He looks up and smiles like any happy hobbyist." This impression of a knowledgeable fancier was confirmed by Menjou's opening line: "Good evening. I'm Adolphe Menjou—and it seems you have caught me in the act. So I'll confess. I'm a philatelist, a stamp collector." Menjou's own status as a stamp collector or even just a collector of fine things might very well have been known to the audience, lending a personal, refined touch to the opening.

His subsequent line added further connotations of worldliness: "There is a world of interesting fact concerning this hobby . . . the fabulous value of certain famous collections . . . the fantastic prices paid for some of the rare issues . . . the men from all walks of life who have been and are interested in the hobby—presidents, kings, merchants . . . yes, even . . . actors." Such dialogue unpretentiously solidified his image as an educated, cultured man. Further, because it was the case here, it more broadly implied that much of the other knowledge he imparted on the show was his own. Thus, *Favorite Story* was able to draw on its host's established cultural image to lend credibility to the show and to enhance the perceived quality of its episodes.

As noted, Menjou often entered the actual episodes at the beginning and again before the middle commercial break. "Strange Journey" serves as an example. After Menjou introduces the tale in standard fashion and exits the map room to indicate the cut to a commercial, the story begins. Walking past tracks, Menjou approaches a train station, and a man hurries past, almost knocking over the host. Menjou, facing the camera, asks "What makes people hurry?" then notices that the man left behind a briefcase. Menjou begins rifling through it, and the man returns angrily, tearing the briefcase away. In the process, the case opens and papers are strewn about, including one with the word "Fraud" conspicuously written across it. After gathering his papers, the man storms off, and Menjou comments, "Too bad we didn't get a look at those papers. I bet there is a story in that briefcase," then bestows a knowing smile. The episode cuts to onboard the train and begins to follow the man's story, leaving Menjou behind until the next commercial break. The episode returns with a couple nervously boarding a freighter: they are embezzlers presumably guilty of killing the man seen in the beginning, their boss. As they sail off, Menjou looks toward the freighter from the shore and says, "Bon voyage. Nine weeks at sea. A nervous thief, a jittery wife, and a suspicious captain." He then turns to the camera and remarks, "It should be a strange journey." In these moments, Menjou is posed as the informed, all-knowing narrator, imparting his considerable knowledge to the audience.

Menjou's direct involvement in the story also frequently implied a type of authorship. In the host openings, Menjou would identify the locale for an episode and, as soon as he entered the story, he would make an issue of trying to locate actual plot elements on that site. In *Favorite Story*'s first episode, "How Much Land Does a Man Need?" Menjou walks around the episode setting and speculates about what he sees, "Where's the story in the troubled land of Trebezan? With this old lady? In this broken fence?" He then bends down and sifts through dirt, commenting, "Here's where we'll find it. Here's our story." From a close-up of Menjou's hand sifting the dirt, the image dissolves to the main character's hand doing the same, and the episode's narrative begins. Menjou regularly implies responsibility for story selection in these hosting sections, as well. In "The Face of Paris," he remarks, "[I've] got my finger on a story. This is a story which came to me; I didn't have to go out and search for it!" Script instructions also indicate acting directions for Menjou that echo notions of authorship: "[N]ow he glances at the camera with a crooked smile, as if he had just decided to let the audience in on his cognitions. . . . He looks up slightly askance, as if he were making up this parable." These examples indicate that the show hoped to imply a measure of authorial control by Menjou over the episodes and their execution—what Michele Hilmes refers to as "false authorship" in regard to Cecil B. De Mille's role on *Lux Radio Theater.* Thus, these allusions to Menjou's authorship as well as his integration into the actual diegeses of the stories further deepened the link between Menjou's personal image of knowledge, worldliness, and intellectualism and *Favorite Story*'s attempts to legitimize its content.[37]

Menjou's hosting duties were closely aligned with this constructed persona, and so were the publicity materials for the show. One publicity still mirrored the image of Menjou from the opening of "Strange Journey"; it shows him leaning on a map stand placed in front of a large globe holding a compass and smiling smartly at the camera. In other photos, he is seated at the desk used in the opening, clutching a map, or standing in front of a map on the wall. These strategic publicity photos aligned Menjou's image of worldly knowledge with the very icons of knowledge that the show relied on, the maps. In related publicity material, an ad in a July 1954 issue of *TV Guide* contains the standard picture of Menjou, wearing his homburg and a typical wry smile, with the caption, "Adolphe Menjou, telling one of his favorite stories." As such, the ad identifies him as personally responsible for the stories, in effect, using him to replace the celebrity selectors from the radio version of the program.[38]

Finally, Menjou's performative duties at times extended into acting in the episodes: he portrayed a lead character in twenty-six of the seventy-four aired shows. The majority of the *Favorite Story* episodes presented

Adolphe Menjou in a Favorite Story *publicity still.*
WISCONSIN CENTER FOR FILM AND THEATER RESEARCH.

moral lessons and transformations, and the parts Menjou played most frequently involved the softening of an obstinate, prejudiced, and self-centered older man. In "Vice-Versa," Menjou's character learns to spend more time with his son; in "Gallegher," he adopts a young newspaper assistant he had previously scorned; and in "Turning Point," he comes to understand the challenges faced by the homeless. In each case, Menjou's portrayals echoed the character actor phase of his late film career, when he often played gruff, narrow-minded father figures. Of course, these parts were rather different from his sophisticated, personable hosting persona. In explaining this divergence between Menjou's hosting manner and his fictional performances on *Favorite Story,* one can first see that this latter persona was useful to the narrative structure of the episodes in which he appeared. Much like his film roles, Menjou's typical *Favorite Story* character either personified a brusqueness that acted as an obstacle to other characters' goal fulfillment or his obstinacy acted as a personal obstacle. Menjou's presentations as host, on the other hand, stripped away this caricatured aspect and its humorous undertones, further authenticating the "real" Menjou. Thus, when Menjou rhetorically questioned the audience at the beginning of episodes in which he would star by asking, "Would you please permit me to play the lead role in tonight's story?" the viewer was explicitly presented with a contrast between Menjou's hosting persona and his acting persona.

While I have no concrete proof that viewers understood Menjou's telefilm image in this way, media reviews of the program generally support the impressions of Menjou and the show described above. *TV Guide* discussed the show in a May 1954 issue, and the article's opening line is quite revealing: "Adolphe Menjou was once known as one of the best-dressed men in Hollywood. His wardrobe plus a series of interesting playlets are now on view via *Favorite Story*." Just as much as the show, Menjou himself was on display, and the reviewer's comments on his wardrobe show how essential this was to the show and to anything involving Menjou. The review goes on to note, "The plays are fortunately good enough to establish Menjou's reputation as an actor and a pleasant host rather than a Beau Brummel." The latter part of this comment is interesting as it seems to mark Menjou's emergence from his caricatured roles of the late 1940s. The final line of the article emphasizes one of the fundamental attractions of Menjou as host: "[W]ith Menjou on hand to give the show that star appeal, *Story* should continue to hold its place as one of the better telefilm dramatic series."[39]

Jack Gould also reviewed the show, surely with a different focus than that of *TV Guide,* and his early endorsement of *Favorite Story* is instructive. After viewing the series debut, Gould wrote that the show "may turn out to be one of the best filmed series produced for television." He further proposed that this was "an encouraging omen that Hollywood was coming to recognize that TV could do with sturdy stuff on the screen." This admission is important, given Gould's constant association of New York with live, high-culture broadcasts and Hollywood with low-culture, commercialized entertainment. Thus, in Gould's estimation, some of Ziv's intentions to create a higher-quality syndicated show, or at least the impression of one, paid off. Gould's only criticism involved the integration of commercials:

> The program's host—in this instance the suave and personable Adolphe Menjou—is shown first in a pin-striped suit and boutonniere extolling the merits of a beer. Then he switches into a parka and fur headgear and winds up smack in the middle of Tolstoy and the remote regions of Outer Mongolia. Finally, Mr. Menjou makes it

back from the racks of Brooks Brothers and to the modernistic setting of the cocktail lounge. All that was missing was Tolstoy's doing
a singing jingle.

Quite similar comments about this episode came from Harriet Van
Horne, a critic for the *New York World-Telegram and Sun:*

> Last night I saw the premiere of a program called *Favorite Story*—
> half-hour films adapted from the best in world literature. It's a pro-
> gram of quality and stature. And were it being paid for by anybody
> but a brewery the viewer might be able to lose himself in the lovely,
> abandoned way he loses himself in a good book or play. . . . We were
> introduced to this parable by Adolphe Menjou, the program's "host"
> and general nuisance. Mr. Menjou came on in his impeccable attire:
> pin-stripe suit, gray Homburg, carnation in lapel, cane at jaunty
> angle. . . . He showed [the episode's location] on a map carefully
> avoiding the word "Russian" as a descriptive of either the author or
> the locale. . . . After the commercial we see our hero drop dead—
> from greed. Then back to Mr. Menjou, smacking his moustache over
> another beaker of beer.

Both reviews indicate that Ziv's attempts to present *Favorite Story* as a
prestigious program, and one above typical syndicated fare, largely
worked for the show opener. But the ultimate imperative of the syndicator, to earn profits through selling advertising, would still impinge on
this impression. Network anthology programs tended to use hosts to
bracket off the commercial from the episode, so as not to taint the
credibility of the show with the shadow of crass commercialism. In this,
at least, Ziv did not follow the networks' lead.[40]

Interestingly, *Variety*'s review of this same episode endorsed Menjou's commercial presentation: "His sophisticated approach lends dignity to the rest of the show, and certainly should help sell beer." For this
reviewer, the prestigious elements of Menjou's presented persona
helped to camouflage the commercial nature of the program. These attempts at prestige, however, could sometimes go too far. *Variety* often
criticized the show's writers for Menjou's occasionally overintellectual
introductions and closings—what the trade paper jadedly termed
"double-talk in an attempt at philosophizing." In response to such lines
as, "Sharper than the blade of a bayonet is the pain of loneliness," and
"Pain is the breaking of the shell of understanding. So saith the poet!"

Variety complained, "Something should be done about Menjou's narration. It's beginning to get a little fatuous."[41]

At its heart, *Favorite Story* was still syndicated fare, and the financial challenges of this practice exhibited themselves in the finished product, no matter the rhetorical strategies. And though the opening episode earned Jack Gould's praise, the fact that he reviewed but one episode after that indicates that the show was still critically marginalized. *Variety* did review every episode, with reactions running the gamut from respectful praise to dismissive scorn. *Variety*'s overall view of the series is clear from a review excerpt: "Like most of the other *Favorite Story* fare, 'The Lady and the Law' is strictly a 'B' telepicture, with little quality but lotsa action. It spins by rapidly, but the loopholes leave you feeling they musta tossed away some script pages in order to get under the wire budgetwise." Despite the preponderance of high-minded signifiers packaged into the format of a prestigious genre, *Favorite Story* was still beholden to its industrial circumstances. Nonetheless, *Favorite Story* was apparently popular with stations and audiences; it finished ninth out of the top ten syndicated filmed shows in station sales at the end of 1954. It ultimately ran for two seasons, airing seventy-four episodes, with subsequent reruns in various markets. And although it never broke into the ranks of network prestige, *Favorite Story* did benefit from the resurrected Menjou star image. It relied heavily on connotations of this star persona to lend credibility to its episodes. Menjou's role as host thus went well beyond mere placeholder.[42]

MENJOU AFTER *FAVORITE STORY*

Menjou gained a great deal from *Favorite Story*, as it kept him working and in the public eye in a positive realm. Hal Erickson described, "The 52-week anthology made him a star all over again; while the actor would never qualify for any Mr. Nice Guy award, Menjou suddenly found himself graciously accepting both praise and criticism for his new series from strangers on the street." He returned to feature films after *Favorite Story*, beginning with the thriller *Timberjack* in 1955. He also returned to his character actor persona, principally the gruff elder: for example, *The Ambassador's Daughter* (1956), in which he played a grumpy, if irreverent, American senator in Paris, a role similar to the one he played in *State of the Union*. Menjou also took another role reflexively tied to his political status in Stanley Kubrick's *Paths of Glory* (1957). Here he played a general within a fascist bureaucracy assailed by the film's liberal leanings. Though a more complex character than the strictly villainous general played by George Macready, Menjou's General Broulard is scorned for his narrow-minded actions: he refuses to prevent the execution of three soldiers unfairly convicted of insubordination. The film indicates that Broulard allows the execution to continue in order to set an example for the whole unit, regardless of the injustice of the sentence. One could easily tie this representation to how Kubrick and other liberals viewed Menjou himself, given his role in perpetuating the Red Scare fervor and in ruining the careers and lives of many in the entertainment industry with his rhetoric.[43]

In 1957, Menjou returned to television to host *Target* (1957–58), another Ziv anthology drama. When asked by the *Los Angeles Times* why he would return to television after a three-year respite, he claimed money was the primary reason: "I'm not positive . . . but I don't think I could make a living out of pictures at the moment—if I had to, which I don't. They just aren't making enough pictures these days. If they want you badly enough they'll get you, but they don't want most actors that badly." Menjou was referring here to the production decreases in this post–Paramount Case studio era, but it is probably more accurate to say that Hollywood did not want Menjou that badly. Ziv television once again allowed him to continue his acting career.[44]

In place of the focus on a favorite tale from classic literature, *Target* presented original stories in which the main character is a target of either a kind gesture or, more often, a nefarious intent. Critically, however, *Target* was far less well received than *Favorite Story*. Possibly, it was hurt in comparison by not relying on classic tales that carried at least a veneer of quality. Indeed, *Variety* frequently lambasted *Target* for presenting superficial and clichéd stories. An excerpt from a review of the penultimate episode illustrates *Variety*'s overall view of the show: "About the best thing that can be said regarding Ziv's *Target* series is that it will end next week. Anthology series hasn't had much in the way of quality or class."[45]

After *Target*'s single-year run ended, Menjou appeared in just one more film, Disney's *Pollyanna* (1960). Capping off the final stage of his career, this last film role was fitting: Menjou played a reclusive old man professing complete impatience for children until Pollyanna brings forth his true heart. Menjou also maintained his fervid anti-Communism into this late period, as expressed in one of his many letters to J. Edgar Hoover in August 1960:

I'm inclined to think that it is too late to save our country. There is so much ignorance and apathy. I spoke over television a few days ago and received hundreds of letters from patriotic people who are looking for guidance. They even went to great lengths to propose that I run for political office. I only mention this to show how eager the public is for leadership of the proper kind. I have a strong feeling that if Kennedy gets elected and [omitted] and [omitted] receive high cabinet posts American will have had it. . . . Sorry to sound so pessimistic but we have lost our fight against the Reds in the film industry and I'm really pessimistic.[46]

Whether from ill health or lack of opportunities, Menjou did not act again after *Pollyanna*. He passed away in 1963. While it had seemed probable that his film career would have ended a decade earlier, television opened new doors for Menjou. His age or his image may have been an obstacle to continued steady work in Hollywood film, but given syndication's financial constraints and *Favorite Story*'s rhetorical needs, he was most appropriate for his telefilm hosting role in the early 1950s. Menjou was a faded film star, but he still carried with him the prestigious connotations of Hollywood stardom and a level of name recognition that Frederic Ziv required of his broadcast performers. And through resurrecting the key elements of Menjou's persona from the height of his film career and emphasizing the refined characteristics he supposedly really did embody, *Favorite Story* succeeded in reaching for a cultural status that its industrial conditions seemed to belie.

As such, this case presents a revealing inversion of the typical assumption about film talent on television: that such work was a step down for film actors and that it invariably hindered the status of their star images. In this case, the producers of *Favorite Story* initially felt that Menjou's status was insufficient for their program, and they deemed it necessary to boost Menjou's standing rhetorically in order to suit the needs of their television program. That they did so by assimilating Menjou's "real" film-based identity with certain elements unique to early television production, such as the presentational mode of hosting and the implication of host-as-author, reveals how integral the film star image could be to the shape and success of 1950s television programs. It also illustrates how a successful marriage of anthology host and program could be built out of careful negotiation of a star's image and a show's premise.

It is also quite clear that, as with Faye Emerson, the construction of Menjou's television persona required a measure of authenticity. With Emerson, such authenticity had been tied exclusively to notions of the domestic and the personal. Menjou, on the other hand, exhibited a level of exoticism in his role as host of *Favorite Story;* rather than taking on an "everyday" identity, he was presented as a figure of exceptional knowledge and authority. These contrasts are explained in part by the divergent nature of the programs they hosted. Of course, one cannot ignore the evident gendered associations, as well. Presumably, male film actors were better able to maintain the power and authority of their personae as public figures on 1950s television, whereas female actors were most frequently relegated to a domestic, subordinate image, no matter their true knowledge or power behind the screen. This schism is exceedingly relevant for the next chapter, which looks at the role of film stars on continuing-character series.

CHAPTER 4
STARDOM AND THE SITCOM

When considering film actor participation in continuing-character drama and comedy series on television, the word "star" becomes difficult to apply in its truest sense. No genuine Hollywood star would commit to such a series. The time investment, lesser stature, potential for overexposure, and character stereotyping endemic to series, as well as the potential backlash from the film studios, would preclude any successful film star's even contemplating such a move. Even so, this classification of appearances does yield productive analysis. While a top tier star would not appear, those whose most acclaimed days were behind them, who often had little to lose, assuredly would. Indeed, numerous supporting actors vaulted to television star status as a result of developing popular series. As such, connotations of stardom still persisted within these shows. In a period of network formation and intense competition, the name value of even a second-tier featured player could prove highly valuable, prompting publicity not much different from that which a film star would receive. Further, the clash between the lowly status of series work and the exalted cachet of film personalities only heightened awareness of a lesser or faded star's precedent status and image. Thus the very concept of stardom itself became a frequent topic of critical responses to series work.

This performance category diverges from the previous ones discussed in several revealing ways. Series work was not presentational (and thus directly personal) like variety, talk, and anthology hosting, nor was it so elevated in status as some other television fare, like the anthology drama. It was, nonetheless, subject to the same medium-specific conditions as these forms, from commercial demands to connotations of intimacy and immediacy. These factors would help to dictate and even delimit the type of film actors who could thrive in series work. Such would prove especially true for film actresses, who found limited opportunities within prime-time dramas but ruled the situation comedy format for much of the 1950s. Most striking about this work is that even though these actresses were not playing "themselves" in the way that Faye Emerson and Loretta Young were in their hosting roles, a sense of personal self still pervaded their character work. Elements of star image, film persona, and television character identity all had to dovetail with prevailing production methods and dominant social discourses for small-screen success to be possible. In this regard, the failures could once again be as enlightening as the successes.

THE ELEVATION OF CHARACTER ACTORS

It is not surprising that character actors and secondary featured players filled the rosters of continuing-character series on 1950s television. Besides the fact that so many were available thanks to shrinking studio rosters and production schedules, their distinctive performance traits were especially suitable for the continuing-character series. In *All About Thelma and Eve: Sidekicks and Third Wheels,* Judith Roof highlights television's success in "capitalizing on the idiosyncratic personalities associated with the performers who regularly played minor or comic characters in film." As Roof describes it, these character actors were filmic figures "without apparent fate, explicit narratives, or prominent star value. . . . Their continuity both within films and from film to film makes them seem unchanging and unchanged, subject to no continuous narrative or social movement." Because of these characteristics, there was little chance for these actors to become leading players in fully developed, feature-length film narratives. These qualities, however, were ideal for television's short-form continuing-character series, which, unlike serial formats such as the soap opera, fundamentally refuses forward narrative progression and relies on the predictable recurrence of readily identifiable character constancy. Thus, Stuart Erwin was able to transfer his amiable oaf identity from countless features into one of the most iconic of early television's many bumbling fathers on *The Stu Erwin Show* (ABC, 1950–55); *Life With Father* (CBS, 1953–55) capitalized on the more distinguished patriarchal demeanor that Leon Ames had developed in films like *Meet Me in St. Louis* (1944); and Walter Brennan's crusty codger routine anchored the rural family of *The Real McCoys* (ABC and CBS, 1957–63).[1]

Such replication meant that the continuing-character series also bore striking similarities to classical-era B film and programmer series, whose utility was fading as the studios slashed production. Indeed, the low-budget telefilm essentially became the new B film. This shift was foreshadowed early in commercial television's life when movie cowboy William Boyd began presenting reedited versions of his old Hopalong Cassidy movies on NBC in 1949. Boyd also created an original *Hopalong Cassidy* telefilm series for syndication (1951–52), bringing veteran character actor Edgar Buchanan on board. Singing cowboy Gene Autry followed Boyd's trail by producing the Western *Gene Autry Show* (CBS, 1950–56) under his Flying "A" Productions banner. Minor and independent film studios, who had previously thrived on non-A production, similarly began to focus their efforts on telefilm production. For instance, Johnny Weissmuller had gained fame as Tarzan in a series of six films for MGM (1932–42) and six more for RKO (1942–48). He next exchanged his loincloth for safari fatigues as the adventurer "Jungle Jim" Bradley in thirteen Columbia-distributed films (1948–53). In 1955, Columbia utilized its telefilm subsidiary Screen Gems to produce a 26-episode syndicated version of *Jungle Jim* starring Weissmuller. Film and television also shared *The Adventures of Superman* (syndicated, 1951–57); the pilot episode of the George Reeves hit was actually a low-budget theatrical release by independent Lippert Pictures. What was once intended for the second half of a double bill in theaters could now be caught at home.

This B-level reputation lent the telefilm series in particular the stigma of being second-rate fare, which meant that no star with an active feature film career in leading roles would be inclined to commit to one. But from the reverse perspective, it meant that many of Hollywood's secondary actors could boost themselves into leading positions via the continuing-character series. Ralph Bellamy, whose A-film specialty was the second-lead nice guy who loses the girl to the more dashing leading man, also made a mark starring in five B films as Ellery Queen. Out of frustration with the ceiling on his career, he left features and from the mid-1940s on worked primarily in the theater. But he also starred in one of television's first of many detective series to come, *Man Against Crime.* The televised version of radio's *Beulah* (ABC, 1950–53), for better or worse, did not spawn imitators, but it did give leading parts to Ethel Waters, Louise Beavers and, briefly, Hattie McDaniel, all of whom had toiled as the subordinate mammy character in features. Of course, playing a lead mammy was probably no better than playing a supporting mammy—in fact, Waters departed *Beulah* in anger at its degrading scripts—but it was not an opportunity they would have found regularly in feature films. In contrast to Waters, Eve Arden expressed her pleasure in 1952 with going from limited work as the sidekick friend in features to being a central focus as the star of *Our Miss Brooks* (CBS, 1952–56): "In a personal way, television is a little more satisfactory. I dribble through a picture being made for theaters, working two days and then being idle for two weeks. This gets to be a bore. Maybe if I were the star of the picture, and everything revolved around me, the work would be more stimulating."[2]

Unfortunately for Arden and other actresses, a prime-time show was much less likely to revolve around a woman than a man, due to cultural stereotyping within the series genres that reigned in prime time, where women were largely denied primary narrative agency. A man could play a cop or detective, like Lee Bowman in *The Adventures of Ellery Queen* (ABC, 1951–52) and Frank Lovejoy in *Meet McGraw* (NBC, 1957–58). Or he could headline as a lawyer, as Gary Merrill and Raymond Burr did in *Justice* (NBC, 1954–56) and *Perry Mason* (CBS, 1957–66), respectively. Various adventure series offered work for Dan Duryea (*China Smith*, syndicated, 1952, 1954), George Brent and Dane Clark (*Wire Service*, ABC, 1956–57), and Lloyd Bridges (*Sea Hunt*). Numerous cowboys also rode in from the film world, including Ward Bond (*Wagon Train*, NBC, 1957–61) and Rory Calhoun (*The Texan*, CBS, 1958–60). Conversely, only a handful of established film actresses carried prominent noncomedic roles on series television, and they were mostly relegated to the vagaries of syndication: examples included Lois Collier in *Boston Blackie* (1951–53), Gail Davis in *Annie Oakley* (1953–56), and Ella Raines in *Janet Dean, Registered Nurse* (1954).

Film actresses were largely limited to anthology programs if they wanted to display dramatic skills. Yet comedy did give them an arena in which to thrive. In fact, the list of female sitcom stars in the 1950s reads like the table of contents from a 1940s issue of *Photoplay:* Ann Sothern, Betty Hutton, Eve Arden, Joan Bennett, Ida Lupino, Donna Reed, Joan Caulfield. Men were well represented in this genre as well, with Ray Milland, Ronald Colman, Robert Young, William Bendix, Pat O'Brien, Peter Lawford, and Robert Cummings among the many Hollywood actors who generated laughs on the small screen. As this listing indicates, 1950s television comedy could be very accommodating to Hollywood stars, especially those whose film successes were confined to the previous decade, but its unique standards could also limit who appeared, for how long, and in what guise.

While classical Hollywood executives couldn't envision designing a feature-length narrative around Eve Arden's wisecracking friend character, her quips supplied ideal threads for the weekly 26-minute patchwork of jokes in *Our Miss Brooks*. (Granted, a feature version of *Our Miss Brooks* was produced by Warner Bros. in 1956, but only after television had uncovered the narrative potential within Arden's persona). Further, even as *Variety* criticized the film for being "merely an elongation of what viewers can get weekly for free on their home set," the reviewer also noted that the film was much more goal- and resolution-oriented than the television show: Connie Brooks finally snares the long-pursued Mr. Boynton. Audience reluctance to pay at a theater for what they could get at home free of charge doubtless affected the film's box office take, but these narrative changes surely did as well. Indeed, an alteration in the nature of Arden's character and the situation itself was required in order to transfer the show from television's sitcom conventions to Hollywood's feature film conventions.[3]

Thus, in key ways, early television comedy was distinct from the chief modes of classical feature film comedy. Drawing from radio, 1950s TV comedy took two primary forms: (1) vaudeville-based, comedian-centered comedy, manifested in variety shows like *Texaco Star Theater;* and (2) plot-centered comedy, manifested in the sitcom, from early ethnic comedies like *The Goldbergs* (CBS, NBC, DuMont, and syndicated, 1949–55) to later domestic ones like *Father Knows Best.* The variety show style ran counter to primary classical film traditions because of its presentational structure and direct address to the audience, its emphasis on connotations of liveness and immediacy, and its embrace of organizational fragmentation and rupture—with all of these elements anchored around a central comedian. The sitcom style had more in common with film forms in terms of telling linear, character-based stories within a self-enclosed, continuous world. The demands of broadcasting's weekly formats, however, required suitably repeatable situations and characters, a focus on small-scale issues resolvable in less than thirty minutes, and a circular narrative pattern of destabilization and restabilization each week, rather than a progressive, goal-oriented drive toward closure that could fill two hours. This is not to say that the situation comedy's distinguishing elements were foreign to classical cinema. But they were more evident in B-film series like Columbia's *Blondie* (1938–50), which relied on the reiteration of relatively mundane situations, and in vaudeville-rooted comedies such as the Abbott and Costello films, which allowed for presentational gag-based humor, than in A-list romantic and musical comedies.

These two comedy formats were not always distinct on early television, especially for the first half of the 1950s. George Burns and Gracie Allen, Jack Benny, and Jackie Gleason all developed hybrid shows that bridged the variety and sitcom formats, with separate proscenium and stage spaces serving different comedic forms and functions. These comedians also developed vivid personalities that could operate both in the presentational space as well as in the representational context, albeit in varied ways. For example, Benny's monologue was driven by jokes about his stinginess and vanity, and the comedy sketches he acted in were specifically developed around those aspects, as well. This familiarity made it easier for Benny to shift his program more toward sitcom form as the decade wore on, helping it to survive all the way until 1965. Jackie Gleason, on the other hand, fostered on his eponymous program (CBS, 1952–59) a clear distinction between his slick, confident hosting persona and the varied range of clowns and cutups he portrayed in sketches. Such performative variability and spontaneous jesting served Gleason well in the variety-comedy arena; by the mid-1950s, he had become one of the highest-paid performers in entertainment history.

These qualities might have also contributed, however, to his failures in movies prior to television and in the two situation comedies he tried in the 1950s. Gleason was briefly contracted to Warner Bros. in the early 1940s, but studio executives never saw the rotund Gleason as leading-man material. Nor did his minor film roles fully exploit the dynamic, personable energy that marked his nightclub performance successes. Gleason brought that energy to television in his first appearance on *Toast of the Town* in 1948. Watching that evening was Irving Belcher, producer of the hit radio show *The Life of Riley* (ABC and NBC, 1945–51), who was most impressed and recommended Gleason for the role as television's Riley. Radio's Riley had been played by character actor William Bendix, but he declined to move to television in 1949, fearing it would limit his film career. Gleason had no such concerns, so he took the role, but the show did not resonate with audiences and was canceled after a single season. The role was so identified with Bendix that Gleason had a tough task in making Riley his own going in. Even more problematic was the confining framework of the situation comedy, whose prescriptive narrative structure limited Gleason's ability to exploit his most dynamic comedic talents.

More curious was the failure of *The Honeymooners* in a sitcom format. The ongoing saga of Ralph and Alice Kramden and neighbors Ed and Trixie Norton had been the most popular sketch within *The Jackie Gleason Show*, and the sitcom version is beloved today. But during its 1955–56 seasonal run as a half-hour sitcom, audiences responded with relative indifference. Granted, strong competition from NBC's *Perry Como Show* hurt the program and, just as crucially, its lead-in, the Gleason-produced musical variety *Stage Show* (CBS, 1954–56). But it is also possible that audiences at the time favored the modularity of Gleason's variety show persona to his singular performance as Ralph Kramden. Comedy historian David Marc perceptively describes the talents on display with the former:

> The live-from-New York, comedy-variety format played directly to Gleason's strengths, allowing him to wisecrack as emcee, to engage in off-the-cuff chats with guests and to move in and out of short sketch material that emphasized physical humor rather than narrative resolution. . . . The Gleason style was utterly suited to 1950s comedy-variety: the vaudeville trappings, including a live audience; the emphasis on slapstick, constant close-ups, blackout segues, splintered segments and so on.[4]

Unfortunately for Gleason and vaudeo stars like Milton Berle, the linear storytelling approach began to rule television comedy as the 1960s approached, and live variety formats were progressively phased out. The urban, ethnic style of humor associated with vaudeo was thought to be less palatable to midwestern and rural America, a consideration that became more relevant with every passing day as television sets spread across the nation. Critics and audiences alike showed a preference for the assurance of predictable, regularized characters and continuous storytelling. Networks additionally appreciated the economic value of sitcoms: they lacked variety shows' added cost of high-priced guest stars, and they were adaptable to film production methods, which enabled profitable circulation in the syndication market. For their part, sponsors increasingly saw the situation comedy as an appropriate format for their advertisements. Domestic sitcoms especially did not traffic in the abrasive humor and off-color jokes that vaudeo shows were thought to tend toward. They were thus a safer association for a corporate image, and they presented an appropriate context for a unified, repeatable set of middle-class associations for products. As Susan Murray describes it:

> [T]he continuing character and setting of the [sitcom] format provided the advertisers with a more stable milieu in which to insert product identification. Indeed, instead of relying on the flexible personas of comics such as Berle, who would perform as any number of characters, advertisers were provided with lead characters in sitcoms that remained consistent in their identity and whose "lives" were set in middle-class domestic settings.[5]

For comedic performers, this emphasis on domesticity meant that individual characters had to be embodied and star personae had to be sufficiently narrativized to interlock with sitcom storytelling standards. The success of *The Phil Silvers Show* (CBS, 1955–59) stands as an example. Silvers had toiled as a comic-relief character actor in feature films of the 1940s; like Eve Arden, he rose no further than the role of the star's friend. Referencing the name of a character he played in Fox's *Diamond Horseshoe* (1945), Silvers described his feature film function as follows:

> For nine years I played the same character: Blinky, the good-humored, bespectacled confidant of Betty Grable or John Payne. . . . Ten minutes before the end of the last reel, I told Betty she wasn't really in love with Cesar Romero. It was George [Montgomery] she *truly* wanted. Or vice versa. You could be damn sure of one thing: It was never Phil Silvers.

Tiring of Blinky, Silvers turned to theater in the early 1950s, striking gold with a play about the chaos of early television called *Top Banana*, in which Silvers played a thinly veiled Milton Berle figure and won a Tony for his efforts. CBS vice president Hubbell Robinson, Jr., subsequently viewed Silvers emceeing a radio and TV correspondents dinner in Washington, D.C., in 1954 and was wowed by his improvisational skills. Only days later, CBS contacted Silvers with interest in developing a comedy show around him.[6]

While Silvers's recent successes might have pointed the way toward a live variety show, CBS was increasingly leaving that genre to NBC, hoping instead to supplement its supremacy in the more economical filmed sitcom format. For this format to work, Silvers and writer Nat

Hiken had to devise a narrative skeleton that could exploit the comedian's proficient line-delivery abilities and expert timing. Silvers described this challenge in his autobiography: "It's not how funny are you; it's how many weeks can you be funny? What will the twenty-third show be like? Does the format give you opportunities for variety in location, people and situations?" The format they settled on placed Silvers in the army as a garrulous, madcap sergeant, scheming and hustling his way through the military. It was a perfect marriage of an engagingly simple, easily repeatable situation and Silvers's virtuosic comedic skills. Marking an important, if not sudden, historical turning point in television comedy, *The Phil Silvers Show* finally ended the legendary Tuesday evening reign of its 8 P.M. competition, *The Milton Berle Show*. What would prevail henceforth would be the filmed sitcom, still offering colorful personalities and a sense of theatricality, but whose humor arose from consistent situations and character relationships, not isolated gags and disparate sketches.[7]

These developments helped to make mid-1950s television comedy more appropriate for true actors, not just vaudeville comedians and comic relief specialists, because their talents were geared toward adapting performative skills to story and character. Nonetheless, there was a circumscribed style of portrayal called for in the period's sitcoms, which were becoming suffused with depictions of idealized domestic spaces and everyday activities—deemed to be the most appropriate context within which to sell consumer products to viewers. Sitcom stars had to mold their character creations to the consistency of a weekly sitcom's representations and its regularized production methods, as well as to early television's preferred connotations of intimacy, immediacy, and accessibility. They had to create personages whose demeanor and lifestyle resonated with the desired target consumer: the white middle-class viewer. These factors combined to encourage a strong meshing between star identity and character identity—or, even more so, a subsuming of star identity *within* character identity, in order to present a seamless, naturalistic selfhood with which audiences could identify in both onscreen and offscreen spaces. Just as the domestic sitcom purported to embody an everyday reality, so too would its featured performers.

It is not surprising, then, that the biggest stars to attempt sitcoms in the 1950s almost exclusively failed. *Hey Mulligan* with Mickey Rooney, *The Halls of Ivy* (CBS, 1954–55) with Ronald Colman, and *The Betty*

Hutton Show (CBS, 1959–60) all lasted only a single season, whereas a number of pilots featuring A-list veterans, including Claudette Colbert, Ginger Rogers, Joan Crawford, and Bette Davis, never even got to the series stage. Of course, the majority of shows of all sorts from this period disappeared quickly, and there was a complex of issues in play for each show, as will be illustrated shortly with the Hutton vehicle. Nonetheless, it is possible that having former A-list film stars as continuing-character series headliners was inherently problematic. These individuals had only been able to reach the heights of film stardom because of the depth and complexity of their combined onscreen and offscreen images. Perhaps the formal reduction of these outsized personae and their containment within the repetitive format of the weekly television series was fundamentally discordant. Further, the dissonance between the everyday, domestic nature of the sitcom and the connotations of eminence and extravagance attached to stars—even former ones—may have also created disharmony. Finally, it can be assumed that not all stars, whether from the film world or otherwise, had personae that lent themselves well to sitcom narration.

Such premises can explain the experience of Ray Milland. Milland's film career peaked in 1945 with his Oscar-winning role in *The Lost Weekend* but then tailed off in the early 1950s. His agents at MCA talked him into trying a Revue-produced sitcom on CBS: *Meet Mr. McNutley*. The program began in 1953 as the tale of a wacky, distracted dean of English at a women's college. MCA was presumably hoping to capitalize on Milland's successful comedic turn as Professor Vernon K. Simpson in 1949's *It Happens Every Spring,* but reviewers largely dismissed the sitcom's slapstick-oriented role as inappropriate for an actor with Milland's image and stature. *Variety* wrote that "the absent-minded prof, in the suave and handsome form of Milland, doesn't hold water," and a *TV-Radio Life* article opined, "The name of the show was just as ridiculous as asking a star of Ray's talent to play what amounted to a jerk." John Crosby went so far as to call the show "an unqualified disaster." The producers, paying heed to these reactions and the show's middling ratings, instituted an overhaul for the second season. Professor McNutley transformed into Professor McNulty, professor of dramatics at a coed college, and the show was retitled *The Ray Milland Show.* Producer Harry Tugend explained: "We changed the title because, to me, *Meet McNutley* sounded like a corny comedy. *The Ray Milland Show* seems to have more dignity." The renamed, toned-down professor still did not resonate

Ray Milland in Meet Mr. McNutley. *CBS/Photofest.*

with audiences, however, and the show was canceled. Possibly it would have been more successful had the program begun with the more appropriate premise at its end, but the incongruity of the first season was apparently too much to overcome. When Milland was asked by *TV Guide* in 1959 to look back on the show, he reportedly replied, "Please! Let's not talk about that. Not a word!"[8]

Sitcoms were more appropriate vehicles for secondary stars whose stature was already suited to series work or for stars whose personae could mesh well with the format. Robert Young had been a serviceable secondary lead player during his 1930s MGM days (he later complained that he was only offered roles Robert Montgomery turned down as beneath him). Upon switching to RKO in the mid-1940s and then freelancing, he seasoned into a versatile character actor and occasional lead standout endowed with a distinguished, quiet strength. Like many others, he was frustrated by the stagnancy of his career in the late 1940s, so he first turned to radio, starring in an NBC sitcom called *Father Knows Best?* beginning in 1949. The show posed Young as a dignified, if occasionally exasperated, head of, in its introduction's words, "the typical American household." The program became a hit, but Young initially resisted attempts to take it to television because of how the move might affect his film career. He told the *Washington Post* in 1950, "Simple economics dictate that as long as I can steal a buck making pictures I won't go into television, at least not until a sponsor will pay as much as a motion picture producer." Such pay was more commensurate by 1954, especially when Screen Gems tendered Young the extra financial enticement of joint ownership and production control of the property. To first test out the viability of making a video version of *Father Knows Best?* Young made his television debut on a May 1954 *Ford Theater* episode entitled "Keep It in the Family," which was similar in spirit to his radio show. Young was happy with the result and willing to commit to a television series.[9]

The titular question mark and any connoted uncertainty over father's wisdom were dropped for the TV version of *Father Knows Best,* and the show established a template for the quiescent domestic sitcom that would come to dominate the medium. It was also a paradigmatic case of star and character becoming tightly enmeshed in a form that was ideal for sponsor Scott Paper to sell home paper products to consumers. Jack Gould's review of the premiere is telling in this respect: he reported that the show "was so engagingly realistic that a viewer had no difficulty in associating himself with one or more of the Andersons." The result for its stars was near-total association with their characters. Robert Young expressed concerns about this to *TV Guide* in 1960:

> At first, when I began to realize how seriously people took me in *Father Knows Best,* I was badly frightened. Understandably, perhaps, I began to think the character was *me.* My wife finally brought things into focus. She advised me to know who I was and who Jim Anderson was, and not to confuse the two. However, the average viewer doesn't make that distinction. As far as he's concerned, Bob Young and Jim Anderson are one and the same man.

Ray Milland and Ray McNutley would never have been mistaken for the same man, given the clash between Milland's stately persona and standing and the inane character he played. But Robert Young's patriarchal maturity and featured player status meshed perfectly with television's genial Jim Anderson.[10]

These conditions also indicate that standards of masculinity could play a role in affecting crossover sitcom opportunities. Most of the stars who turned to sitcom work were either older or more foppish than Hollywood's typical male stars of the period. As a case in point, Jeff Chandler had starred as Mr. Boynton on the radio version of *Our Miss Brooks*, but producers declined to bring him to television, deeming him too virile for the visualization of the character. Instead, he went on to a productive career in Hollywood films. An arguable exception to this rule would be Robert Cummings, who played Bob Collins, a womanizing bachelor and photographer surrounded by beautiful models, in the successful *Bob Cummings Show* (NBC and CBS, 1955–59). But Cummings had made his mark in Hollywood with a quality of subdued affability, not robust masculinity. He told the *LA Times* that as a result "Hollywood was never hot about me" and that he was "always second choice" at the studios. Additionally, although his television character was a male chauvinist, Cummings played him with a certain affected, even effeminate style. Perhaps this absence of virility in the sitcom is not surprising, presuming that the period's standards of normative masculinity could not comfortably bear mockery. The many weak-willed, bumbling fathers on 1950s sitcoms were not supposed to be paragons of manhood; the typical male movie star was. Such gendered social formations would also prove challenging for female stars in comedies.[11]

FEMALE STARS AND SITCOMS

The kind of identity meshing that Robert Young spoke of could be especially problematic for women, who have long faced a bias against their participation in comedy. Prevailing norms of middle-class feminine propriety mitigated against women serving as comedic spectacle and enacting the excesses typically displayed in bawdy, vaudeo humor. Not surprisingly, women were limited in number on variety-comedy shows, and the handful to perform regularly, like Martha Raye and Imogene Coca, tended to distort their facial expressions and bodily movements to extremes as if to separate themselves definitively from norms of femininity. One is struck, however, by the significant number and popularity of women in situation comedies in the 1950s, especially those former film actresses like Lucille Ball, Marie Wilson, and Joan Davis who excelled in slapstick-oriented roles. In fact, Michele Hilmes claims that the term "situation comedy" emerged into common use in the 1940s predominantly with reference to a number of female-centered, storytelling-based radio comedies. By the mid-1940s, the networks had determined that women made up the majority of the listening audience, and sponsors appreciated that the name recognition and talents of comedians like Davis and Eve Arden drew in these listeners. Even so, a generic compromise was necessary to circumspectly contain their potentially transgressive talents. Hilmes writes:

> Situation comedy could surround the female comedian with an innocuous, domestic situation, with jokes arising from the interaction of characters and the resolution of comic narratives rather than the often-risqué double entendres of gag comedy. It could substitute female authority in the sphere of home or private life—a fairly palatable place for women to exert control—for female authority as host in the context of a variety show, a place in the public sphere much less hospitable to feminine power.

Any signs of transgression in the comedic excesses of the actress could be contained by the narrative frame of sitcom storytelling and ideologies of domesticity, albeit in exaggerated form.[12]

These standards continued when the popular comedies were brought to television, yet the visual versions complicated even further the tensions stemming from the fact that these were primarily actresses from the film world appearing. Sitcom sponsors intended to sell utilitarian consumer products to middle-class Americans and therefore wanted their goods attached to relatively commonplace images, not to Hollywood pretension, in the belief that necessary identification would be more attainable. A substantial negotiation of star images was required, as was evident in the development of *I Love Lucy*. Like Faye Emerson, Lucille Ball had careened through varied roles in her film career without developing a concretely identifiable central persona: she went from an earthy "Queen of the Bs" figure at RKO to a more glamorous second lead in musicals and sophisticated comedies at upscale MGM. Ball subsequently turned to a career in broadcasting as the star of radio's *My Favorite Husband* (CBS, 1948–51), playing the screwball Liz Cooper alongside Richard Denning. The show was a modest success, and CBS hoped to add it to the network's television schedule with the stars intact. But Ball wanted Denning replaced with her real-life husband, Desi Arnaz. The couple felt the show could then be revised into a fictional showcase of their real personae as married performers, with Arnaz as bandleader and Ball as movie actress. However, this idea was rejected by ad agencies, with one claiming that he could only pick up the show if the Ball and Arnaz characters became types "with whom the average person can associate—everyday people."[13]

Ball's role, therefore, would require a denial of the glamour and sexuality that had been constituents of her 1940s film persona and an approximate return to her *My Favorite Husband* character. The Arnaz character did remain a bandleader—thereby complying with the reassuring ethnic stereotype of the joyful entertainer—but his ethnicity also required that Ball's character be even more infantile than Liz Cooper in order to compensate for Ricky's deviant masculinity. In uncovering this transformation, scholar Alexander Doty further points out that, especially through the early years of *I Love Lucy*, the image of "Lucille Ball, film star" occasionally erupted during moments where Ball sang, danced, or displayed herself erotically in ways that "Lucy Ricardo, television character" supposedly could never carry off. The resulting tensions, however, were always alleviated through the subsequent reinforcement of Lucy's infantile, domesticized image.[14]

The phenomenal popularity of *I Love Lucy* led to numerous attempts to replicate its success. NBC's primary entry into this CBS-dominated arena was *I Married Joan* (1952–55)—an intriguing turnabout as star Joan Davis's successes in radio had opened the door for shows like *My Favorite Husband*. Davis was a vaudeville-style physical comic, largely limited to comic relief in feature films owing to her rubber-faced looks and a transgressive "body that acts as though she can't do a thing with it," in the words of one fan magazine. She primarily carried a narrative identity as a zany "man-chaser" (who, of course, rarely caught one), and she brought this identity to radio with success on hybrid sitcom-variety shows like *The Sealtest Village Store* (NBC, 1942–48). Davis's transition to television was helped by the fact that early 1950s sitcoms still evinced vestiges of variety-comedy, making her knockabout style amenable to the period's sitcom standards. Further, in a change from her radio appearances, Davis's character was married, allowing for a domestic situation to contain her authority. Like Lucy Ricardo, Davis's Joan Stevens was a rebellious, uncontrollable wife, but also like Lucy, Joan's rebellions were limited, and she would inevitably be repositioned as the subordinate object of ridicule by episode's end.[15]

Despite the outlandishness of their sitcom characters, both Ball and Davis were strongly associated with their parts in publicity for the shows. In Ball's case, her real-life marriage to her costar and the hyperreality of events like the birth of little Ricky/Desi, Jr. lent myriad parallels. Also, the oft-reported claim that Ball's motivation in doing the show was to be able to spend more time with her husband reinforced the notion that despite her evident desire to be a public performer, it was really domesticity she craved. This notion paralleled episode endings that would reinforce Lucy's love for Ricky and her contentment with the marital bond. Further, as Heather Osborne-Thompson has shown, Ball's considerable production control over the show was heavily downplayed in publicity in favor of images of domesticity; she was portrayed primarily as a motherly overseer to the everyday operations on the set, content to let her husband run the show. Osborne-Thompson writes, "In all of these ways, the images of Lucy Ricardo—a childlike, erratic housewife who couldn't be trusted with adult responsibilities—and of Ball—a successful television star with a penchant for comedy but no head for the TV business—became intertwined."[16]

On the other hand, Joan Davis's status as an astute businesswoman who strategically designed her own career was emphasized in publicity, seemingly in contradiction to her irrational television character. She also got divorced in 1948 and became a single mother, unlike her married and childless television character (though the part of Joan's young sister was played by Davis's real daughter). Publicity about Davis's production activities, however, portrayed her as near-maniacal in her work habits and thus plagued by nervous exhaustion, creating a strong association with her energetic, uncontrollable nature onscreen, especially in relation to female transgression of acceptable boundaries. In fact, the press emphasized these factors as an explanation for the dissolution of Davis's marriage and, after the cancellation of *I Married Joan* in 1955, the subsequent decline of her career. Ball was able to tame her potentially unruly image and foster one of the most successful careers in television history. Davis did so only for a time; despite originating a template for performance that ostensibly made Ball's career possible, she is largely forgotten today.[17]

Not all of these female-led sitcoms were entirely domestic in setting. The first half of the decade witnessed a significant trend of "single working girl" sitcoms, which would seem to contradict the need to relegate women solely to domestic roles. In fact, sitcom format dictated that each and every week these women would still be single, thus operating outside of their "natural" roles as wives and mothers, in addition to having some measure of autonomy within the public sphere of the workplace. Even so, some of these shows still presented regressive, compliant images of women, such as Marie Wilson's kooky, dumb blonde secretary in *My Friend Irma* (CBS, 1952–54), who wants nothing more than to be domesticated. Wilson had originated this character on a radio program of the same name (CBS, 1947–54) and then carried her into two Hal Wallis–produced features, *My Friend Irma* (1949) and *My Friend Irma Goes West* (1950). These films, though, were largely vehicles for Dean Martin and Jerry Lewis instead of Wilson. Only the small-screen version could integrate Wilson as a starring figure.

In fact, the majority of the working girl sitcom stars were either supporting actresses or B-movie and programmer specialists from Hollywood. For most of them, some measure of aberrant femininity had been responsible for their marginalization within the hierarchy of feature film stardom; they did not conform to bourgeois standards of femininity and thus could not headline in bourgeois modes of storytelling. They were, however, able to headline in the early 1950s television sitcom during a time when the format still bore the marks of its working-class vaudevillian ties yet contained them within repetitively recuperative storylines. Further, the specific identities that these actresses had established in film made possible their roles as nonconforming women.

Eve Arden stands out in this regard. Pigeonholed as the icy, sardonic sidekick in feature films, Arden longed for roles with more emotional depth and hoped that radio and television could provide them. One could question how much *Our Miss Brooks* truly gave Arden that opportunity; to some extent, Connie Brooks was Ida Corwin from *Mildred Pierce* (1945) in the classroom. But the teacher role let Arden pose as a compassionate person, and her lead status lent her character the narrative agency to capitalize on her feisty spirit in pursuing Mr. Boynton and overcoming her blustery boss, Mr. Conklin. This empowerment was an advance on her film roles, and Arden was definitively less conventional than most women on 1950s television. Rather than resorting to the slapstick antics that many of her early sitcom colleagues did, Arden's Miss Brooks controlled situations with her wit and intelligence and was nearly always savvier than the men around her. Plus, despite Miss Brooks's very conventional desire to settle down with Mr. Boynton, her wisecracks were often directed at mocking and questioning the societal pressures placed on women. The latter was a strong carryover from Arden's film persona—as Ida Corwin, Arden had uttered the famous rejection of motherhood, "Alligators have the right idea. They eat their young"—which enabled such verbal license for her television character.

Ann Sothern's filmic past allowed her to manage similarly unconventional single, urban, working female roles in *Private Secretary* and *The Ann Sothern Show*. Though she had played relatively diverse parts throughout her Hollywood career, Sothern was most identified with Maisie, the character she played in a ten-film programmer series for MGM from 1939 to 1947. Every film follows the same template: Maisie, an unemployed showgirl, comes to a new town and happens upon a job, a love interest, and some central conflict. In the end, the conflict gets resolved, and Maisie embraces her new beau, only to start from scratch in the next film. Through it all, Maisie is brassy, resourceful, independent, outspoken, sexually alluring yet accessible, and largely liberated from any obligations to society. She was a unique creation, made possible by a repeatedly proven popular formula, the slack oversight generally given to rank-and-file series by studios, and a set of female screenwriters. While the film series ended in 1947, the actress had already established the character on CBS radio, voicing Maisie there from 1945 to 1947 and in syndication from 1949 to 1952. She also freelanced in a variety of film roles, but a bout with hepatitis beginning in 1949 brought a three-year hiatus to her film career. Despite regaining her health by 1951, Sothern received only supporting-role offers from the Hollywood studios. She opted instead for a television sitcom, because it could provide her both a lead role and production control, the latter attained with the founding of her own company, Vincent Productions. The sitcom Sothern subsequently produced, *Private Secretary,* premiered on CBS on February 1, 1953, and across four years and 104 episodes Sothern portrayed Susie McNamara, single woman and personal secretary to a Manhattan talent agent.[18]

Susie shared some traits with Maisie, particularly the ones that made her most unconventional for a 1950s female sitcom lead. She operated outside of the domestic sphere with an independent, no-nonsense attitude, and she was much more resourceful and clued-in than the men who surrounded her. These qualities and Sothern's own warm, down-to-earth performance style would have provided a familiar reference point for audiences tuning in to *Private Secretary,* which likely gave Sothern the entry to bring this incomparable woman to television in the first place. Yet Susie's character would never have been confused with that of the itinerant traveler Maisie. Susie was an educated, middle-class, professional career woman, more refined and less sexualized than Maisie, though still romantically available. She repeatedly, however, chose to sacrifice potential romantic commitment in favor of her career, making it clear that not even a well-off woman like Susie could have both. Sothern's age—she was forty-four when *Private Secretary* began—minimized the transgression of sacrificing her natural maternal role; according to cultural convention she was nearly past being able to fulfill that role anyway. But the show also emphasized that Susie was perfectly happy with her decision to forgo marriage and family for her career. At the same time, there was an implied domesticity to Susie's office activities, as she kept the office running like a household and completed wifely tasks for her boss. One publicity article even referred to Susie's role as "office wife." Lisa Parks notes the importance of the title in this respect: Susie is denoted as a *private* secretary, not a professional one. Parks writes, "The only successful working woman allowed in 1950s television culture was tempered by a nurturing domesticity." It was also important for this situation to take place in an urban setting connected to the world of entertainment, where an independent career woman (especially one played by a long-visible film star) was a more viable proposition.[19]

Likewise, the constant enmeshing of Maisie, Susie, and Sothern in publicity naturalized this unique depiction. Sothern was portrayed as plucky and determined like Maisie, hardworking and professionally committed like Susie, and resistant to convention like both. But Sothern's real personality was even more resolutely connected to Susie than it had been to Maisie. Whereas many 1940s publicity articles defined clear distinctions between Sothern and Maisie, most television publicity collapsed Susie and Sothern. A *TV Time* article quoted Sothern as saying of her choice to portray Susie, "She seemed kinda like a girl I might be," and it ended with "to meet Ann Sothern is to know Suzie [*sic*]." Viewers seemingly internalized this meshing. Much as Eve Arden was flooded with letters from real teachers and was made an honorary member of the National Education Association, secretaries across the nation wrote Sothern personally for advice about their jobs, and she appeared on the cover of *Today's Secretary* magazine in 1954. This identification also translated into the ever-important sales of consumer products, as tie-in merchandise like dresses, spectacles, and office supplies sold in profitable amounts. As long as Susie, and Sothern, could be incorporated into the cultural and economic order of 1950s television, limited straying outside of dominant social discourses could be accepted.[20]

Ann Sothern in Private Secretary. NBC/Photofest.

Private Secretary stayed strong in the ratings but ended prematurely in 1957 owing to a financial dispute between Sothern and producer Jack Chertok. Sothern launched a similar show the next year, in which she played Katy O'Connor, assistant manager of a New York City hotel. Less popular than its predecessor, *The Ann Sothern Show* still presented the actress as an independent, career-oriented woman who outshined her male boss, played by Ernest Truex. In an attempt to goose the middling ratings and recapture old magic, the second season saw the older Truex ushered out and replaced with Don Porter, who had previously played Susie Mc-Namara's boss. This reinstated some romantic tension, but Sothern told *TV Guide* that the meekness of Truex's character had also been judged as problematic: "The simple psychological truth is, people don't want to see me dominating a man." She expressed a similar sentiment when responding to Hal Humphrey's 1960 observation that she was the last of the great sitcom comediennes on the air: "It's a man's world now. It's populated mostly with broad shoulders and slim hips, and apparently the women in the audience like it that way. Women like to be dominated."[21]

By that time, a more docile version of sitcom femininity—represented by Jane Wyatt of *Father Knows Best* as the archetype—had come to permeate the format. Most of the "unruly women" were off the air by 1957, some never to be seen in series again. Joan Davis, for one, failed to find a new vehicle after the end of *I Married Joan*. She did shoot a pilot in 1956 called *Joan of Arkansas,* in which she played a female astronaut, chosen at random by a government computer searching for "one perfectly normal American adult" to become the first person in space. Of course, the computer malfunctions and only accidentally chooses Joan. A similar set of malfunctions would have had to take place at the networks to place a woman in such a masculine occupation in the late 1950s. Even Lucy was sent to the suburbs in 1957, and in the following seasons, she only appeared in occasional hour-long specials. By the late 1950s, the serenity of the domestic sitcom and its contented and conforming wives ruled the airwaves. This transition does not mean there was no longer space for established film actresses in the sitcom format; rather, that only a certain type could prevail, as the comparative experiences of Donna Reed and Betty Hutton illustrate.[22]

REED SUCCEEDS, HUTTON HITS BOTTOM

On September 24, 1959, ABC premiered its struggling sophomore sitcom *The Donna Reed Show* in a new time slot, Thursday nights at 8 P.M., a space the subsequently successful program would occupy until 1966. One week later, on October 1, 1959, CBS debuted the brand-new sitcom *The Betty Hutton Show* in that same time slot. This show, however, was a flop, generating only thirty episodes. One show launched its star-actress to the status of television legend; the other essentially brought its star's entertainment career to an end. Why did one transitioning film actress succeed on a late 1950s sitcom whereas the other failed in direct competition when given the same opportunity?

The Donna Reed Show featured its title star as Donna Stone, the prototypical domestic sitcom wife: tolerant of the constant demands of her husband and children and highly capable of running the household yet content to stay within its confines. Also quite typically, publicity for the program meshed Donna Stone's character identity with Donna Reed's star persona to naturalize the depicted family and gender structures. The newspaper supplement *American Weekly* did exactly this within a 1962 profile of the show:

166

The [off-air] Donna Reed is not superficially different from the Donna Reed who performs on the air. Both Donnas are possessed of serene, even sunny dispositions . . . and the ability to meet nearly every situation with poise and grace. Both appear to be normal, average, well-adjusted women. It is as though all that corn, consumed in Donna's Iowa childhood, distributed itself into complacent cells of un-neurotic well-being throughout her lovely body.

This description of Reed could have been lifted outright from any number of 1940s studio publicity articles about her filmic image. During Reed's days as a contract player and marginal star at MGM and Columbia, publicity focused heavily on her Iowa farmland background and her supposedly wholesome yet practical personality. This image dovetailed with Reed's supporting and starring roles as the sincere, plainspoken and gracious girlfriend or wife in family pictures and romances. Not even a strikingly off-cast, Oscar-winning role as a prostitute in 1953's *From Here to Eternity* could dislodge her superficial persona as the model wife and mother.[23]

Biographer Jay Fultz concludes that a frustration with this typecasting and the apparent ceiling on her level of film stardom led Reed to consider appearing in a television sitcom by the mid-1950s. As for what kind of show she would do, Fultz claims that a Screen Gems producer saw a photograph of a beaming Reed with her children and "knew that television should present Donna as she actually was: a wife and mother." The fact that this image was originally commissioned as a publicity photo in conjunction with a 1952 film indicates that the transition from film to television would not be difficult for Reed. If the ideal domestic sitcom instructed its female audiences on the proper, socially accepted ways to behave as wives, mothers, and consumers, it seems inevitable that Reed would have found success in this genre.[24]

On the other hand, when we look closely at Betty Hutton's image, it seems almost impossible to believe that anyone ever thought that she was a good fit for television. Hutton reached the height of her film career in 1950, when she was one of Paramount's highest-paid stars, enjoyed a career-defining role in *Annie Get Your Gun,* and was named *Photoplay*'s Top Actress. Hutton's performative trademarks were her boundless energy and excessive exuberance, but her extreme behavior and the implied lack of control over her body pushed the boundaries of acceptable femininity. This image became a significant problem for Hutton in the early 1950s. She went through two very public divorces in 1952, one from her

The Donna Reed
Show *family.*
ABC/Photofest.

first husband and one from Paramount, the latter allegedly because the studio refused to hire her new husband as a director, after which the major movie studios blackballed her for insubordination.

Thus television became a significant option for Hutton, and she dove into the new medium with a fittingly big splash in 1954 as the star of television's very first spectacular: an *Annie Get Your Gun* knockoff entitled "Satins and Spurs." Unfortunately, the program was a critical and ratings failure, and many reviewers reacted quite derisively to Hutton's performance. The *New York Times*'s Val Adams commented, "[Hutton] held her singing down just short of blowing a tube . . . and did a type of dancing rarely seen on television. Evidently NBC is not taking the industry's [censorship] code book too literally." While the scope, depth, and public setting of the big-screen musical may have furnished sufficient space within which to contain Hutton's image of excess, the intimacy, diminution, and private setting of television apparently did not.[25]

Hutton was devastated by the failure of "Satins and Spurs," and she immediately announced her retirement from entertainment. This was

168

only the first of Hutton's many retirements across the 1950s, and each was followed shortly thereafter by a theatrical engagement or a variety show appearance. Correspondingly, her public image became just as unstable as her career from this point on, especially without the studio system apparatus around to control her problematic image as it carefully had in the 1940s. Both scandal sheets and legitimate magazines alike began to explain her dynamism as a by-product of emotional deficiencies, particularly a frantic need for acceptance and an overwhelming insecurity. The scandal magazine *Uncensored* reveled in such depictions; one 1955 article related, "Unless the applause equals the noise Betty makes, she's the unhappiest girl in town . . . just let Betty think she didn't score and a real show goes on, one her admirers never see and would shudder at if they did." Such descriptions indicate a disturbing instability behind her excitement, an irrational volatility that one would not ordinarily welcome into the living room.[26]

Nonetheless, Hutton gained weekly entry into America's living rooms in 1959 with *The Betty Hutton Show*, in which she played Goldie, a showgirl-turned-manicurist who is so beloved by one of her regular customers that when he dies, he bequeaths to her his entire multimillion dollar fortune plus guardianship of his three children. She then struggles from episode to episode with both the sudden fortune and single parenthood. This scenario alone, no matter who starred in it, was decidedly unconventional at a time when domestic sitcoms were supposed to feature an approximation of the cohesive, middle-class suburban nuclear family so desired by sponsors and networks. Also anachronistically, the program was strikingly reflexive, and Hutton drew on conventions of presentational theatricality in her performance. She frequently looked at the camera to volunteer her reactions, as if directly addressing the viewer, and her facial mugging seemed more appropriate for a variety show than a sitcom. As Hutton friend Ben Carbonetto put it, "She tried so hard and it showed. . . . It was as if she was playing to a live audience, looking for immediate feedback." Given that the popular press had reported so heavily on her insecurities, viewers were already positioned to read Hutton's mugging not as screwball comedy but as frantic desperation.[27]

Hutton's public image also suffered from reports of chaos on the set of the show, as she insisted on creative control of everything from writing to directing to designing. Three producers and two directors quit in frustration, and by the season's midpoint, Hutton was largely producing

The Betty Hutton
Show *family.*
CBS/Photofest.

the show alone. The television press heaped criticism upon Hutton for this; a *TV Guide* profiler described Hutton's "all-out campaign to have things her own way" and wrote of Hutton's reactions to press coverage of her backstage troubles: "To press her too hard on this point is to shorten the fuse on a critical mass of explosive Hutton atoms. Betty begs the press . . . like a small child precariously living out a daydream which a little reality can bring crashing around her ears." Though there are substantial misogynistic connotations within these comments, it is the case that what Hutton was creating simply would not work for late 1950s television, neither aesthetically nor culturally, and *The Betty Hutton Show* was canceled after only one season. Except for a handful of guest appearances on television in the coming years, Hutton's entertainment career was over.[28]

In retrospect, one wonders how *The Betty Hutton Show* ever got on the air in the first place. Perhaps the allure of a name as big as Betty Hutton's was too strong for CBS and sponsor Post Cereals to pass up.

One can assume that the network also saw the show as appropriate competition for *The Donna Reed Show*, pitting one of Hollywood's biggest former stars against a supporting player whose show had struggled in its first season. But the volatility of Hutton's star image coupled with the raggedly uneven show that resulted from trying to contain that image within the confines of the television screen and a sitcom narrative was no match for the domestic serenity of Donnas Reed and Stone. At the very least, CBS and Post should have recognized that 1950s television was more equipped to accommodate complacent cells of unneurotic well-being than a critical mass of explosive Hutton atoms.

FILM STARDOM IN SITCOM FORM

Hutton's experience and the demise of the effervescent female-centered comedies that had reigned during the early 1950s might lead one to assume that nothing but serene suburban wives were allowed to occupy the airwaves thereafter. Yet there is still the curious case of Ida Lupino's *Mr. Adams and Eve* (CBS, 1957–58). This series featured former film star and independent film director Ida Lupino as the glamorous Hollywood movie star Eve Drake, wife of more sensible costar Howard Adams (who was played by Lupino's real-life husband Howard Duff).

Whereas *The Adventures of Ozzie and Harriet* (ABC, 1952–66) tried to show how the Hollywood-based Nelsons were no different than the typical American family, *Mr. Adams and Eve* instead highlighted the abnormal lifestyle of its star couple, a factor that would seem to violate the basic principles of the domestic sitcom. Indeed, the show was partly set in the public sphere of the film industry, and Lupino acted out a glamorous star image. All of the program's episodes revolve around Howard and Eve's life in Hollywood, from "This is Your Life," which features Eve on the famous television program, to "Suspension," in which the couple is punished by their studio for refusing to do an assigned picture. In a period increasingly filled with suburban family sitcoms like *Leave It To Beaver* (CBS and ABC, 1957–63) and heading away from the reflexivity that had marked comedy earlier in the decade, this self-conscious depiction of the public and private lives of flamboyant film stars is quite striking.

It is also worth noting how extraordinary it was for a female film star to be showcased in such a manner at any point. To some extent, Eve Drake and Howard Adams were similar to other famous screwball couples on 1950s television, including George and Gracie and Lucy and

*Howard Duff and
Ida Lupino as
Howard Adams
and Eve Drake.
CBS/Photofest.*

Ricky. Like Gracie and Lucy, Eve frequently upset the serenity of the household with a variety of screwball antics, but she was inevitably put back in her place by her male counterpart at the end of each episode. The ways in which Eve overstepped the boundaries of typical female roles, however, and the scope within which she operated notably diverged from either Gracie's or Lucy's activities. Many of *Mr. Adams and Eve*'s episodes deal with Eve's public persona, her glamorous Hollywood life, and her successes in show business rather than her failures—quite unlike the persona of Lucy Ricardo, whose repeated attempts to enter the world of show business and stardom usually end in failure and a return to the home. Instead, Eve escapes the confines of domesticity precisely because of her professional success and film stardom. Without question, she is an inept housewife, but that is because she is busy making movies and living the life of a glamorous star. Eve represents a significant exception in a medium that generally demanded its female public performers adopt more private identities. The question thus arises, why was Lupino able to explore a portrayal

172

closed off to such actresses as Lucille Ball and with a performative flamboyance apparently closed off to someone like Betty Hutton? And how did the program manage the relatively transgressive, public identity presented by Eve Drake? Further, the specific topic of the sitcom raises an additional relevant question: what does *Mr. Adams and Eve*'s satirical depiction of film stars indicate about how television was presenting the concept of film stardom by the late 1950s?

THE MANY FACES OF IDA LUPINO

Throughout a Warner Bros. film career that won her the tag of "the poor man's Bette Davis," Lupino played a variety of roles, but she was best known for playing hardened and tough yet emotional females in a string of crime dramas, including *They Drive By Night* (1940), *High Sierra* (1941), and *Road House* (1948). Describing her typical character as the "female victim-turned-survivor," profiler Judith Redding defined her film persona as "the tough girl forced by circumstances to get what she wanted by whatever means necessary." In keeping with this image of hard-edged toughness, Lupino frequently denied a connection to typical Hollywood standards of glamour and femininity. She told one newspaper about the Hollywood life: "It was not for me. I didn't like anything about it—the acting, the daily facials, the so-called glamour." Similarly, film critic Jerry Vermilye described her as "finding the glamour side of the acting life totally distressing," and the *New York Times* retrospectively defined her in 1965 as "a movie star who happened to hate stardom. A glamour queen who loathed glamour."[29]

Lupino ended her Warner Bros. contract in January 1947 and, like many who left Warner Bros., she yearned to control her own work. Thus, along with then-husband Collier Young and friend Anson Bond, Lupino formed Emerald Productions, a low-budget film production company. The company's first release was *Not Wanted* (1949), a controversial film about illegitimacy. Lupino cowrote the script and, when the scheduled director had a mild heart attack just before shooting, she also took over as director. Lupino and Young left Emerald in 1949 after a dispute with Bond and formed The Filmakers with writer Malvin Wald. Lupino subsequently directed a number of films for the company, including *Never Fear* (1950), a drama about polio victims; *Outrage* (1950), a story of a girl's molestation; and *Hard, Fast and Beautiful* (1951), about a young tennis player and her scheming mother. These films gained her a directorial reputation for controversy and social realism, and they also earned her industry respect, evidenced by her invitation to present the Best Director award at the 1950 Oscars. In 1953, Lupino directed her most famous film, the suspenseful *The Hitch-Hiker*. That same year, she directed and starred in *The Bigamist*, thereby becoming the first woman to direct herself in a theatrical feature. Filmakers planned to enter television production, but the company folded in 1954, succumbing to the financial challenges of independent production.

Lupino's theatrical directorial efforts, reliant on social-realist treatments of women's issues and the travails of vulnerable men and women, have generated a good deal of critical attention aimed at assessing their status as feminist texts. Traditional critics have expressed disappointment with her work; Molly Haskell sums up Lupino's films as "conventional, even sexist" because of their passive heroines and their reliance on melodramatic plots that strongly reinforce prevalent ideologies of marriage and gender roles. Conversely, Claire Johnston has argued that although the films do not explicitly attack sexist ideology, ambiguities and distortions within their narratives leave a space for feminist interpretations.[30]

Lupino herself publicly rejected a feminist identity as a director and said that her intent as a filmmaker was simply to present "high quality, low budget, independent films on provocative subject matter, to tell 'how America lives,' and to be commercially successful at it." She was also notorious for comments that would make feminists cringe, including: "[A]ny woman who wishes to smash into the world of men isn't very feminine. . . . Baby, we can't go smashing. I believe women should be struck regularly—like a gong. . . . If a woman has a man who loves her, she better stick close to home." She even described her own directorial talents as passive in nature, equating them with domestic submissiveness: "I would never shout orders to anyone. I hate women who order men around—professionally or personally. I think it is horrible in business or in the home. I've seen bossy women push their men around and I have no respect for the gal who does the shoving or the man who lets himself get pushed around. I wouldn't dare do that with my old man."[31]

A number of critics have argued that Lupino had to take such positions in order to be accepted as a woman working in a patriarchal industry and culture. Mary Celeste Kearney and James Moran explain how the press frequently seized upon Lupino's masculine-coded status as film and television director and, at the same time, undercut it with references—often supplied by Lupino herself—to her femininity and submissiveness. They write: "Despite Lupino's being gendered masculine as a director of typically male genres, there were just as many comments in the media (if not more) that she still had a 'feminine touch,' comments which demonstrate an attempt to offset the threat of a woman performing a 'man's job'."[32] Thus, although Lupino potentially held a transgressive position as female film director, this image was most frequently overshadowed by the depiction of her subservience to male control. The repeated circulation of these issues in press descriptions of her film directing reveals a complex, tangled image.

While this image has been explored through Lupino's independent films and her status as a female film director, only a handful of scholars have given similar attention to Lupino's directing work for television, especially as this material presents greater challenges to analysis. Because of the production circumstances of the medium, few television directors have had the opportunity to put a personal imprint on their work. Thus, although she directed hundreds of episodes and averaged about eight televised hours on television a year across the 1960s, Lupino's work is very difficult to assess from an auteurist or feminist standpoint. It is relevant to note here that, because directing did not supply much money, Lupino did sustain a notable acting career on television and, significantly, she had a substantial measure of production control over her acting appearances in the 1950s. The challenges of her status as a potentially powerful woman in a male-dominated industry were remarkably evident in some of these roles.

Like many of her peers, Lupino was initially hesitant to move into television, but, especially with Filmakers struggling, it seemed a viable opportunity. Cameraman George Diskant, who had worked with Lupino on *The Bigamist,* was currently at work on *Four Star Playhouse* and told her she should get involved, so when David Niven personally invited her to fill a guest spot, she agreed. She made her television debut in December 1953 on a *Four Star* episode entitled "House for Sale." After a number of guest appearances across the next season, Powell, Niven, and Boyer asked her to stay on as permanent fourth member, where she remained until the program's demise in 1956.

Across the run of *Four Star Playhouse,* Lupino appeared in nineteen episodes. A striking number of these depict melodramatic relations between Lupino and the male leads, including five tales involving men either stalking or attempting to kill her character and four episodes detailing marital betrayal, either by her character or the male lead. These episodes have at their core issues of female strength and stability, with Lupino playing the unstable victimizer as often as the persevering survivor. For instance, in "House For Sale" Lupino's character successfully battles an escaped killer, while in "The Listener" she murders her husband and then is nearly driven insane by her fear of being caught. In "One Way Out" she smartly turns the table on her scheming husband, who attempts to trap and kill her; in "The Case of Emily Cameron" she is a crippled wife who blames her husband for her condition and tortures him mentally for it.

The latter was one of two episodes that Lupino herself wrote and performed in for *Four Star Playhouse,* and it was a tour de force of both scripting and acting. Presenting the story of a troubled marriage from each spouse's perspective, the episode allowed Lupino to play both a victimized wife and a shrewish manipulator. The conclusion of the tale reveals the latter characterization to be the true one, and the husband in the end humiliates and rejects Lupino's character. Emily Cameron offered her an intriguing portrayal, and it is not surprising that Lupino would script such a complex, double-edged character for herself. As both controller and controlled, this depiction was an echo of the oscillating roles she played throughout the series. Of course, with her aggressive side condemned at the end of this episode, the message sent was that a domineering woman deserves to be punished. Indeed, both the character's vacillation and the story's resolution mirrored Lupino's own attempts in the press to shape her image as female film director. Just as her star image shifted from authoritative to submissive and back again in the press, so did her characters on *Four Star Playhouse.*

The other *Four Star Playhouse* story that Lupino both wrote and acted in was "Stand-In," wherein Lupino played the bitter stand-in of a flamboyant but aging Hollywood star. The episode was quite critical of filmdom hypocrisy, and *Variety* surmised that Lupino based the tale on "some of the stories that she has heard about strutting stars of Hollywood who faded into oblivion when their day was done." Lupino also starred in a similarly themed yet comical *Four Star* episode entitled "Award." Here she played a bombastic Hollywood star who fails in her Broadway premiere. She blames the critical press for her failures, but a director friend, played by Franchot Tone, explains that she's too shallow for acting on the stage, where "you have to do it all yourself" and "acting is truth," not the falsities of Hollywood. She soon awakens to this idea and admits that her studio-created biography is a sham, that she is really a blue-collar girl at heart and that only within that identity can she find the truth needed to act in the theater. This resolution very much echoed Lupino's own identity as an actress who dismissed the trappings of Hollywood and embraced realism. Also, these episodes were fitting precursors to *Mr. Adams and Eve*, which similarly mocked life in Hollywood.[33]

MR. ADAMS AND EVE

After completing her commitment to *Four Star Playhouse*, Lupino turned to the continuing-character sitcom *Mr. Adams and Eve*, which premiered on CBS on January 4, 1957. Conceived by Collier Young, written by Sol Saks, and distributed by Four Star Productions, the sitcom was underwritten by Lupino and Duff's own production company, Bridget Productions, with Fred De Cordova acting as producer on most episodes. As already mentioned, *Mr. Adams and Eve* presented Lupino and then-husband Howard Duff essentially playing a version of themselves, a Hollywood star couple named Howard Adams and Eve Drake. Given the show's premise and its stars, reflexivity became a central focus of the program and its publicity. The program's publicity was similar to other celebrity-focused sitcoms in claiming that what viewers were seeing was a depiction of some version of their real lives. However, rather than showing how the featured couple shared the same routines and values as the typical American family, *Mr. Adams and Eve* instead focused on the extravagant lifestyle and reckless behavior of its twosome. In fact, neither sponsors nor the networks were initially interested in the show for this very reason. A *Time* magazine profile on Lupino claimed that she and Duff met resistance from an advertising executive who said that a show about their celebrity lifestyle was doomed to fail because their characters "would not be identified with the next-door neighbors." The article then detailed, "The Duffs looked the adman over and told him, in effect, that it was all right, since they would not particularly care to be identified with their next-door neighbors."[34]

What the couple would be identified with was their "real" selves, as successful, affluent film stars: many articles on the program insisted that most of the program's plotlines—and even a few props—came straight from the stars' own lives. In a *TV Guide* article titled "Mr. Duff and Ida: A Hollywood married couple are themselves (more or less) on TV," the magazine described a persistent feeling that Duff and Lupino were "putting on the funniest *documentary* on TV." In a similar vein, *LA Mirror* critic Hal Humphrey wrote, "The similarity between the plot of the TV show and Ida and Howard's own marriage is considerably more than coincidental." The show itself took full advantage of these publicized connections. From the opening credit sequence, the producers of *Mr. Adams and Eve* put forth the program as a skewed glimpse into the actual married life of Duff and Lupino. The opening presents animated versions of the Lupino and Duff characters on a film set (daringly displaying the single bed that they share, incidentally) as a voice-over explains: "This is Mr. Adams and Eve. They play movie stars who are husband and wife. Starring Ida Lupino and Howard Duff. And in real life, they actually are husband and wife. It's *Mr. Adams and Eve.*"[35]

Significantly, Eve is often the driving force for these plots, both creating farcical situations and resolving them. In "Dear Variety," Eve reads a ten-year-old copy of *Variety*, but mistakes it for that day's edition. A front-page article describes the closing of the studio that employs Howard and Eve and the firing of the studio head, J. B. Hafter, by the studio's New York executives. Eve responds with an angry editorial in *Variety*. When the New York executives see the editorial, they have no idea who decided to fire Hafter; but, because they read about it in *Variety*, they assume he must deserve to be fired and do so. Eve later realizes her mistake and publishes another editorial praising the executives for changing their minds and reinstating Hafter. They again presume that this must be the right thing to do, and all is set straight.

As this episode and the earlier "Stand-In" indicate, Lupino did not hesitate to mock the shallowness and pretension of Hollywood in her television work. In a number of episodes, she even presented her own image for mockery: two such episodes, "Typical" and "Howard and Eve and Ida," are most striking in terms of the documentation of Lupino's star image and its complexities. The plot of "Typical" begins with Howard and Eve's agent proposing that the Hollywood couple try a television series as a typical family in a standard domestic comedy. Eve responds dismissively, "No, no, we'll never, never do TV," but then bristles when her agent agrees, saying the couple could never pull off a typical family portrayal anyway, given their entrenched movie star habits. Eve reacts to this with indignation and decides she wants to try to be a typical domestic housewife for a day. She and Howard thus get up at 7:30 in the morning to start the day like "normal" people. Eve exclaims upon arising: "I wanna

Howard and Eve are stunned at how early "typical" people wake up. CBS/Photofest.

be nice and normal. I want to be doing what every typical, average American woman is doing. Eve Adams, housewife and woman."

Not surprisingly, Eve utterly fails at being typical. She has no idea how to find her way around the kitchen, make coffee, do the laundry, or even associate with the neighbors, and she grows more discouraged with her domestic inadequacies as the episode heads toward its climax. But in the penultimate scene, after Eve hysterically berates herself for not being typical, Howard grabs her and tries to reason with her by reminding her of her celebrity status: "You're illogical, inconsiderate, and unpredictable. You can't do what fifty million other women are doing every day of their lives. But when you're in front of a camera, you're great, and those fifty million women forget about their laundries and their kitchens when they see you, the glamorous, exciting Eve Drake." With this speech, Howard repositions Lupino's character from "Eve Adams, housewife and woman" back to her proper identity as "the glamorous, exciting Eve Drake." Of course, Howard also reinforces his control over Eve with his final speech, displaying masculine rationality over her irrationality. Eve is therefore rescued from typical domesticity but cemented into typical femininity.

Significantly, this episode's plot trajectory is the polar opposite of the typical episode of *I Love Lucy*. Eve moves from a successful stage performance during the episode's opening to trying and failing to be a housewife back to being a performer again in the end. Thus, rather than a Lucy-like return to domesticity, Eve experiences a restorative return to glamour and stardom in the end. This does not mean that *Mr. Adams and Eve* is a transgressively feminist text and *I Love Lucy* is not. Indeed, Patricia Mellencamp has argued that the humor drawn from Lucy's shenanigans can be seen as displaced "anger at the weekly frustration of Lucy's desire to escape the confinement of domesticity"; these attempts to escape scatter moments of feminist liberation throughout plots that typically relegate Lucy to housewifery. On the other hand, while *Mr. Adams and Eve*'s main female character does operate capably outside the realm of domesticity, she too is contained by her husband and patriarchal control, as seen in the denouement of "Typical"—and, indeed, in the very title of the program, which accords only Howard the respect of an appellation.[36]

In addition, the publicity on *Mr. Adams and Eve* functioned in much the same manner as had the publicity that tried to subordinate Lupino's feminist power as a film director. A 1957 *TV-Radio Mirror* article on *Mr. Adams and Eve* entitled "Where Adam is King" offers an illustration. The article begins, "Eve can be happy as a queen, says Ida Lupino, who finds it pays to let husband Howard Duff be 'the boss' at home," and continues to describe how much Lupino enjoys letting Duff be the commanding presence in their home. While most other publicity articles stressed the similarities between the program and the couple's real life, this one made sure to point out that though Eve drove the drama on the small screen, Howard controlled events in their real lives. This emphasis on submission indicates that Lupino's acting career followed much the same pattern of her public image as film director: occasional eruptions of potential feminine power quashed in the end by dominant ideology and Lupino's own rhetorical embrace of the latter.[37]

It is also clear from this publicity that despite the claims of the sitcom being a "documentary," there were significant dissimilarities between Lupino's publicized "real" life, her star persona, and the character of Eve Adams. Whereas Eve is an impetuous, impulsive, even unsteady screwball figure who perpetually plunges her domestic world with Howard into disarray and who insists on being treated like a luminary in both her public and private life, Lupino's reigning persona as a film star was that of a tough, hardened woman. A *Family Circle* article on Lupino in 1958 described her "real" personality as that of "a nononsense hard driving gal with no patience for detours or delays," and the *TV-Radio Mirror* profile referred to her as a "domestic stabilizer" in the Duff-Lupino household. These characterizations also echo her publicized image as film director, in keeping with the tone of the gritty independent films that she helmed, such as *The Hitch-Hiker* and *The Bigamist*. Such publicity images were obviously designed to muffle the transgressive power of Lupino, and Eve, within patriarchal society. The schism that existed between Lupino's persona and Eve suggests that what is ultimately, and quite self-consciously, documented in *Mr. Adams and Eve* is the artificiality of publicized star images and the duplicity of the mechanisms that construct them.[38]

Fittingly, the most frequently iterated theme in *Mr. Adams and Eve* involves the conflict between studio publicity about the stars' lives and the reality of those lives. At least seven episodes directly address this in their plotlines. In "The Life Story of Howard Adams and Eve Drake," their studio boss hopes to make a feature film about the stars' lives, but the scriptwriter cannot reconcile the various versions of their biographies that he's presented with. In "That Magazine," Howard and Eve carefully rehearse an ideal version of their daily lives in preparation for a magazine profile, only to have their performance go awry when the reporter arrives. An episode entitled "Academy Award" contains just such a critique of the contrivance behind the performance of media stardom. The show opens with file footage of crowds milling around outside the RKO Pantages Theater, as a voice-over introduces the viewer to "the glamour capital of the world." Meanwhile, Eve and Howard ride in a limousine on their way to the Oscars, as both have been nominated for the respective top acting awards. Both also insist that they'll be perfectly happy if one goes home empty-handed and the other wins, and they agree that if they do win, they'll make sure not to change or take themselves too seriously. The Oscar ceremony is a comic affair: the acting award presenters are depicted offscreen, represented only by vocal caricatures of James Cagney and Bette Davis, and after Eve wins for Best Actress, Howard loses out to the twelve-year-old star of a juvenile delinquency picture.[39]

Despite her pre-ceremony assurances, subsequent scenes show that Eve cannot help gloating over her victory and gleefully milking the star treatment that comes with it, especially on the film set the next day, where Howard is left feeling ignored and belittled. The couple is subsequently approached by real-life Hollywood gossip columnist Sheilah Graham for a story about "the marriage they said would never last," the kind of story that, Graham jokes, "usually breaks in the fan magazines about a month after the couple have split up." Correspondingly, Howard and Eve appear on "Ned Darrow's People to People" as they try, and fail, to perform sufficiently as a happy star couple while their agonized press agent watches. This thinly veiled send-up of Ed Murrow's celebrity chat show *Person to Person* calls attention to the potential contrivances of that show and even the possibility that what is presented as authentic by television is actually manufactured performance by the featured stars.[40]

An episode entitled "Howard and Eve and Ida" similarly exploits the fragmentation of Lupino's image by presenting her both as Eve and as Ida Lupino the movie director, hired by the studio to shoot a star vehicle for Howard and Eve. The episode begins abstractly, with Howard seated on a darkened stage. He comments that he has a problem in that there are *two* women in his life. A spotlight then reveals Ida Lupino in two different costumes on either side of him, as Howard says, "Over here is Eve Drake, and over here is Ida Lupino." He then entices the audience by telling them to "stick around and see how it turns out," adding, "Personally, I'm scared stiff." The episode's story then begins with the director of Eve and Howard's latest film derailed by an illness. They need a replacement, and after turning down the names of George Cukor, Charles Vidor, and George Stevens, they come up with Ida Lupino. Eve objects to this choice, describing the female director as a tyrannical hack, but it soon emerges that her primary objections are based on the fact that Howard used to date Ida and on her perception that her career was held back because of her resemblance to Ida (which no one else in the episode recognizes). Eve spends most of the episode battling against Ida and, aside from their obvious facial resemblance, the two are thoroughly contrasted within the episode—directly so in split-screen moments with Eve decked out in excessive, theatrical glamour, including a fur coat and elaborate hat, and Ida in a simple dress and bookish glasses. Contrasts are also evident in their character behavior: Eve is shown to be a hysterically jealous actress, while Lupino is depicted in her capacity as a skilled film director, discussing script changes with Howard, planning out potential shots with an assistant, and craning up and down in the director's seat.

Despite their conflicts (which are solely generated by Eve; Ida is not even aware of them), Eve sees through her jealousy in the end and acknowledges that Ida is a great director. Her change of heart occurs in response to a creative battle between Ida and studio head J. B. Hafter. The film they are shooting is a working-class drama called *Man on the Docks*, but Hafter announces his intention to include a gratuitous dream sequence involving a scantily clad Eve. Ida adamantly argues for her artistic vision over Hafter's desires for sensationalism and commercialism. He bellows in response, "All I wanted was a little glamour," but Howard and Eve support Ida's vision of the film, and Hafter relents.

This conflict is an intriguing centerpiece in the episode, in part because it depicts Ida's intellectual and creative superiority over Hafter. In demanding that she drop the disputed scene, Hafter insists, "I am the boss here." He tells her to shoot the dream sequence or be fired. She refuses, and Hafter is made to look like a fool for his blustery demand. Ida's assertiveness in this depiction is thus quite striking. As previously noted, part of Lupino's image was as an actress and director on the fringes of Hollywood, and the critical stance of "Howard and Eve and Ida" supported that dimension as well. With its comparison of Eve and Ida, the episode mocked the excesses of Hollywood (much as *Mr. Adams and Eve* did every week). Through her battle with Hafter, Lupino the director was shown to be outside of such excesses. In arguing against the inclusion of the seminude scene, her director-character said she agreed to do the film only because it was "hard-hitting and real," and if she was forced to change the film she would walk away from it. These assertions intertwined both Lupino's own artistic credibility and her independence from Hollywood. Further, given that her directorial career was largely based in television at this point, this portrayal also inherently underscored the credibility of television as a place that *did* make room for the maverick spirit of Ida Lupino.

It must also be noted that only when Eve finally defends Ida is the director's job, and the film, saved. Only Eve and the authority of her stardom can truly dominate Hafter. Eve uses her star power to eliminate the glamour scene, yet it is that very quality of glamour that gives her the privilege to do so. With this resolution, *Mr. Adams and Eve* acknowledges a level of power in its female star that Lucy, Gracie, and

Harriet never openly received. Of course, only when Eve overcomes her feminine hysteria is she lucid enough to use her power in a positive way. Thus, as when Eve capitulates to Howard at the end of "Typical," the potency of the image is tempered by its acquiescence to prevailing gender assumptions. But, as Lupino herself did, the character of Eve at least exerts pressure on the boundaries of those assumptions.

The cleverness with which these episodes are executed, not to mention their very existence, attests to the richness of Lupino's persona in this period. In fact, after the episode's story has unfolded, we return to the same stage for the closing shot, as Howard remarks, "Now my problem is, which one do I go home with?" As he rises and turns to walk off, both female characters follow, he puts his arms around them, and all three walk off together; he takes home both Lupino-versions. The joke here is profound (not to mention somewhat racy), and the real and fictional divisions in the show truly do collapse. Howard Duff did indeed live with multiple versions of Ida Lupino, as far as her public image was concerned. She was "Eve Adams, housewife and woman" and "the glamorous, exciting Eve Drake" and the independent film director Ida Lupino and the television star Ida Lupino and the "poor man's Bette Davis." And she was all of these splintered, sometimes conflicting images *on television.*

THE ATYPICAL IDA LUPINO

Given the period's sitcom conventions, it is striking that Lupino and Duff were able to play the character types that Lucille Ball and Desi Arnaz could not sell a few years earlier and that Eve Drake's filmdom glamour and distance from the domestic sphere were the central topics of this program. A number of historical catalysts could explain these factors, but two stand out. I would first argue that Lupino's star image made possible a portrayal not available to an actress like Ball. Lupino had repeatedly tested gendered limitations and ideologies in the entertainment industry in her multiple capacities as director and actress in both film and television, and she succeeded in challenging them while showing that she would still work within them. As a result, the complexities represented by the image of the movie-star housewife Eve Adams were roughly the same complexities presented by the image of Ida Lupino from her first moment behind a camera. Both Ida Lupino (the star image) and Eve Drake (the star character) operated in the public sphere and exhibited power therein, but both

184

also acknowledged the limitations of their power, with Lupino doing so primarily through public pronouncements and Eve doing so through her relationship with Howard. Thus, just as Lupino could direct films and television programs without being expelled by the dominant patriarchal industry, she could also portray a more transgressive role on a domestic sitcom without contention. In this manner, Eve was a farcical version not just of a typical movie star, but of Ida Lupino herself, and this "funniest documentary on TV" truly did reveal an aspect of Hollywood reality in a way much more complex than any publicity article could consider.

Second, this case must be viewed in light of the history of film actors on 1950s television. Only when film actor appearances on television had become relatively common could the mocking portrayal of Howard Adams and Eve Drake resonate. "Typical" ends with Howard proposing that he and Eve really could play themselves, a movie star couple, on a sitcom. He then dismisses this idea by saying, "No, nobody'd ever believe it," referring both to the couple's inability to act "typical" enough for television's demands and to Eve's initial comment that they would never stoop to appearing on the small screen. The irony of this comment is obvious. Back in 1950, when Ball and Arnaz pitched their original idea for *I Love Lucy*, no one truly could have believed it, because it was not a possible scenario. But by 1957, the very fact that Lupino and Duff—and Ann Sothern, Ray Milland, Ronald Reagan, Dick Powell, and so on—were on television made the parodic humor that much richer and relevant. Many film actors *were* appearing on television, and this show could therefore directly present a combination of film and television identities.

In fact, this program was unique in collapsing distinctions between film and television. The character of Eve, as well as Lupino's own "guest-starring" role in her film director identity, repeatedly calls forth the notions of Lupino as both film·and television star and director. Recalling Howard's speech to Eve near the end of "Typical," he tells her that "when she's in front of a camera" she is at her glamorous best. Even though the fictional dialogue refers to a film camera, the television camera that recorded this exchange and the rest of the series was implicitly acknowledged as well. Furthermore, when Howard refers to the fifty million housewives who watch Eve, it is not difficult to interpret this as a reference to television viewers at home, not filmgoers in theaters. Thus, this portrayal signals that film and television were getting closer as performers moved more fluidly between the two media. As the distinctions between film and television performers were becoming more diffuse in the latter half of the 1950s, *Mr. Adams and Eve* could take advantage of this milieu by addressing the multiplied identity of its stars from week to week. Stereotypical Hollywood pretension was still thoroughly mocked, but in a way that acknowledged the shifting relationships between both media. Given that Lupino herself had such a mix of identities across the two media, this presentation is especially appropriate.

Despite embodying such insights, *Mr. Adams and Eve* had limited popular appeal. The advertising executive who warned against picking the show up may have been right, as the program never attracted a sizable percentage of the viewing audience. Though it did last for two seasons, *Mr. Adams and Eve* never appeared in the top twenty-five shows in weekly ratings, and *TV Guide* considered it only "quasi-successful." The industry, on the other hand, certainly appreciated *Mr. Adams and Eve*. Lupino received an Emmy nomination in 1957 for best comedy actress (she lost to Jane Wyatt for *Father Knows Best*), and the show earned numerous feature stories and favorable reviews. *Variety* praised the program's "sophisticated" concept and commended it for offering viewers a "chance to depart from the well-worn rut of situations in the average ... series." Similarly, *TV Guide* called it "quite refreshing" for "a season during which the situation comedy on TV has often fallen to the level of the comic strip." Such industry praise was not enough to extend the show beyond two seasons, though, and *Mr. Adams and Eve* aired its final episode on July 8, 1958.[41]

The real Ida Lupino's identity, even as it was an artificial construction, was crucial to her role as Eve Drake. Lupino's own shattering of boundaries—both actress and director, both television star and film star, both feminist and dismissive of feminism—helped to make possible a role not open to other female sitcom stars of the 1950s, especially late in the decade. In addition, *Mr. Adams and Eve* emerged in the surging wave of regular film star appearances on television, a factor that complicated the previous cultural and industrial divisions between film and television and in turn impacted the nature of stardom. Indeed, while early television perhaps had to sharply separate glamour and domesticity with regard to its stars, the combination of the two in a show like *Mr. Adams and Eve* indicates that by the late 1950s, glamour had, in a

186

sense, become more domesticated through increasing appearances of film stars on television.

I am not arguing that *Mr. Adams and Eve* itself helped to alter conceptions of stardom in any measurable way; rather, that the show could only exist as a result of the ongoing awareness of shifting star images that resulted from the meshing of film stardom with continuing-character television. *Mr. Adams and Eve*'s metatexuality was profoundly indicative of the ways in which star images were beginning to fragment, the sites of authority on film stardom were splintering, and public discussions of these developments were flowering in media discourse—primarily because of stars like Ida Lupino, Eve Arden, Ann Sothern, and Robert Young moving to television. As the experiences of Ray Milland and Betty Hutton indicate, however, these changes were not necessarily all positive for stars. Milland surely diminished his cultural stature with his turn as Professor McNutley, and Goldie drove Hutton's entertainment career to its virtual end.

Bearing these outcomes in mind, we should also note that Ida Lupino played a version of *Sunset Boulevard*'s Norma Desmond in a *Twilight Zone* (CBS, 1959–65) episode entitled "The Sixteen-Millimeter Shrine" that aired one year after the cancelation of *Mr. Adams and Eve*. Here Lupino plays Barbara Jean Trenton, an aging Hollywood star who spends the bulk of her days privately watching her old films from the 1930s unspool on a 16 mm projector. Rod Serling's customarily eloquent introduction classifies her: "Movie great of another time, once-brilliant star in a firmament no longer a part of the sky . . . struck down by the hit-and-run years and lying on the unhappy pavement, trying desperately to get the license number of fleeting fame." A family friend implores Trenton to realize that she can no longer live in the past and tries to give her a dose of reality by ushering in her Golden Age costar, Jerry Herndon. But Trenton is only horrified by Herndon's now-aged appearance: he is saddled with Coke-bottle glasses, dentures, and a shock of white hair. She subsequently retreats to her projection room, gazes up at Herndon's youthful image on the screen, and whispers, "There you are, Jerry. There was a strange old man here who said he was you. I wish I could be up there with you. I wish." Echoing *Sunset Boulevard*'s famous ending shot, the close-up of Trenton then goes out of focus. Unlike Norma Desmond, however, Barbara Jean Trenton does not merely enter the movies in her mind; the paranormal powers of the fifth dimension enable her to become a part of the bygone world of her wishes: as she then appears in the projected image, gathered with her costars, rooted in the filmic past. And only in that filmic past on the screen could Trenton's star image be frozen, left untouched by television's ceaseless exposure. For Lupino and countless others, there would be no such mystical escape.[42]

CHAPTER 5
THE STAR IN THE STORY
ANTHOLOGY DRAMA GUESTS

No genre reflected early television's varied industrial structures and shifting cultural standing quite like the live anthology drama. It was an essential component of television's early efforts to sell itself to audiences, critics, and sponsors as a culturally valuable and financially viable entertainment format. Conversely, the genre was discarded once the mechanisms of network control were cemented into place by the early 1960s, and its demise was lamented by many cultural critics, who viewed the anthology drama's marginalization as evidence of the dwindling public worth of the medium in general. It is important to note that the catalysts behind the initial growth and eventual disappearance of this foundational genre are largely the same forces that both fostered and later ended significant film star participation on television. As such, the story of the rising and falling fortunes of the anthology program must be told in order to understand why film stars were first attracted to television in the early 1950s and why many no longer found a place on the medium only a decade later.

The history of the anthology drama typically has been outlined in terms of its producers, primarily Fred Coe, Worthington Miner, and Martin Manulis, and writers, including Paddy Chayefsky and Rod Serling. Such histories depict a genre dependent on these creative artists (as well as the shows' being live) for its image of prestige and quality. Within these studies, the role of actors on the anthology drama has largely been ignored. Yet Hollywood guest stars were essential to the critical and popular status of these dramas, and their images were cardinal components of the publicity strategies that defined the genre. Indeed, the anthology drama became the most common outlet for Hollywood guest star appearances. Exactly why the format and these stars were so compatible is revelatory of the industry position of both during the 1950s. What did the anthology drama offer to film stars that made the genre such an attractive destination for them across the 1950s, and how did the format change across the decade in order to attract this growing pool of top-tier film talent?

THE DEVELOPMENT OF THE TELEVISION ANTHOLOGY DRAMA

The anthology drama genre thrived on radio in the late 1930s and 1940s. Shows such as *The Lux Radio Theatre* (NBC, 1934–55) and *The Screen Guild Theatre* (CBS and NBC, 1939–51) presented adaptations of material from films, often featuring the original stars, and programs like *Mercury Theatre of the Air* (CBS, 1938) and *Brownstone Theatre* (Mutual, 1945) tackled stage and literary adaptations. While versions of such dramas appeared on television from its earliest experimental days, the 1947 premiere of *Kraft Television Theatre* (NBC and ABC, 1947–58) on NBC foretold the long-term viability of the genre on TV. *Kraft* was the first commercially sponsored anthology drama to appear on television, and its success with sponsor, ad agency, network, and audiences alike cemented the anthology drama's position within television. *Kraft's* ad agency, J. Walter Thompson, wished to pattern the show along the lines of *Lux Radio Theatre* and drew from a number of the conventions of the radio anthology drama. Even so, *Kraft* and other early anthology programs differed from their radio ancestors in several important respects. First, many radio anthology programs could tout the highest-level Hollywood stars in their audio plays: radio interests fervently pursued Hollywood cooperation to lend glamour to programming and to foster increased advertising revenue. For a short period, the major studios rebuffed these overtures fearing the competitive threat of radio. By the mid-1930s, however, the studios regularly exploited radio, especially for publicity purposes. The studios subsequently lent most of their contract players to such shows as *Hollywood Hotel* (CBS, 1934–38) and *Lux Radio Theatre,* granting virtually free publicity to the studios and lending Hollywood star power to radio. Similarly, a number of these anthologies based their properties on Hollywood films, with *Lux Radio Theatre* specifically designed for this purpose.[1]

Early television's anthology programs, on the other hand, were granted no such cooperation. The high-caliber film stars who regularly appeared on radio anthologies were not available based on either studio prohibition or personal disinclination. In regard to the latter, film stars were reluctant to appear on these programs because their production was almost exclusively centered in New York and performed live, plus the salaries anthologies could offer were barely enough to cover the cost of a flight from Hollywood to the East Coast. As producer Worthington Miner, supervisor of *Studio One*, described the situation: "Our budgets were pitifully small. . . . We'd been forced to adopt a top salary of \$750 a show, including two weeks of rehearsal. That wasn't going to buy us Cary Grant or Humphrey Bogart, or Lauren Bacall even. At that price we had to discover our own 'stars of tomorrow' just as much as *Toast of the Town*." Production values were also low on many of these shows, especially compared to the standards set by feature films. Teresa Wright dismissed the genre in 1953 after appearing in only a handful of episodes. She told *Time* magazine of her disdain for anthologies: "They're mostly soap operas. It's just like making a cheap film."[2]

Thus, out of both convenience and necessity, early anthology programs turned primarily to theatrical talent and unknowns getting started in the medium. Director George Roy Hill explains, "Here in New York, there was almost a repertory company of actors who did all the live shows: *Danger, Philco Television Playhouse, Studio One, Kraft*." Among them were two actors who would soon become film legends: Grace Kelly and Charlton Heston. Kelly began her performing career in New York modeling and acting for the stage. *Philco* director Delbert Mann admired her stage work, and he cast her in a January 1950 episode of the drama. She would appear in twelve different teleplays in that year alone, from *Actors Studio* (ABC and CBS, 1948–50) to *Studio One*. For the next two years, Kelly mixed anthology and film work, most notably receiving a starring role in *High Noon* (1952), but she left television acting behind for good after the 1954 film successes of *Dial M For Murder* and *Rear Window*.[3]

On the other hand, Charlton Heston would continue to act in anthologies even after a series of substantial film hits, claiming that he simply found live television performance to be highly gratifying. Like Kelly, Heston's acting career began in New York with a combination of stage and anthology television work. He appeared in twelve episodes of *Studio One* from 1949 to 1952, and his late 1949 performances in adaptations of *Jane Eyre* and *Of Human Bondage* caught the attention of Hollywood producer Hal Wallis, who was based at Paramount Pictures. Wallis wanted to sign Heston for feature work, but the actor refused to sign an exclusive contract, as he feared being prevented from doing the stage and television acting that he enjoyed. Wallis agreed to nonexclusivity, which meant that despite being housed at a major studio as early as 1950, Heston was still free to carry on with television work. It also made him one of the very first indigenous television actors discovered on the new medium to launch a substantial feature career. By 1952, he was earning a decent salary in television, receiving $2,000 per appearance at *Studio One*. But he claimed what drove him to keep working in television even after anchoring such box office hits as *The Greatest Show on Earth* (1952) and *The Ten Commandments* (1956) was the thrill of live performance and the versatility of the anthology format. When questioned in 1958 as to why he continued to do television anthologies even then, unlike his A-list colleagues, Heston told columnist Bob Thomas:

> I can't explain why other actors don't do it—perhaps some of them don't have stage training and are afraid of doing live shows. I do it because I enjoy doing it, because I think an actor should keep working, because I can reach an audience I wouldn't be able to reach with a movie. And in TV, I can do roles that I wouldn't get a chance to do in films.

These sentiments would resonate for many actors throughout the 1950s, though early television's conditions would prevent many film stars from learning this firsthand for a few years.[4]

In addition to the anthologies' inability to draw from prominent film talent, they also could not rely on movie properties for stories, including scripts written specifically for the cinema, because the studios would refuse to provide their competitor with story material. Furthermore, Hollywood usually retained the film rights for any book or play that had already been turned into a movie, and the prospect of intense competition with television discouraged the studios from leasing adaptation rights to television. One might assume that the live transmission of anthology dramas would allow TV producers to circumvent this rule, but most live broadcasts were also kinescoped—put on film for either transmission on the West Coast or for syndication purposes—which technically qualified them as film productions under copyright law. *Robert Montgomery Presents* initially strove to be a television version of *Lux Radio Theatre*, presenting abridged versions of properties that had been prominent film successes, including *The Letter, Kitty Foyle, The Philadelphia Story*, and *Dark Victory*. By 1951, however, increasing use of kinescoping and studio copyright threats curtailed these efforts and the show had to turn to other material.

As a result, the television anthology drama in its early years relied heavily on theatrical talent and story material. *Chevrolet Tele-Theater* (NBC, 1948–50), *Ford Theatre, Philco TV Playhouse, Actors Studio,* and *Studio One* all borrowed heavily from Broadway plays, which, combined with live production methods, also affected the style of the anthology drama. As Marc Daniels, a director on *Ford Theatre,* explained in 1949: "Legitimate drama in television is basically theater. It is true we use the camera techniques of moving pictures and the time element of radio, but all the other factors of production most closely resemble the theater." Accordingly, then, anthology drama publicity of this period placed emphasis on the story as the main area of interest for potential viewers. Said Edmund Rice of the J. Walter Thompson agency: "Our aims in the very beginning were to build in our audience the habit of tuning in to *Kraft.* The actors were not top stars and the play was usually unfamiliar, so we attempted to get our audience to expect a good story." Thus, for both properties and talent, the networks and ad agencies frequently drew upon the prestige of Broadway theater, borrowing the theater's high-culture connotations to combat any notions of early television as crass, undeveloped entertainment.[5]

Despite this rhetoric, anthology dramas were so abundant by 1951 that a glut of similar types of stories filled the air, as most were adaptations of Broadway plays and classic literature. The critics who had initially praised these dramas for their prestige and quality now began to blast them for their lack of creativity and originality. Famed anthology producer Fred Coe told of his early challenges on *Philco Television Playhouse:* "We took Broadway plays, trimmed them to an hour and cast them with Broadway players, topped by a Broadway star. Within a couple of months it became obvious that this could not work out. We were running out of material! . . . [T]he Broadway cupboard was bare almost before we started." Coe recognized that anthologies could not subsist for very long on material written for another medium, and he pioneered the move to original stories written especially for television. He hired writers like Paddy Chayefsky, Tad Mosel, and Horton Foote to write for *Philco* and gave them free rein to create their own stories specifically for television. Those writers would go on to achieve legendary status within the medium and indirectly encourage greater participation by film stars.[6]

Spurred by Coe's moves and the overarching need for more material, anthology dramas underwent a shift to original writing. Correspondingly, in terms of anthology drama publicity and criticism, the focus was no longer on the story but on the centrality of the writer. No longer so reliant on the status of another medium, anthology drama producers now tried to foster prestige based around the notion of the television writer, a person writing solely for the televisual medium, thereby lending the genre credibility as an arena for individual, distinctive artistry. Consequently, as the prestige of the dramas and the ambitiousness of the story material increased—along with salaries for guest appearances—the number of film stars willing to appear on anthology dramas grew as well, to the point where a number of anthology programs began to originate from the West Coast in order to take advantage of the stars' increasing willingness to appear.

One program whose history mirrored these developments was *Lux Video Theatre*. Broadcast from Hollywood throughout its audio run, *Lux Radio Theatre* had been on the air for sixteen years before its television counterpart began in October 1950. The half-hour video version originated from New York, however, and because of the standard copyright conflicts, it presented stage plays and original dramas each week rather than film adaptations like its radio ancestor. *Lux Video Theatre* also did not feature the same caliber of film stars that *Lux Radio Theatre* could, evidenced by the fact that the radio program's slogan, "Lux presents . . . Stars from Hollywood," was condensed to simply "Lux presents . . . Hollywood" for television. And indeed, by 1953 producers decided to relocate the television version to Hollywood in order to take advantage of the star talent now more willing and available to appear. This move brought appearances by stars like Ronald Reagan, Edmond O'Brien, and Edward G. Robinson.

NBC then grabbed the show from CBS in 1954 and added film actor James Mason as host to lend filmdom connotations (although after an unsuccessful turn, he was replaced the next year by Otto Kruger). Other changes to the show included expansion to an hour and the inclusion of interviews with the featured stars. *Lux* producers also finally worked out a deal with Paramount to adapt some of their feature properties and thereby reclaim some of the program's radio luster. This deal brought Dorothy McGuire as star of "To Each His Own" and Miriam

Hopkins in an adaptation of *Sunset Boulevard*. In exchange, Paramount received the opportunity to plug current features through both clips and star appearances at the teleplay's end. For instance, William Holden appeared in early September 1954 to tout *Sabrina*, while the following week guest star Thelma Ritter ad-libbed an introduction to clips from *Rear Window* when James Mason muffed his lines and couldn't continue.[7]

Although *Lux Video Theatre* did thereby boost its level of star attractions, there was one anthology it could not match. *General Electric Theater* tried to distinguish itself from all other shows by featuring more Hollywood film stars than any other anthology, and stars were the primary selling point for the show. As a case in point, a two-page *Variety* advertisement consisted of nothing more than the program title and a lengthy list of film stars who had made appearances. *General Electric Theater* was produced by MCA's Revue, which put at the program's disposal a considerable roster of top-name talent. Myrna Loy, James Stewart, Joseph Cotten, Anne Baxter, Fred Astaire, Fred MacMurray, and Alan Ladd all made their dramatic television debuts on the program, and other notable guest stars included Rosalind Russell, Bette Davis, Gene Kelly, Barbara Stanwyck, and Cornel Wilde.

To accommodate the widest possible range of stars, *General Electric Theater* oscillated between live and film production, sometimes letting the talent choose its preference, and producers shot on both coasts for a substantial portion of the show's run. Another strong lure was high salaries; the top stars could command as much as $10,000 for just a few days' work. As a result, the *New York Times* wrote, "The video outfit has about as much star power for its filmed and live shows as most Hollywood studios have under contract these days." Of course, such star power was very costly, and it made *General Electric Theater* one of the more expensive series on the air. But it also paid off in the ratings; from 1954 until 1961, its penultimate year on television, the show remained firmly lodged in the Nielsen ratings' top twenty. Further, the prestige inherent to these respected names was transferred to General Electric's image as sponsor.[8]

Even programs that were not originally developed with an explicit connection to the film world in mind were affected by this increased use of Hollywood talent, as illustrated by the history of the DuPont-sponsored *Cavalcade of America* (ABC and NBC, 1952–57; the show was later renamed *DuPont Cavalcade Theater* and *DuPont Theater*). Beginning in 1952, *Cavalcade* presented tales of great events in American

Bette Davis stars in "With Malice Toward One" in 1957, while Alan Ladd makes his television debut in "Committed" in 1954 on General Electric Theater. *CBS/Photofest.*

history. Touting a focus on the story, not the star, most of the featured performers were newcomers to entertainment; the few recognizable guest names across its first three seasons included Cecil Kellaway, Ray Collins, Ann Doran, and Fay Wray. This choice was partly economic, but also related to corporate image. DuPont, a chemical company, hoped to bolster its image as a contributor to American society, and company executives preferred having the corporate name attached to hallowed tales with long-standing prestige within American culture rather than star images with often fleeting popularity.

DuPont did find, nonetheless, that audiences responded favorably to more familiar talent in *Cavalcade*, according to audience survey reports filed by John Dollard, employee of Television Studies, Inc. For example, in his report on the January 1955 episode "The Marine Who Was 200 Years Old"—filed under the category "interesting finding not predicted"—Dollard noted the significant number of surveyed viewers who commented positively, without prompting, about Ward Bond, the biggest star to have appeared on the program by that point. Dollard wrote, "Apparently the fame of an actor really does make some difference in the impact of a *Cavalcade* play."[9]

This finding became vital by the end of that season, as ratings for *Cavalcade* continued to trend downward. DuPont actively sought out new directions for the show, soliciting proposals from various production companies and talent agencies to take over production of the program. MCA's proposal stated that "the inclusion of *stars*, either live or on film, will give *Cavalcade of America* the added impact and public acceptance which it needs in order to fill the sponsor's requirements." Stars that MCA claimed they could get for the show included Claude Rains, Franchot Tone, Teresa Wright, and Paulette Goddard. A representative of *Cavalcade*'s advertising agency, Batten, Barton, Durstine and Osborn, wrote, "It appears that 'Cavalcade' lacks that extra degree of showmanship, and excitement and interest to make enough people want to tune to it at the expense of another program." Consequently, the first listed solution is "we should have an MC, stars, or both," citing the dramatic proportion of the highest-rated shows that featured stars. In subsequent deliberations, DuPont executives eliminated Jack Denove Productions from the list of potential new producers because of Denove's "greater difficulty in delivering stars." Ultimately they settled on independent producer Don Sharpe, partly on the basis of his ability to obtain notable stars at reasonable cost.[10]

These examples illustrate why anthology producers were so keen on convincing Hollywood stars to act on their programs. In turn, the appeal of periodic appearances in respected anthology dramas, with self-contained and varied episodes often written by critically lauded playwrights, attracted numerous high-level Hollywood actors. Many stars echoed Charlton Heston's comments about the excitement and variety of anthology work in explaining why they were so willing to commit to these programs. June Allyson told *TV Guide* that she planned to take advantage of the variety of roles that her eponymous anthology program would enable her to play: "I repeat, I am not going to play the girl next door. In one episode I am going to play a conniving socialite who deserts her husband. And there goes the sweet June Allyson we all knew and loved. Good." Esther Williams, too, tried to break out of her swimming-pool roles in the mid-1950s and hoped that anthology participation would help her do so. As the *New York World-Telegram and Sun* put it, "Esther believes that a few acting roles in 'the new medium' may persuade the movie boys that it's time she came up for air." Of course, film stars were not stereotyped in the classical era so resolutely as one would assume; Allyson in particular had enjoyed a number of off-cast roles during her film career. But television and its participants could use such condemnations of film industry conventionality in order to bolster the new medium and the anthology genre rhetorically. Indeed, television compared itself favorably to film by claiming that only the boldness of the small screen and the artistry of anthology programs could enable the genuine talent of Hollywood film actors to come forth. Such discourse could benefit not only the television programs but the image of its stars, as well.[11]

In fact, many of these actors likely felt that anthologies were markedly inferior to feature films, yet they were compelled to defend the format in order to justify their participation. Decades after making more than thirty appearances on 1950s anthologies, Laraine Day admitted that she would have much preferred acting in features because "the quality of television was nowhere near what was happening in the movies." She nonetheless conceded that for actresses like herself and second leads such as Franchot Tone, anthologies were a necessity given that work in Hollywood was increasingly tough to find. The genre "kept us alive," in her words. Even Teresa Wright, who had previously dismissed the quality of the anthology drama, found herself guest-starring in anthologies as a primary career. She made more than thirty anthology appearances following her 1953 comments, but only four feature films across the rest of the 1950s. It may not have been the outlet she preferred, but it was the one that enabled her to perform on a regular basis, and this was the crucial factor. Wright told the *Hollywood Citizen-News,* "The important point is that an actress must work—and I don't mean just to eat. You either create or you wither."[12]

ANTHOLOGIES BECOME SPECTACULAR

By the decade's midpoint, legitimate stars found anthology dramas to be more commensurate with their star status, especially once the influence of the spectacular began to affect the most prestigious entries in the genre. Spectaculars were extravagant programs with lavish production values and unpredictable scheduling practices, akin to a special treat inserted into the programming schedule. NBC began programming these shows during the 1954–55 season, *TV Guide* noted, "to forestall the possibility of viewers growing tired of standard TV fare and to spur the growth of new audiences." As historian Vance Kepley has established, NBC's Pat Weaver felt that unique programming was needed at this stage of television's development to bring in new audiences, encourage affiliation from stations and participation by sponsors, and sell TV sets for parent company RCA. Kepley writes:

> [Weaver's] variety programs, dramas, and the like would feature talent that no syndicator, let alone local station, could hope to afford. He exploited live programs to make affiliates dependent on the Radio City feed and to differentiate television's product from that of a competitor, the film industry. . . . Only a line-up that featured special attractions would encourage families to invest in that all-important box for the living room.

This programming was certainly a huge expense for what amounted to a small number of programs each season, but Kepley argues that Weaver was content with them as a loss leader: "Just as a grocer might sell some products at a loss to attract buyers into the store, Weaver's profligate ways were constructing the future market for NBC." Here was also a way for networks to take programming control away from sponsors and ad agencies, a key shift that took place across the decade and changed network broadcasting. Finally, NBC's spectacular strategy was intended to overcome the increasing ratings and ad billings supremacy of CBS, which was thriving on a schedule of lower-budget continuing-character series. Weaver believed that special programming could redirect attention, viewers, and ad dollars away from CBS, especially if he could attract upscale audiences who were turned off by CBS's more lowbrow approach.[13]

NBC's first spectacular was the musical "Satins and Spurs," a $200,000 production that aired on September 11, 1954, and starred Betty Hutton. "Satins and Spurs" was a critical and ratings flop, but this dubious beginning did little to stem the tide of spectaculars, and NBC forged onward with *Producers' Showcase*, a combination of the spectacular and the anthology that aired every fourth Monday. The October 1954 premiere featured Ginger Rogers in "Tonight at 8:30," and subsequent airings offered Humphrey Bogart, Lauren Bacall, and Henry Fonda in "The Petrified Forest," and Fredric March and Claire Trevor in "Dodsworth." To its roster of regularly scheduled monthly spectaculars, NBC also sprinkled in occasional features of *Max Liebman Presents* (1954–56) and *The Hallmark Hall of Fame* (1951-present), as well as frequent Bob Hope specials, which brought forth such guest stars as Greer Garson, Ann Miller, Lana Turner, James Cagney, and Dorothy Lamour.

Initially, CBS was reluctant to join NBC's spectacular trend: the network believed that predictable, habitual, and economically sound weekly programming was the way to ensure consistent viewership, rather than occasional, variant, and expensive specials. But, as critics lavished praise upon NBC for its high-quality efforts, CBS was compelled to respond with some measure of competition for both financial and image reasons. Thus, CBS's early offerings included *Shower of Stars* (1954–58), which showcased stars like Betty Grable, a "Christmas Carol" performance featuring Fredric March and Basil Rathbone, and *Ford Star Jubilee* (1955–56), which premiered with a Judy Garland special. For its part, the more frugal ABC arrived very late to the specials table, not presenting what the industry trades considered spectaculars until 1957. Even then, it was still lagging behind; ABC had few resources to compete with its bigger counterparts and little desire to follow their programming model.

Overall, the number of specials increased as the decade continued. During the 1957–58 season, ABC presented two specials; CBS, twenty-two; and NBC, fifty. And 1959 continued the run of big-name stars on network specials. The advertising trade paper *Sponsor* wrote of the reasons for such a drastic increase in star-based specials:

Humphrey Bogart, Lauren Bacall, and Henry Fonda in a May 1955 Producers' Showcase adaptation of The Petrified Forest. NBC/Photofest.

Bigger and better stars and properties are being attracted to TV for the first time because of the appeal of the specials format. . . . For the first time in the short history of specials, [stars are] able to get the price they've been asking for the past couple of seasons. And for the first time they are personally excited at the prospect of a major vehicle which gives them the best showcase in terms of reaching mass audiences with a quality production.

Many of these specials were oriented toward musical-variety performance, at precisely the same time that the musical genre was declining in Hollywood. Thus television supplied an essential new performance space for artists who found their talents less in demand in feature filmmaking. ABC primarily presented musical-variety programs with such featured stars as Bing Crosby and Frank Sinatra, while CBS and NBC aired specials starring Fred Astaire, Esther Williams, Jane Powell, Ginger Rogers, Rosalind Russell, Maurice Chevalier, and Gene Kelly.[14]

Thus, by 1956, anthology dramas and spectaculars succeeded in bringing a substantial caliber and volume of film stars to television.   201

Favorable salaries, prestige, production location, and formats—all converged to attract stars whose stature would have precluded participation only a few years earlier. Unfortunately, although ratings for these programs were occasionally as spectacular as the genre's name denoted, they were more often a disappointment, especially in light of the substantial investment needed to set them apart from ordinary fare. It was such ordinary fare that outstripped specials and anthology dramas in the ratings—and in the network ledgers—week after week. Audiences showed a preference for predictability in their living rooms and advertisers followed. But before these genres were ushered out, one anthology show would have considerable impact for both television and film stars.

PLAYHOUSE 90 ON THE AIR

The mid-1950s witnessed a shift toward larger, more lavishly produced anthology dramas, changes that were influenced by the rising prominence of spectaculars with high production values and big stars. As the scope of these occasional specials widened, so did the parameters of many of the regularly scheduled dramas. With its hour-and-a-half running time, live method of production, slate of original scripts, and ample budgets, CBS's *Playhouse 90* was introduced in 1956 as the summit of television quality and prestige, the culmination of all anthology shows and dramatic spectaculars that had preceded it. Unfortunately, all summits have a downslope, and *Playhouse 90* emerged just as the anthology genre was entering a period of terminal decline. Therefore, the story of this program reveals both the height of the anthology drama's prestige and the depth of its ultimate failure. Further, *Playhouse 90* appeared during a period when Hollywood film actors were most willing to appear on television. Given the program's level of prestige, one would thus assume that *Playhouse 90* had access to the cream of the Hollywood talent crop. But this was not the case; even television programming at its most prestigious could not draw on Hollywood's elite. To compensate, *Playhouse 90*'s producers relied on a casting strategy designed to elevate not only the cultural status of the program but also that of film stars who appeared on the program.

Playhouse 90 was expected to have an advantage over spectaculars in that it was being slotted into a regular time, every Thursday night at 9:30 EST, rather than appearing sporadically. CBS saw this slotting as an effective way to adapt NBC's critically acclaimed spectacular strategies to their own preference for regularly scheduled shows. As CBS president Frank Stanton explained, "One trouble with the 'specials' is that people haven't known where they are." Audiences would now know exactly where and when to find such esteemed fare. To clear the time slot for *Playhouse 90*, CBS removed *Four Star Playhouse* from the Thursday evening schedule. By replacing the more pedestrian half-hour filmed program with the extravagant *Playhouse 90*, the network could proclaim the new show as a regularly scheduled cultural experience that would enrich the lives of viewers with nothing less than the very best that television could make available—and all for free in anyone's living room. The ambitious scale of the show, however, combined with its initial plans for live performance, created a substantial challenge in terms of production scheduling. Each live episode required approximately six weeks of preparation time, including three weeks for rehearsals. To make it easier on the crews and producers, the network decided to broadcast live only three times a month, with the fourth show of the month put on film courtesy of Screen Gems, thereby allowing for a break in the hectic production schedule.[15]

Playhouse 90 launched in fall 1956 with a full season of twenty-nine live and ten filmed shows. With budgets ranging from $125,000 to $175,000 per episode, the show was expensive, even occasionally challenging the budget levels of the spectaculars and specials. To subsidize these costs, the network turned to a method of sponsorship wherein multiple sponsors would pay for portions of a program, instead of having a single sponsor underwrite the entire program. Based on the program's ninety-minute running time, CBS aimed for five sponsors, who were expected to bring in a total of $355,000 per episode ($228,000 for airtime, $127,000 for production costs). CBS was responsible for funding unsponsored time and any budget overruns—which were incurred quite frequently. Martin Manulis was the sole producer for the show's first two years. He left in 1958 to head the television production unit at 20th Century–Fox, and CBS settled on a rotating set of producers to replace him, thereby lessening the production burden carried by a single person.[16]

No matter the year or the producer, *Playhouse 90* strove for all of the markers of highbrow culture available to television. The program's casting director, Ethel Winant, recalled: "Everything we had learned the previous ten years came with that show. It was the best of *Philco* and *U.S. Steel,* the best writers and directors. It all came together and produced this magical moment. That was *Playhouse 90.*" In such a manner, publicity underscored the show as evidence of preeminent material on the frequently disparaged medium. CBS's own publicity primarily touted the show as the embodiment of quality and art, not profit potential:

> [T]here was no compelling reason in the Summer of 1955 to disturb the CBS Television Network program schedule. . . . Business was fine. But in television there is an even greater risk in accepting the routine and failing to anticipate the changing taste of the audience. The broadcaster must constantly be prepared with fresh, provocative new programs to strengthen whatever weakness may develop in any segment of his weekly program schedule.

Such publicity material also tried to suggest that money was no object in this endeavor, that only programming of artistic merit was of concern to CBS. The network claimed it had invested $228,000 in the program before any individual show preparations even began, and it discounted those who might say that such an endeavor was not worth the money. CBS stressed that though the show might even fail in its ambitions in particular weeks—"For every occasion it works out, there may be three when it doesn't, with the inevitable loss of time, effort and money"—a bit of lost revenue was well outweighed by the quality of those episodes that succeeded. The network also claimed that the ninety-minute running time was indicative of the program's quality, and it praised the unique nature of the material.[17]

In terms of the latter, *Playhouse 90*'s publicity frequently emphasized the supposed benefit of television as a vehicle for profound, character-based material, in contrast to the shallow, action-oriented fare released by Hollywood. CBS indicated that the show would take on "the challenge of enlarging the area and dimensions of television drama by presenting the kind of material that achieves its power through the development of character and the interplay of motive and personality." In so defining the show, this publicity also presented the overall benefits of television to American culture: "It is the process by which the worlds of science and politics, history and contemporary affairs, music and art have been brought within the focus of the tiniest schoolhouse and the most remote rural household."

While CBS trumpeted the expensive show from an "art for art's sake" standpoint, we must consider as well the industrial motivations behind the emergence of such a program during this period. CBS was interested in both reclaiming network control over programming from advertising agencies *and* staving off any government regulation of its efforts. One resulting strategy was to create a show like *Playhouse 90*, over which the network had nearly full control and which with its quality would prove that only a network could produce a program of such great cultural worth. CBS hoped for just such an impression to result from its decision to air the majority of *Playhouse 90's* episodes as live productions, despite the steady decline in that mode as the decade continued. But "live" was not only an aesthetic or economic choice; it was also a marketing label, a rhetorical trumpeting of the unique artistic potential of television. CBS had more than just money invested in *Playhouse 90*.[18]

HOLLYWOOD FILM STARS ON *PLAYHOUSE 90*

Given CBS's attempts to draw on connotations of theatrical prestige, one might assume that *Playhouse 90* was produced in New York. In fact, the program was shot on the West Coast, largely because Hollywood represented access to nationally famous stars. Indeed, as part of its attempts to attain high-profile status and attract renowned performers, CBS decided to produce the show at its Television City studios in Hollywood. Former *Playhouse 90* director Arthur Penn summarized the implications of this choice:

> CBS in all their wisdom in setting up *Playhouse 90* decided that they would [have shows emanate from the West Coast] because they would have access to the big movie stars. So what happened was the transition from New York theater and the New York actors to the Hollywood actors and the Hollywood names. When I went out there to do the "The Miracle Worker," it was an accepted fact that it was going to be with people from the Hollywood community.

Playhouse 90 thereby represented the culmination of the trend toward using Hollywood talent in anthology dramas. *Time* magazine emphasized this strategy in an October 1956 article, explaining that producer Martin Manulis had "skirted the globe" to track down the Hollywood stars he wanted, some of whom were on location shoots. Casting director Ethel Winant similarly claimed that *Playhouse 90* was "designed as a show to use Hollywood stars. That was the whole point." In conjunction with this motivation, Winant explained that one of the program's primary visual icons, a glittering, spiked star presented during credit sequences and advertisements, was designed to conjure up the notion of the luminous film star. The producers also had the featured player of each episode appear a week earlier to introduce the preceding episode, in order to entice the audience with the prospect of star performances to come.[19]

According to Winant, CBS hoped to feature at least one Hollywood film star per episode. Cast listings for the first season confirm that *Playhouse 90* did initially rely heavily on Hollywood actors in leading roles. Out of the thirty-nine episodes in this first season, only five did not present established Hollywood actors as lead players. Notable stars appearing in this season included Paul Henreid, Claudette Colbert, Mickey Rooney, Edmond O'Brien, Franchot Tone, Ann Sheridan, Farley Granger, Teresa Wright, Gilbert Roland, Eddie Bracken, Jeanette MacDonald, Joan Blondell, Errol Flynn, Sylvia Sidney, and Ethel Barrymore. The show's second season brought appearances by Sterling Hayden, Margaret O'Brien, Joseph Cotten, Mary Astor, Joan Bennett, Paul Muni, James Mason, Buster Keaton, and Agnes Moorehead, among others. It is also interesting to note that Dana Andrews, who had claimed repeatedly that he would avoid television because of its commercialism, made his live television debut on *Playhouse 90* in March 1958. The prestige of this program apparently did separate it from the run-of-the-mill commercial material on TV; thus otherwise hesitant talent deemed it a "safe" venue on which to appear.

Those listed above were undoubtedly prominent Hollywood names, yet the highest tier of film stars would not appear on *Playhouse 90*. As director John Frankenheimer noted: "We couldn't get some actors that we wanted—we couldn't get Cary Grant, we couldn't get John Wayne." Casting director Ethel Winant agreed that actors like Grant, Marilyn Monroe, and Clark Gable were simply unattainable for *Playhouse 90* (or virtually any other television program). Despite the unlikelihood of securing these stars, production records indicate that their names appeared repeatedly on proposed casting lists for each episode. In fact, Winant commented in a 1959 memo to Fred Coe, "I think that men such as James Stewart, Bill Holden and Glenn Ford are completely unrealistic in today's market but I always like to have their names on a list because I think it seems more classy that way." As the reference to "today's market" indicates, asking price was one major block to getting these names. Because of industrial changes in Hollywood and the

rising power of the talent agent, film and television star salaries were

rising precipitously. Additionally, the fact that the show maintained a
heavy schedule of live productions discouraged some stars from appearing. Winant confirmed that a number of important actors could
not handle the demands of live production and were deterred by the
unfamiliar production methods.[20]

Thus, although *Playhouse 90* was cloaked in connotations of Hollywood stardom, it was really the middle-tier Hollywood star who was
featured most often, as most in the upper tier would still not appear
even on a show of such substantial credibility and prestige. Close
scrutiny of certain episodes and their promotion, however, reveals that
the program's casting philosophy was not oriented around leeching off
of the filmdom status of a star; instead, it uncovered how that particular actor could be utilized uniquely for television. Ethel Winant termed
this approach "stunt casting"; that is, off-casting a well-known film
actor and then publicizing that performance as prestigious and artistic
because of its uniqueness. With this method, *Playhouse 90* could favorably promote itself not only in opposition to the rest of television, but
also in opposition to the film medium.[21]

The implication was clear: whereas Hollywood forced actors into
repetitive, superficial and slight roles, because the movie capital
cared more about profits than anything of cultural worth, *Playhouse
90* stipulated that the true talents of the actors mattered more. As
such, the show could allow its actors, removed from the artificial requirements of Hollywood film, to explore roles that revealed their
genuine skills. While off-casting had always been important within
the Hollywood studio system, it became central to *Playhouse 90's*
casting decisions and publicity. Rather than varying a star's performances only on occasion to keep a persona fresh, *Playhouse 90* used
off-casting as a regular strategy to define its very purpose, to present
actors in ways that one supposedly could not see in movie theaters.
Drawing upon this notion, *Playhouse 90* publicity claimed that the
show was not beholden to the established rules for how to utilize actors. As *TV Guide* explained, the show refused to "yield to convention
on the score of casting according to 'type.'" *Playhouse 90* trumpeted
this off-casting as a marker of creativity, pure artistic motivation, and
cultural worth. In doing so, the program's creators could underscore
the public service being provided by CBS and the producers of *Playhouse 90* (and simultaneously elide the fact that the show did not obtain the high caliber of star to which it aspired).[22]

Of course, these claims were exaggerated. As discussed earlier, CBS was not striving altruistically for artistic quality; the network wanted regularized viewing, increased network control over programming, and freedom from regulation to result from these efforts. Furthermore, CBS's strategy was not far removed from the film industry's motivations for off-casting: Hollywood too tried to increase attendance, impress spectators, and garner critical accolades through off-casting its stars. Thus, film actors could still find in Hollywood what *Playhouse 90* was offering. In case the actor's attempt to broaden his or her persona failed, however, an off-cast role on an anthology program would be less risky for a star's reputation and career in most cases than a similar role in a big-budget feature film. An off-casting failure in film could have substantial financial penalties and might thereby considerably limit the actor's attempts to move beyond, or even maintain, his or her persona in the future. A misstep on television, however, could be written off due to the circumstances of live production, and an appearance in another drama even a few weeks later could restore the actor's luster. Further, viewers would probably tune in to view the performance anyway, not knowing before the single run of the live program if the performance was effective. The stunt-casting strategy would have thus fulfilled its mission: to garner both curious viewers and sponsor underwriting.

Playhouse 90's very first episode exemplifies the success of these strategies. The premiere episode was based on a Rod Serling–penned spy story entitled "Forbidden Area" and aired on October 4, 1956. The episode presented a range of stars, including Charlton Heston, Diana Lynn, Victor Jory, and Vincent Price, but most significant was the casting of teen idol Tab Hunter, in only his fourth dramatic television appearance, as a Soviet spy on a mission in the United States. *Variety* wrote in its review that Hunter's performance "may have been a revelation to his film fans." Unfortunately, their reaction to his off-casting was negative: the reviewer noted that Hunter "looked more like the kid next door than the character he played." In the second season of *Playhouse 90*, however, Hunter returned and this time found success with even more dramatic off-casting. In "Portrait of a Murderer," Hunter portrayed a serial killer and was praised for his performance by *Variety;* the reviewer commented that he was "no soxer's idol" in this story of "penetrating depth." Hunter expressed great satisfaction at these opportunities and had endless praise for television. As he, or his publicist, told Hedda Hopper in 1958: "[I]t isn't motion pictures that have given me great parts. It was TV. . . . In TV they seem to have more imagination about casting. . . . I want to be treated as an adult actor. I'm a product of Hollywood publicity, and publicity has exceeded the output of the product. I want pictures with substance." Thanks to *Playhouse 90*'s mission to showcase itself as an artistic alternative not only to the rest of television but feature film as well, Hunter found substance there, however fleeting it was.[23]

The second episode of *Playhouse 90* also off-cast its featured film actor, and the expert execution of this episode definitively established the program as a critical triumph. Broadcast on October 11, 1956, Rod Serling's "Requiem for a Heavyweight" detailed the story of a washed-up boxer who had nowhere to turn now that his career was over. Jack Palance starred as the slow-witted and weathered boxer; Ed Wynn, as his sympathetic trainer; Keenan Wynn, as a corrupt manager; and Kim Hunter, as a social worker who tries to help the boxer. Besides having made occasional television appearances, Keenan Wynn, Palance, and Hunter were well-established film actors by this point: Wynn had appeared in more than thirty films, Palance was nominated for best supporting actor Oscars in 1952 and 1953, and Hunter won the 1951 Oscar for Best Supporting Actress for *A Streetcar Named Desire.*

While these actors were indicative of *Playhouse 90*'s desire to rely on Hollywood players, the most notable piece of casting for this episode was the choice of Ed Wynn as the trainer who tried to do whatever he could to shield his boxer from the harshness of life beyond the ring. Ed Wynn was a well-known comedic vaudeville and radio star, and he had appeared occasionally in films. Known for a slapstick, "baggy pants" comedy style, Wynn briefly found a home on television in 1949 with *The Ed Wynn Show,* which lasted only a year. Thereafter, he appeared mostly as a guest on variety programs hosted by show business friends, such as Red Skelton, Ed Sullivan, and George Gobel. Producer Martin Manulis saw him play a rare dramatic role in the 1956 film *The Great Man* and recommended that he be cast in "Requiem." Putting such a playfully comedic actor as Wynn in a serious dramatic role was a risk— but exactly the kind of risk Ethel Winant and CBS coveted.

In rehearsals preceding the show's broadcast, Serling and the others involved in producing the show were quite concerned: Wynn was having trouble with his lines and his famous lisp, and many doubted his dramatic acting abilities. Despite these problems, Manulis insisted on leaving Wynn in the role. Son Keenan Wynn recalled in his autobiography:

"He had to have Dad in that role. For the producer, the 'draw' is important, the advertised attraction that commands the big audience." The casting decisions that *Playhouse 90* relied on so heavily were too important to change, and the show aired with the cast intact.[24]

The elder Wynn's performance did indeed help turn the episode into a ratings success, and critics showered the show with praise. *New York Times* reviewer Jack Gould headlined his review, "TV's Creative Ability Demonstrated on *Playhouse 90*," and singled out the performances for their quality. *Variety* also praised the performances and wrote that Wynn in particular displayed "a fine talent as a straight character actor." The stunt casting had worked: Wynn's profile had helped the show gain exposure and his performance itself had succeeded admirably. The success of the show in return greatly benefited Wynn himself. Keenan Wynn said of the evening's broadcast, "At eleven o'clock that night, Ed Wynn had re-established himself. A whole new career had opened up for him."[25]

The guest star who had introduced this episode, Eddie Cantor, appeared in the following week's episode and replicated Wynn's experience as a comedian cast in a serious role. In "Sizemore and Son," Cantor played the father of a returning GI in "the most dramatic play of his illustrious career," according to *Variety*. The trade paper reviewer further wrote that Cantor's performance "proved that serious acting can well become his métier after one of the brightest careers in comedy and song." Similar reactions resulted from a number of film actors' appearances across the next two seasons. Midway through *Playhouse 90*'s first season, Peter Lawford appeared in "Sincerely, Willis Wayde" as a ruthless member of a tycoon family coldly rising to control the family business. Despite criticisms of his overacting, *Variety* praised Lawford's "laudable try at a serious role."[26]

In addition, a number of actors whose film careers were in a severe slump found meaningful parts on *Playhouse 90* in 1957. Mickey Rooney's career had flatlined in the early 1950s, and the former child star tried to reinvent his persona with a series of film roles showcasing his skills as a serious character actor, including *The Bold and The Brave* (1956), in which he starred as an American soldier in Italy during World War II, and *Baby Face Nelson* (1957), where he played a Prohibition-era gangster. *Playhouse 90* granted Rooney a similar opportunity to broaden his range of portrayals and flaunt his acting skills with the starring role in "The Comedian," which aired on February 14, 1957. In

Mickey Rooney starring in "The Comedian" for Playhouse 90, with Mel Tormé and Kim Hunter. CBS/Photofest.

this episode, Rooney played an egomaniacal, crass, raging television comedian who nearly destroys everyone around him. This tour de force performance earned Rooney an Emmy nomination and helped the episode win the Emmy for Best Single Program of the Year in 1957. Critics similarly validated the actor's effort; *Variety* praised Rooney's performance for adding "another facet to his remarkable career—a powerful maturity as a heavy." This single performance briefly revitalized Rooney's career and made audiences forget his Andy Hardy roots.[27]

Positive reviews also resulted from the casting of Sterling Hayden during the second season of *Playhouse 90*. Hayden had trouble finding work at this point in his career, as he had been denounced for his six-month membership in the Communist Party in 1946. When testifying before the House Committee on Un-American Activities in 1951, Hayden admitted his past affiliations and named other Hollywood personalities as Communists. As a result, both sides of the debate in Hollywood castigated him, and thereafter, he found quality roles hard to come by. He made his live television debut on an October 1957 *Playhouse 90* episode entitled "A Sound of Different Drummers," a futuristic

Orwellian allegory about a perfect society run by a book-banning government. Here Hayden played a government worker who finds himself among the underground rebels and freethinkers and is transformed by his passion for their plight—and, inevitably, for a female member of their group. Giving a performance of great sensitivity and emotion, Hayden captured the attention of a *Variety* reviewer, who wrote: "[Hayden] turned in the top performance of the season, leading to the inevitable question of how come Hollywood never really discovered this guy. In all probability a victim of type-casting in the extreme (seems he's played nothing but cowboys or cops), Hayden revealed himself to be an actor of depth, force and perception."[28]

Peter Lorre realized a similar benefit in his numerous *Playhouse 90* appearances. *TV Guide* featured an article in connection with his November 1957 appearance in "The Jet-Propelled Couch," wherein Lorre played a psychiatrist and mentor to a fanciful doctor played by Donald O'Connor. The article highlighted Lorre's satisfaction at being able to play sympathetic, average characters on television, in contrast with his customary eccentric film characters, and it quoted him as saying, "There comes a time when you have to find the integrity to stand up and refuse to play certain kinds of roles." Strongly implied throughout this publicity piece is that only television in general, and *Playhouse 90* specifically, could engender the kind of artistic integrity that enabled such varied roles; the profit-obsessed movie studios could not. Lorre also benefited from off-casting in such *Playhouse 90* episodes as the aforementioned "Sizeman and Son," in which he played an empathic neighbor, and he appeared in an adaptation of Fitzgerald's *The Last Tycoon* as an aging film director unable to get work in the movies because of his reputation as an alcoholic. This role allowed Lorre a great measure of sympathy within a disparaging portrait of callous, money-grubbing Hollywood.[29]

Furthermore, this episode's depiction of Hollywood serves as a singular example of how *Playhouse 90* positioned itself against the film industry, and the casting described above is cardinal evidence. CBS touted in publicity material that the show strove to "use the best performers in unorthodox ways," and another publicity vehicle, the fan magazine *TV-Radio Mirror*, extolled the fact that "[w]ell-known names basked in a new light and actors in a rut climbed out." Off-casting brought prestige for both the program and the actor, as it meant allowing these stars to present their talents in a way that Hollywood supposedly would not allow. CBS could trumpet its efforts as a public service, thereby helping the network's cause to maintain and even increase network power and autonomy. The guest stars could also battle any negative connotations stemming from their appearances on the small screen with the defense that they were merely trying to explore more complex facets of their acting careers in an opportune environment.[30]

Although anthology dramas at this point sought to make extensive use of film stars, most upper-level stars still would not appear, not even on the most prestigious drama on television. Nonetheless, in its mission to position itself as an employer of top-ranked talent, the producers of *Playhouse 90* found in specific casting decisions a way to show off acting talent and to assert a corresponding superiority over Hollywood on a number of levels. William Boddy has discussed how the producers of anthology programs played into "taste hierarchies and ontological claims for the medium" in publicizing the quality of their shows, especially from the standpoint of their live status. Critics espoused these same claims, and the networks then made "tactical use of the critical status of the nationwide live broadcast as the privileged ontological and aesthetic television form." *Playhouse 90*'s use of stars served a similar rhetorical purpose. The show primarily relied on another medium's stars to fill its roster of onscreen talent, but it presented and publicized them in such a way as to validate the unique artistry of the televisual medium, an artistry supposedly tied to allowing actors to display their genuine acting skills, not just their box office potential. Unfortunately, such a rhetoric of artistry would not be enough to protect the show from the shifting economic structures of television.[31]

THE END OF *PLAYHOUSE 90*

Many today have the impression that *Playhouse 90* represented the height of "Golden Age" success on television. And indeed, if one were to look at much of the contemporaneous publicity and critical rhetoric around the show, this impression would be bolstered. *TV-Radio Mirror* said of the show, "The only guarantee is excellence," and influential critics like Jack Gould, Gilbert Seldes, and John Crosby praised the show over virtually all other programming on the air, heralding such live dramas as the only true art on television. A look at the many awards the show received across its run further illustrates its critical potency. From 1956 to 1959, *Playhouse 90* won virtually every award for which it was eligible, including the Golden Globe for Best Television Program,

Quigley Publications' Best Network Program and Best Dramatic Program, *Look*'s Best Dramatic Series, Screenwriters Guild awards for Best Television Episodes, and yearly Emmy awards for Best Dramatic Series.[32]

And yet, reviews of *Playhouse 90* were not always positive. In fact, many episodes were criticized quite harshly for not living up to the promise of the series' conception. Perhaps more crucial, the critical fawning over *Playhouse 90* was never matched by widespread audience interest on a consistent basis. Ratings soon plunged, especially after its first-season splash and even more so once ABC's *The Untouchables* (1959–63) arrived to dominate its time slot. *Playhouse 90* never finished a season in the top twenty-five of the Nielsen ratings, and CBS had problems maintaining full sponsorship throughout the show's run. As a result, the cost overruns were substantial; during the 1958–59 season, CBS reported losses in the millions because of unsold time. Former CBS programming executive Guy della Cioppa described the situation succinctly: "We were losing money hand over fist on *Playhouse 90*." By early 1959, only halfway into its third season, *Playhouse 90* was on life support.[33]

One strategy to boost ratings and attract sponsors might have been to try even harder to saturate the show with famous talent, but while the desire to do so was there, the money was not. Star salaries were skyrocketing by this point, driven up by the preponderance of spectaculars. As the decade continued, *Variety* noted the increasing levels of star salaries, and by 1959 the trade paper frequently focused on how this cost worked to the detriment of both spectaculars and anthology dramas. Revealingly, *Variety* argued that stars did not guarantee success anyway: "the mere pacting of a star doesn't necessarily mean you've got a hit on your hands," noted one observer. Even so, this critic also commented, "Of course, grabbing off a Marilyn Monroe is something else again." A star of Monroe's caliber could make a difference, but not even the most prestigious show on television could hope for such a luminary.[34]

By 1960, the costs were too great to sustain *Playhouse 90* on a full-time basis. CBS first turned to airing the program only every other week, then to airing it more irregularly as a special feature, a move that countered the founding philosophy of the show. John Cowdin, CBS publicity relations chief, claimed the purpose of the sporadic scheduling was "to give the series a more glamorous publicity build-up," the better to compete with other specials. Ironically, a show initially devised as a predictably programmed special was relegated to erratic scheduling after only a few years. *Playhouse 90* lived out its final days as a summer replacement series and aired its last episode on September 19, 1961.[35]

Part of the problem was that *Playhouse 90* had emerged in a period when anthology dramas and spectaculars were losing their value within television's shifting industrial and programming structures. In fact, television producer Mort Abrahams told *Variety* in July 1956 that if *Playhouse 90* proved unsuccessful and the similarly lavish *Producers' Showcase* continued its ratings decline, the entire genre of live anthology drama could permanently suffer. Abrahams's comment was prescient, as only a handful of these programs were left in *Playhouse 90*'s wake. The genre that kept alive the careers of Laraine Day and her colleagues was quickly disappearing. It was inevitable that film star appearances would decline, as well.[36]

THE DEMISE OF THE ANTHOLOGY DRAMA

Significant industrial changes lessened the practicality of live anthology dramas for the networks. Especially for CBS and NBC, specials and live dramas were important early in television's life to draw in new and skeptical viewers, sell television sets, and control affiliates. But by 1957, nearly 80 percent of homes in the United States owned a television set and the network-affiliate system was well in place. Now, the networks strove to regularize viewership, control costs, and reap syndication profits. Standardized filmed programming and a high volume of low-budget continuing-character series provided the most cost-efficient path to those ends. ABC never had the resources to compete with the big-budget fare of the other two networks and thus began even earlier to contract with Hollywood studios to produce filmed programming. For all three networks, the end result was less costly filmed programs produced on Hollywood studio lots in a mode akin to B-movie production.

This move to film had a corresponding impact on the cachet of television, as far as film stars were concerned. *Playhouse 90*'s status as a live production constituted a major component of its cultural prestige; as live programming in general disappeared, so did much of the critical respect for the uniqueness of televisual form. Not surprisingly, the filmed episodes of *Playhouse 90* received disproportionately negative criticism, and the fact that they were filmed was almost always highlighted as a factor. Significantly, the casting of certain episodes of *Playhouse 90* also echoed the contrast between live and filmed. The bulk of the famous names to appear on the program did so on the live episodes, with lesser names like Linda Darnell, Jan Sterling, Ralph Meeker, and Richard Baseheart filling out the roster of filmed episodes. In fact, this disparity became a point of contention between CBS and Screen Gems, the company that produced the filmed episodes, when Screen Gems complained that the network did not provide their production unit the budgets necessary to bring in high-caliber stars for its episodes. This withholding was actually sound business practice on CBS's part: it was in CBS's best interests that the filmed episodes remain lower in quality and endowed with lesser star power, in order to sustain the valuable connotations of high culture associated with the live episodes. Thus, with the network seemingly unwilling to improve the quality of the program's filmed episodes and given the increasing financial pressures put on the live episodes, *Playhouse 90* and similar anthology programs floundered. Without the prestige of live television and its highbrow connotations, actors were much less motivated to appear on or even host the few filmed anthology programs still on the air by the early 1960s.[37]

The proliferation of recent feature films on television also hastened the anthology program's demise. The Screen Actors Guild had reached an agreement with the major studios in 1960 that set standard residual payments for post-1948 features sold to television. This agreement resulted in a flood of recent, major features on television the following year and a new source of income for established film actors. Even *Playhouse 90*'s presentations of actors like Joseph Cotten and Joan Bennett paled in star attraction to TV-aired feature films with Cary Grant and John Wayne, and while the new practice affected ratings for anthology programs, it also discouraged some film actors from appearing on new television programs. Why would Cary Grant want small-screen fare competing against his televised feature films? Film actors could now profit from television without having to perform in new programs for the medium.

A final hindrance to the anthology program was the oft-cited distress that anthology program content caused for sponsors. Advertisers did not like the fact that the dramas were often complicated stories presenting problems without clear-cut solutions. Such was commonplace for *Playhouse 90*, which employed controversial story lines in such episodes as "The Plot to Kill Stalin" and "A Town Has Turned to Dust," an allegory of the murder of young Emmett Till. While the ambitious subject matter and perceived quality of such episodes were praised by

216

certain critics and viewers, they did not sell a greater amount of cigarettes, natural gas, or tissues than a much cheaper Western or sitcom could. Therefore, sponsors saw little reason to continue support for the genre. For actors, however, this sanitization removed a major incentive for appearances: less controversy meant less critical attention, thereby eliminating one of the major attractions of television—especially for publicity-starved film actors in career lulls.

The same trends that made *Playhouse 90*'s demise inevitable also altered many of the conditions that had made television an attractive option for film actors since the mid-1950s. The majority of film stars had appeared on TV only periodically, especially in anthology, spectacular, and variety programs, and these genres were at full strength in the mid-1950s. With the decline of these programming types by the early 1960s, and especially with the disappearance of the anthology drama by the end of that decade, there were fewer appropriate outlets for willing film actors. The resulting landscape of television was summarized dourly in November 1960 by Pat Weaver, pioneer of the big-budget specials: "Television has gone from about a dozen forms to just two—news shows and the Hollywood stories." "Hollywood stories" did not mean blockbuster films with well-known film stars, of course. On the contrary, it meant Westerns and detective shows shot on Hollywood backlots.[38]

Of course, by the late 1950s, these two forms did appear to be the type of programming that audiences preferred—or at least those audience members whose preferences advertisers and networks cared enough about to cater to. A single anthology show could vary widely from week to week in both type of material and quality, whereas audiences knew exactly what they were going to get from their favorite continuing-character series each week. A popular transitional text in this regard was NBC's *Wagon Train*. It was partly a continuing-character Western, as each week Ward Bond and Robert Horton would drive the titular vehicle toward its next stop on the way to California. But each episode also brought the group encounters with a new crop of guest characters and a different set of adventures. This enabled anthology-style stories and guest appearances by stars like Bette Davis, Jane Wyman, Joan Blondell, Mickey Rooney, and Sterling Hayden, and it set forth a guest-star template for many series to come. Nonetheless, it was the continuous elements that would dictate the form that series programming would take. Ultimately, the stability of the series won out over the variability of the anthology.

According to many critics, it was economic demands by the networks that won out over the creative potential of the live anthology drama. It was not surprising to see journalists like John Crosby and Jack Gould lament this fact: they had always decried what they perceived as the drive for profits over high-culture aims in television. More striking were comments from many stars who had previously accepted the inevitability of that conflict in commercial television yet who now saw the balance irretrievably tipped toward corporate interests rather than creative interests. Like Charlton Heston, Jack Lemmon had maintained an active anthology schedule throughout the 1950s even as he distinguished himself in feature successes like *Mister Roberts* (1955) and *Fire Down Below* (1957). Also like Heston's, Lemmon's career duality ended in the early 1960s. Lemmon told the press in 1960—probably not coincidentally after his smash-hit *Some Like It Hot* (1959)—that he was walking away from television: "The professional incentive is gone, if you know what I mean. There's less and less live drama, and I wouldn't want to be caught dead in a film show. . . . When I look back on my TV work, I see it as one of the most professionally rewarding periods in my career. But an actor wouldn't find on TV today what I found then. I say this also as a viewer." Lemmon was surely not the only star who felt that way.[39]

In fact, even more vociferous invective came from Robert Montgomery, one of the pioneers of both film star appearances on television and anthology drama production. NBC canceled *Robert Montgomery Presents* in 1957 because of low ratings, and Montgomery's television career ended shortly thereafter. But he did not go away quietly. Montgomery spent the next decade lambasting the oligopolistic network control of television and the ways in which commercial demands had demolished the creative potential of the medium. His complaints culminated in a 1968 publication, a self-proclaimed "ill-tempered book" entitled *Open Letter From a Television Viewer,* in which Montgomery indicted everyone from advertisers to politicians for letting the cultural promise of early television evaporate. He did not, however, indict viewers; instead, he blamed the networks' "free-wheeling oligopoly" and even political conspiracies for television's refusal to provide quality fare:

As we were all informed and believed when television was new, it has the greatest potential for good of any communications instrument ever invented. Most of us still feel that this is true. At the same

218

time, I think there are now millions of people who, like me, believe that television lost its way and fell among evil companions who have not only prevented it from realizing its potential but have turned it in another direction.

Whether or not evil conspiracies were at the root of television's changes, there is no question that the industry changed markedly from the time when Montgomery first turned to NBC to when he was turned away. And one of the major consequences of these changes was that the services of Hollywood film stars were no longer so essential.[40]

The end of *Playhouse 90* echoed the multitudinous demise of live programming, the anthology drama, and the frequency of established film actor appearances on television. A *Variety* reviewer seemed to understand these implications when he wrote of the final regularly scheduled *Playhouse 90* episode, "It was not a very graceful way for *Playhouse 90* to exit the regular Thursday night scene, cueing, in a sense, the end of an era for TV." But *Playhouse 90*'s inception also represented the culmination of an industrywide trend toward more spectacular shows with expensive talent. The genre initially sought numerous markers of prestige, from original writing to liveness to the stunt casting of stars, and these qualities, plus such advantages as rising salaries and the relocation of these shows to the West Coast, drew a number of film actors to anthology lineups. When the corresponding industrial benefits of these strategies disappeared, so did a major space for film actor appearances. Yet this demise represented more than just the dissolution of a single genre. The networks' move into the infamous "vast wasteland" of 1960s programming and the film studios' help in producing this programming helped bring to a close the fluid movement of actors from film to television that had become so familiar a sight to 1950s audiences.[41]

While the most famous Hollywood stars would not appear on a show even of *Playhouse 90*'s caliber, spectaculars and anthology programs were still an essential arena for established Hollywood talent in the mid-1950s—to the point where *TV Guide* commented in 1956 that television viewers were "now conditioned by spectaculars to the biggest name stars." Accordingly, the early 1960s shift away from such shows forced viewers to recondition themselves: no longer would such a high number of established film actors appear on television in so concentrated a period. Myriad changes in programming styles and production modes, in both film and television, and the resulting considerable shift downward in the cultural status of television had a direct effect on film actor appearances on television. A 1956 *Variety* editorial predicted the changes to come: "Hollywood performers will shortly have to make up their minds between television and motion pictures. The time for playing both sides of the street is coming to an end."[42]

CONCLUSION

The programming changes that caused the demise of the anthology program lent television a substantially negative image by the early 1960s. Newton Minow's famous 1961 "vast wasteland speech" signified the plunging cultural status of television, and the topic was frequently addressed in the popular press, as journalists and intellectuals alike opined that television had sold its soul to advertisers. While television had always had negative critics, most cultural observers had held out hope throughout the 1950s that the medium could at least present a combination of popular mass culture and more highbrow fare such as anthology dramas, spectaculars, and current affairs programs. By the early 1960s, however, it was clear that such a balance would not be sustained. The preeminence of programs from the Golden Age may have been as much a factor of marketing as of actual quality, but these shows were replaced by programs perceived to have considerably less artistic and cultural merit, making perceptions as important as reality in shaping how people felt about television. With lowbrow connotations cemented to much of TV's programming, any recognized film actor concerned about star status now had little reason to turn to television.

Even if star motivations for crossing over had stayed strong in this period, the changing nature of television brought less need for the medium to utilize well-known film actors. To understand this effect, we must first consider the progression of the medium across its initial years of commercial operation. A reliance on the popularity and name value of Hollywood stars was an important strategy for television in its first decade to secure both attention and stature for the new medium. But once television had established itself as comparable to film and radio as a legitimate entertainment medium, and once the industry had saturated the market with TV sets and affiliated stations, there was less need to rely on connotations from other established entertainment forms for validity.

Further, the rising salaries of well-known performers hindered much of the remaining impetus toward recruiting film stars. *TV Guide* reported in 1957, "The bidding to court the top names has become so frantic that the guests can almost name their own fees." The magazine quoted one actor's telegram to a producer: "I spit at $25,000. I act at

$100,000." Such demands greatly affected the budgeting system in television, especially given that the condensed timetable for series production could not support a ballooning salary structure. Investment in talent began to affect the budgets and resulting quality of individual programs. Critic Hal Humphrey accordingly lamented the budget cuts required to afford big names: "TV's executives have run into the realization that stars cost big money, so in trying to hold the budget down they scrimp on other things like writers, sets, etc. I don't think it will be too long before they also discover that viewers not only like to see big name stars, but a story and production to match their talents."

Similarly, *Sponsor* suggested that producers needed to start relying on programs suffused with ideas rather than notable names to combat the rising salaries that were sapping programs of their quality and financial balance. *TV Guide* also indicated support for this idea with their review of Four Star Productions' *The June Allyson Show*, which featured "the biggest and most expensive stars in the business," including Bette Davis, Jane Powell, Ginger Rogers, and Harpo Marx. The reviewer complained about the shallow stories being performed and wrote, "It costs so much to hire [these guests] that there is bound to be very little left over for a decent script. It shows on the show."[1]

In addition to the imbalance that talent price tags caused for budgets, industry observers commented that these expensive names simply were not bringing in ratings and ad billings sufficient to warrant their costs. The bottom line spoke quickly, according to *Variety:* "[I]f Nielsen says not enough people are watching them or paying a proper-cost-per-thousand allegiance to these entries, it's a sure bet the sponsor is going to reevaluate this thinking and possibly return to bread-and-butter stuff. The fare may be more pedestrian, but the risks are fewer." Such an attitude would explain why Spencer Tracy had trouble finding takers for his offer of doing a live spectacular in 1959 at the exorbitant price of $350,000. *Variety* cynically noted that the new hero on television was no longer the Western cowpoke; it was now the cost accountant, "the guy with the knack for whittling down those below and above-the-lines charges and who can bring a show in for maybe $5,000 or $10,000 less than the original estimate."[2]

A number of emerging young television actors, such as *Maverick* (ABC, 1957–62) star James Garner, proved that building a new name could pay off just as much as presenting an old one. *Television Digest* saw

Garner's immediate success as "[o]ne of the most potent arguments" for going with new faces. Other relative unknowns who proved successful were Chuck Connors (*The Rifleman*, ABC, 1958–63) and Clint Eastwood (*Rawhide*, CBS, 1959–66). This situation was not necessarily new—unknowns had been gaining success in television since its earliest days—but with the increases in salaries and the great success of these young performers, the trend was growing considerably during this period. One industry observer told *Broadcasting*, "Now [producers] are simply manufacturing Westerns and such on an assembly-line basis—they don't need stars. All they need is profits."[3]

Although financial success had obviously always been central to television's operations, the drive for profits and ratings came to dictate network decisions more than ever before, and anything that did not serve these factors did not last long. A 1959 feature article in *Broadcasting* highlighted ABC's pioneering role therein, pointing out that the network's main objective was simply for "a high average rating for all shows through the week," not for a respectable range of programming. On the other hand, CBS president Louis Cowan claimed that his network strove for "responsibility, stability and balance" in programming, and NBC's Robert Sarnoff touted his network's "totality of service" in providing a broad range of programming to audiences, regardless of ratings. These latter responses were obviously public relations rhetoric, but ABC didn't even bother with such illusions: the network's vice president Oliver Treyz unabashedly admitted to programming whatever would keep the ratings high in all time slots. ABC's president Leonard Goldensen spoke in similar terms to *Forbes* magazine in that same year: "People like what we're giving them. First we build a habit factor, get them used to watching us. Then we can do something about upgrading programming. We're not interested in the critics." The point was no longer to prove that television deserved a place in American culture alongside radio and the movies; it was now to make television a habit in order to maximize revenue. If the use of featured film actors no longer maximized revenue, they would no longer appear on screens.[4]

Changes in the roles of advertisers brought similar aims. By the 1960s, production responsibilities had shifted from sponsors and ad agencies to the networks and Hollywood telefilm packagers like Revue and Screen Gems. The rising costs of programming also brought a shift from single-sponsorship to multiple-sponsorship of programs, and sponsor names synonymous with program names became a rarity. Whereas a company like DuPont might have sponsored an anthology program solely for the prestigious connection, there was now markedly less motivation to advertise on television for that reason alone. The sale of products, not prestige, became the motivating factor. Christopher Anderson argues that these "small-ticket" advertisers were interested in pitching to young families in particular, as they were most likely to use these products. Once again, ABC led the way, as *TV Guide* noted:

> If it's possible to personalize a corporation, ABC can be pictured as a brash young newcomer flexing its muscles and standing up against the more mature and slightly more sedate CBS and NBC. That's the youthful image ABC's leaders have of their company and that's the basis of their programming: to emphasize shows that will appeal to younger audiences, to the 15-to-40 age groups.

ABC chairman Leonard Goldensen expressed similar youth-minded reasoning to *Forbes* in defending the impending cancelation of the long-running, prestigious *Voice of Firestone* (NBC and ABC, 1949–63): "The ratings were down to nothing, it's been killing our whole Monday night schedule, and the audience that likes it, mainly older people, isn't the audience we want anyway. Now we can fill that time with a solid adventure show that'll pull in a bigger and younger audience." This intent surely affected which performers the network chose to feature as well: younger actors were considered to be more in line with what younger audiences wanted to see.[5]

ABC's success with young stars only accelerated these shifts, and berths for older, established film stars were harder to come by. Critic Hal Humphrey described the implications in 1961: "An old movie star can't get himself arrested on TV these days. . . . A whole stable full of fading movie stars are trying to get themselves launched in TV series now, but with no luck. A few years ago they could have written their own contract." Thus, because networks, sponsors, and advertisers at the end of the 1950s had aims and methods significantly different from those of previous years, any established film actors still wanting to turn to television had much less opportunity to do so.[6]

Notably, this fractured connection occurred as the production relationships between film and television grew tighter, and the new oligopoly that arose in the new medium could moderate star power as much as the old studio system once had. By 1960, the Hollywood majors produced approximately 40 percent of network programs, and television became nearly as important as features to the film industry's industrial operations. Yet high-level film stars were rarely part of this merging. While many stars had taken advantage of television's developmental accessibility by producing their own shows and reaping syndication profits in the 1950s, the consolidation of production control and program ownership by the networks and film studios in the 1960s meant that performers were increasingly shut out of these opportunities. Television producers did not have to give over considerable profit participation to stars, because they were no longer deemed indispensable. Hiring an unknown with few demands could prove to be far more practical.

In fact, Hollywood began to use television as a training ground for these unknown actors. *Variety* frequently called attention to a so-called talent crisis in Hollywood film in the 1950s: too few new stars were being developed to replace those older stars who were retiring. The ever-rising costs of feature production on top of exhibitor demands for name stars to place on marquees made turning to unknowns for feature production perilous. A relationship with television could provide the solution. In a 1956 article entitled "TV Replaces Movie Scouts," Hal Humphrey reported the comments of Jerry Wald, vice president at Columbia Studios. Wald claimed that he frequently tuned in to television to scout talent: "TV saves us making screen tests. . . . The TV appearance of an actor serves as the screen test." The investment in a failed pilot or even a season series was quite small compared to the risks inherent in presenting unknown talent in the big-budget features that were coming to dominate Hollywood screens. As *TV-Radio Mirror* put it:

> Putting a youngster in a series which shows on home television screens week after week, a studio can get a reaction quickly. (The studio doesn't have to search for the reaction, either; the postman brings it in every day). If the public's reaction is favorable, studio publicists go into high gear, and gallons of printer's ink pour out. Conversely, if the public seems apathetic, the hopeful is liable to be forgotten, talent or no.

Thus, at the same time that the major studios used television to profit from continuing sales of their libraries of features filled with classic stars, a number of them also used the small screen to develop new talent for future features.[7]

Warner Bros., emerging in the late 1950s as a force in television production, was at the forefront of this trend. Rather than test out new names in the more expensive big-screen medium, the studio found it less risky to put an actor into a Warners television series. First, it was cheaper to hire unknowns. Second, the practice also gave the studio control over that actor's film activities in case he managed to find stardom on the small screen. Interestingly, this meant something of a return to the late 1940s, when the studios still had players under contract and could tightly monitor their relationship to television. The studio even attempted to resurrect some semblance of the old studio system with their television production studio.

The experience of James Garner was emblematic of the Warner Bros. approach. Garner's television career began with a small part on Warner Bros. Television's Western program *Cheyenne;* on the strength of this appearance, the studio signed him to a seven-year contract in 1955 starting at $200 a week. He appeared briefly in the feature *Toward the Unknown* (1956), and his first prominent role was in *Sayonara* (1957) with Marlon Brando. Garner was then given the lead part in *Darby's Rangers* (1958), while simultaneously receiving a script for a Western telefilm pilot, *Maverick.* This strategy was common practice for Warners during this period: the studio would sign an unknown actor, feature him in a Warners-produced television series, try him out in a few feature roles, and then hope for success in either medium. Other actors Warner Bros. contracted and groomed in such a manner included Clint Walker, John Russell, and Efrem Zimbalist, Jr., but none of these actors ever matched the success of James Garner.

Maverick quickly climbed into the ranks of television's most popular shows, with Garner outgunning such old-time heavyweights as Ed Sullivan, Jack Benny, and Steve Allen in the same timeslot. Garner continued making features during the initial seasons of *Maverick,* and leads in such films as *Cash McCall* (1959) gave Warners the opportunity to keep Garner on a relatively small salary while starring him in feature films— another advantage of controlling both the film and television careers of a contract star. Garner's exploding popularity led to considerable conflicts, however, as he began to capitalize on his popularity by making it more difficult for the studio to control his career. Garner especially bristled at the studio's demands on his time and the proportionately low pay. Though his salary had been raised to $1,750 a week by January 1960, he did not get to share in the series' enormous profits to the studio. Thus he felt his earnings were not commensurate with the income that his name drew into the studio's and the network's coffers. Another Warner Bros. star, Clint Walker, had unsuccessfully battled for a contract release, but

Garner got lucky: a technicality in his contract allowed him to win a suit against the studio in 1961 for breach of contract. After leaving the studio, Garner vowed never to attach himself to television again, telling one newspaper, "Wild horses couldn't drag me back to a television series."[8]

Of course, Garner would return to television after his feature career floundered, and his initial success was only the most prominent among a large wave of new faces on television, with *Television Digest* citing a "peak of series featuring actors new to the public" for the 1959–60 season. Obviously, this emphasis on unknowns meant in turn that fewer established Hollywood actors saw the kinds of opportunities on television that had existed in previous years. Film actor Dana Andrews, who years earlier had shunned television, now lamented in 1963 that TV no longer welcomed stars: "Name actors are shunned in favor of some unknown who doesn't want as much money and doesn't know enough about acting to give the producers trouble."[9]

The challenge was doubled for female actresses, who were heavily marginalized by the prime-time reign of male-dominated Western and adventure series. Barbara Stanwyck noted the simultaneous cancelation of shows starring June Allyson, Ann Sothern, and Loretta Young in 1961 and complained, "I don't know who 'they' are, but they've decreed no more women on television. The only woman who will be left next year is Donna Reed. The rest of us have been dropped. . . . And we all had good ratings. . . . 'They' want action shows and have a theory women can't do action." Stanwyck would later get in on the action with her starring role in the Western *Big Valley* (ABC, 1965–69), but for actresses who maintained prominent careers in feature films, the opportunities offered by anthology dramas in the 1950s had disappeared by the 1960s. The primary guest-acting opportunities were now on continuing-character series, whose low-culture status meant that, as the *Chicago Tribune* observed in 1960, "even if the more important women stars of motion pictures want to slip over into television, their very eminence prevents them from accepting lesser roles."[10]

Thus, although it was common by the middle of the 1950s for midlevel stars to work regularly in both film and television, this choice began to decrease as television progressed into its second full decade of commercial transmission. When ad agencies and sponsors ruled program development, there had been a significant number of Hollywood actors on TV. As the networks and Hollywood studios began to take over programming, this situation changed. With the film studios more involved in television, they could set a line of demarcation between features and television. In the mid-1950s, with shows like *Screen Directors Playhouse* (NBC and ABC, 1955–56) presenting episodes directed by such famed directors as John Ford, Leo McCarey, and George Stevens, and featuring such stars as John Wayne, Errol Flynn, and Ray Milland, there were points of close contact between the two media—certainly one reason for Hollywood's ongoing concern about competition with the small screen. By getting directly involved in television production, the studios could have a measure of control over the level and intensity of this competition.

While the film studios were interested in using television as a training ground for talent, they preferred definitive separations between the media. For unknown actors, television was of use to the studios; for established actors, it was to be either a minor avenue for publicity purposes or nonexistent. With increased control over television production, the studios could make those conditions a reality. *Television Digest* highlighted syndicator Frederic Ziv's complaints that while Hollywood studios were turning to a blockbuster strategy to repair problems in the film industry, they took a far different approach with their involvement in television. Ziv said derisively of the standard Hollywood studio production package for television: "[T]hese are not the stars, writers and directors [the studios] plan to use in their TV programs. These people must be reserved for feature film production." On the other hand, unknowns and lesser talents under contract were ideal for telefilm productions. In 1958, James Garner had predicted, "People are still inclined to think a TV actor is farther down the scale than a movie actor. Four or five years from now, that attitude will be changed. People will hardly be able to remember when there was a class distinction between TV and movies." Hollywood had a substantial interest in making sure his words did not come true. But the fact that there *was* a time when this seemed possible reveals that film actors truly did have a substantial impact on 1950s television.[11]

Indeed, as this book has shown, the assumption that only actors with faded or insignificant film careers appeared on 1950s television is false. Granted, in the early years of television, the vast majority of established film actors on television were either secondary-level character actors or ones whose film careers had sputtered: stars who had healthy film careers did not appear, except on the occasional talk show. By the middle of the decade, however, a significant number of higher-level stars with active film careers did begin to do television, especially by appearing in anthology programs and making frequent publicity appearances on variety programs and game shows. It is quite true that most of the film actors who made the permanent move to television, such as Faye Emerson, no longer had a viable film career, and that some, like Adolphe Menjou, needed television to carry them through significant Hollywood lulls. But these circumstances did not preclude the continuation of a film career, as David Niven's 1958 Oscar victory would confirm. For those in need of a career boost, television could be a lifesaver; for those just needing publicity to complement an already thriving film career, television provided a valuable outlet.

Further, 1950s TV had more to offer a film actor than a potential career resurrection or publicity buildup. As television's infrastructure solidified and performer salaries increased, the new medium could offer a competitive income and even a level of prestige through particular types of programming. A star like Mickey Rooney could line his wallet *and* enhance his reputation as an actor by tackling the challenges of a live performance as a controversial character on an anthology drama. Accordingly, television provided the opportunity for an actor to push the boundaries of an established persona, with less risk than attempting such a role in a feature film. Television offered a range of program types and performance modes. Whereas theatrical film limited actors to the portrayal of fictional characters, TV provided these opportunities plus roles as hosts of variety and anthology shows or as guests on quiz and panel programs. Programs like *Playhouse 90* and *General Electric Theater* also offered West Coast shooting locations; spectaculars provided high visibility and substantial salaries; and quiz shows and variety programs brought opportunities for publicity and prominence without raising overexposure concerns. Thus, while a declining career might provide a film actor the impetus to investigate the opportunities offered by television, it was not by any means the sole motivation to turn to the medium.

This circumstance in turn satisfied the bottom line for television: film actors could be very effective at drawing in audiences and selling television sets, and they were easy to organize marketing campaigns around. Stars like Ginger Rogers and Gene Kelly were featured in specials for this very purpose. They could also lend credibility to a program because of their revered status. Such was the case with *Playhouse 90*, which oriented everything from casting decisions to the program's logo around this impression. Even less extravagant programs and genres used this logic: film actors were brought in as hosts and featured players on regular programming in order to bring attention and distinction to shows and to deflect attention away from the commercial base of a program.

It is certainly the case, however, that no film actor could appear on television without a potential loss of star credibility. TV was viewed as a step down from film throughout the decade. The impression that former film stars on series television were washed-up was especially pervasive; thus many actors with healthy film careers were hesitant to appear on the small screen on a frequent basis. But, just as significant, television developed ways to negotiate this challenge. Despite the disparate types of programming and strategies involved, the case studies of Adolphe Menjou and *Playhouse 90* offer similar lessons: producers could draw upon the components of an actor's film career and prevailing persona to lend credibility to the television program. With Menjou, this strategy meant resurrecting the most prestigious elements of his film persona and mapping those onto the distinct characteristics of the syndicated *Favorite Story*, thereby elevating the status of both. With *Playhouse 90*, the show's producers, writers, and casting directors exploited a reverse circumstance: distinctly separating the featured actor from her film persona in order to mark the program as an artistic enterprise unique to both film and television. These cases illustrate that television's production executives were well aware of the perceived stigma of film actor appearances on television and therefore adapted programming methods for the purpose of circumventing or undermining any negative connotations.

Further, the stars themselves could use television appearances to shape the meaning of their images. The actor-producers of *Four Star Playhouse* certainly had the creative control to guide their careers and images as they chose. Dick Powell opted to perpetuate his tough-guy persona, at the same time achieving greater creative success behind the camera than he ever had in film. David Niven stretched beyond the confines of his debonair image and thereby positioned himself for a successful return to film. Most crossover actors did simply carry their prevailing film personae into television. Such was especially the case for those who appeared in continuing-character series sitcoms and dramas. In fact, for some, like Eve Arden and Ann Sothern, the star images they had previously established were crucial to their blazing a unique trail in television history.

While star image represented a figurative association with the film world, there were literal industrial bonds that were just as important for film actor activity on television. The studios initially forbade their contracted actors from appearing on television—which was actually an advantage for unaffiliated actors like Faye Emerson who began in television in its early years. But as the studio system broke down, studios had fewer stars under their control to bar from television in the first place. They did, however, begin encouraging publicity appearances for those stars under contract. As a result, film actors were quite free to move between film and TV by the mid-1950s. By the beginning of the next decade, however, this situation shifted yet again, and an association with a film studio became more advantageous for young unknowns than for established actors looking to exploit television. As these changes illustrate, the varying visibility of film actors on television reveals as much about the inner workings of the Hollywood film and television industries as the careers of the actors themselves.

Indeed, film star appearances were essential to nearly every programming mode in television, from the height of the live spectacular to the depths of the syndicated telefilm, and to nearly every crucial change in the industry, from the moves out to the West Coast to the boundless growth of talent agencies. The rise and fall of film actors on 1950s television also reveals the saga of a classical studio system first in disarray and then in cooperation with a new entertainment industry. Without the breakdown of the studio system, few film actors would have become involved with television, but without the impact of television's subsequent production involvement with the major film studios, it is possible that film stars would have continued to enjoy prominence on TV screens well into the 1960s. Ultimately, the relationship between Hollywood and television has traditionally been read in terms of production associations, but this book proves that the drive to integrate film and television came as much from the talent on the screen as behind it.

The case studies presented here also indicate that despite early television's pressing need for prominent star talent and the willingness of significant numbers of stars to fill this need, television's unique industrial and cultural qualities required performative skills appropriate to the medium. Only those stars who could adapt to those circumstances would succeed. Faye Emerson's naturalistic personality, Adolphe Menjou's worldly affability, and Ida Lupino's self-conscious drollness were

231

perfectly attuned to the intimate scope and domestic setting of television. On the other hand, film stars like Betty Hutton and Ray Milland, who were unable to situate their images and performance styles into the context of television's primary style and production methods, could find that the opportunity to rekindle their fame via television was quite limited. They could also see their reputations diminished significantly in the process.

Finally, the growing acknowledgment of the artificiality of star images likely provided an obstacle to certain stars' continued success. For someone like Betty Hutton, the very fabric of her persona was stitched out of performative excess; any acknowledgment of the artificiality of that excess would cause the intensity of her star image to evaporate. Thanks to the small screen's exploitation of intimacy, immediacy, and authenticity, television relentlessly shredded the illusion of film stardom throughout the decade and accordingly highlighted the new medium's supposed ability to remove the shroud of fantasy surrounding celebrity and grant viewers direct access to the true people beneath. Even when television was trying to be complimentary to film star guests, it was still pulling the veil off the face of stardom that the Hollywood studio system had cultivated for so long.

A final case study analysis of the most iconic set of 1950s film star appearances—on the TV series that starred the most iconic film-to-television crossover actor—proves illustrative. The legendary *I Love Lucy* set the bulk of its 1955 episodes in Los Angeles, with Ricky recruited to star in a feature for MGM and Lucy in tow, continuing her never-ending quest to break into the world of entertainment. Ricky's own fictional celebrity was the basis for many of the program's Hollywood jeers. For instance, during the production of his first feature, *Don Juan and the Starlets,* Ricky is ordered by the studio publicist to take the four featured starlets to a movie premiere and leave Lucy at home; his true home life doesn't mesh with the publicity campaign the studio is developing for the film. This emphasis on falseness is, of course, in contrast to the sitcom itself, which purported to give audiences a glimpse into the real married life of Lucille and Desi.

Allusions to reality also came with MGM's involvement with the series, which enabled cameo appearances by an impressive list of current Hollywood stars, including Rock Hudson, Richard Widmark, and John Wayne, all playing themselves. These episodes have a striking thematic uniformity: the stars are presented as easygoing, normal people unimpressed with their own celebrity status. The concept of stardom itself is characterized as a comedic masquerade that the stars perform only intermittently, yet always amiably, in order to satisfy the starstruck delusions of gullible fanatics like Lucy. Lucy herself participates in just such a masquerade in the May 1955 episode entitled "Harpo Marx." Lucy's New York friend Caroline is in town and desperately wants to meet some of the movie stars that Lucy has claimed are now her close friends. Of course, Lucy has no movie star friends, so she steals the nearsighted Caroline's glasses and poses from afar as a variety of stars, including Gary Cooper and Jimmy Durante. Her costumes consist of the most basic icons of each star's persona, such as Cooper's Western garb and Durante's worn hat, and she parrots the expected lines, "Yup" and "Pleased ta meetcha." The result is a fitting metaphor for a conception of stardom and fandom: Caroline is too blind to see that these are not really the extraordinary people she has always envisioned from their images on the screen; instead, these figures are merely performative collections of easily reproducible icons.

Lucy's desperate desire to know the real stars drives most of the star-cameo episodes. She is a prototypically hysterical, neurotically infatuated, and pathetically naive fan, while Ricky, as a celebrity himself but also a man, is blasé despite his close contact with a multitude of stars. "Honey, they're just like anybody else," he tells Lucy. Most of the episodes present the stars as exactly that: William Holden simply wants to eat lunch in peace at the Brown Derby, and Cornel Wilde hopes to escape the madness of Hollywood by hiding out in a hotel and relaxing with a newspaper. Of course, Lucy enters their supposed worlds of normality and turns them upside-down: Holden ends up covered in cream pie after their interaction, and Wilde flees his hotel, believing that his room has been burglarized based on markers that Lucy leaves behind.

But it is most striking how gracious the stars are to Lucy, despite the extreme disruption she brings into their lives. For instance, when Lucy breaks into Richard Widmark's home in pursuit of a souvenir, the star ends up confronting her at gunpoint with Ricky by his side, goading him on. After Lucy asks him to put the gun down, Widmark responds, "I don't know about that, it would be such a public service to Hollywood," and Ricky adds, "Yeah, you'd get a special Oscar." In the end, however, Widmark just laughs off her legitimately criminal behavior and happily signs an autograph for her. John Wayne is even more tolerant. Lucy

CONCLUSION

Lucy swoons
upon meeting
William Holden.
CBS/Photofest.

steals his footprint display from Grauman's Theater, accidentally destroys the multiple copies he makes to get her off the hook, breaks into his dressing room, and incompetently impersonates his masseuse, but in the end Wayne makes even more copies of the display for her and lifts her up in a joyful embrace when she tries to kiss him.

As this illustrates, the featured stars mocked the excesses of fandom but also displayed a benevolent tolerance of them. Emerging from the mockery of this fandom was the impression that the stars were very accessible, humble people, and though they did not invite such gratuitous behavior, they were nonetheless appreciative of it, despite its occasional excesses. These episodes offered a benign form of ridicule: fans at home could laugh at Lucy's extremist version of fandom (while judging their own as appropriate and welcome), and the stars gained positive exposure and a more intimate bond with their admirers watching on television. The stars were also granted ample opportunities to plug their most recent theatrical releases for MGM. William Holden casually discusses his work on *The Country Girl* with Ricky (1954); Cornel Wilde invites Ricky to see the premiere of *The Big Combo* (1955) with

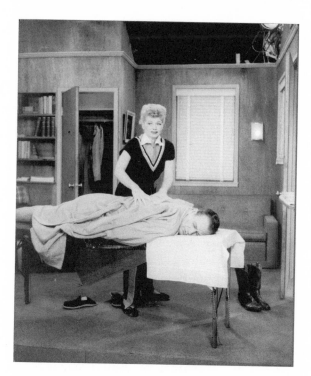

him; and two of John Wayne's features are mentioned, while the publicity poster for his *Blood Alley* (1955) gets prominent display within a scene. It is thus easy to see why MGM would have allowed its stars to make cameos on the program. Even the mockery of Hollywood's publicity games was ostensibly to the studio's benefit.

One star cameo later that season was overtly critical of Hollywood, however, likely because the featured guest was more associated with television by that point and no studio was involved. The second half of the 1955–56 season saw the program's foursome traveling to Europe for Ricky's band tour, and the March 1956 episode entitled "Lucy Meets Charles Boyer" brought them into contact with the *Four Star Playhouse* star. In the course of the plot, Boyer's agent arranges a lunch between his client and Ricky, hopeful that the bandleader will agree to appear in an episode of *Four Star Playhouse*. Ricky actually asks Boyer to pretend he is not Boyer, in order to prevent Lucy from bringing certain disaster into his life because of her celebrity obsession. He accordingly pretends to be Maurice Dubois, a struggling actor who admits that his career is doomed by his strong resemblance to Boyer.

After some inevitably zany plot twists, Lucy hires Dubois to play Boyer in a romantic exhibition intended as a lesson for Ricky. In training Dubois to be Boyer, Lucy turns him into a grotesque caricature of the star, whittling him down to a handful of excessively overwrought traits. For instance, after he politely pecks her hand, Lucy insists that he must kiss her whole arm dramatically: "Oh no, no, Maurice. Charles Boyer doesn't kiss like that. When you kiss a woman's hand, put some schmaltz into it." When he accordingly overdoes it, she sneers dismissively, "I don't know how you ever make a living as an actor." Boyer looks sincerely pained and says, "I often wonder myself." Here the show mocks the absurd one-dimensionality that the film industry has reduced the Boyer image to—such as his smoldering gaze, which Lucy turns into an absurdly overdone leer. And just as clearly, Lucy is a victim of Hollywood's myths: she has bought wholesale Boyer's iconic traits and insists that he, or someone portraying him, must embody them. But in the realm of television, the world he discusses with Ricky and is decidedly most comfortable in, Boyer is just an affable producer and actor trying to manage his career.

Such one-shot appearances must have been very gratifying for stars like Boyer, Wayne, and Holden. In exchange for relatively minor effort and investment in the new medium, they received valuable public exposure and publicity for their current work. Further, by knowingly mocking their constructed star images and the essence of fandom, they came across as down-to-earth, unpretentious people, presumably further endearing themselves to audiences as a consequence. In turn, the episodes that presented them gained invaluable audience attention by capitalizing on the attraction of these star names. Through showcasing the stars in ways that tweaked their film-based images, television could pose itself as the fresher, more authentic, and intimate medium.

But a likely consequence of such appearances was the continued demythologizing of stardom. By foregrounding the question of whether a film star should appear on television or not, uprooting star images from their codified studio system–era bedrocks, and presenting a panorama of film actors in an unprecedented range of performance contexts—all reflexively acting out some version of their star images and all in the private spaces of American homes—early television progressively deconstructed the mythologies of stardom that the film industry had systematically cultivated for decades. Such a circumstance may in fact be a central reason why Hollywood found it so difficult to cultivate new stars in the 1960s. The industry only succeeded again by learning to foster illusions and mythologies more suitable to the television age.

The phenomenon of film stars appearing on television likely even represents a missing link between the epoch of classical film star glamour prior to the arrival of television and the oft-noted decline of such glamour in subsequent decades. Several journalists and scholars have charted this apparent decline; more recently, scholars like Joshua Gamson have pinpointed irony and self-mockery as qualities essential to contemporary celebrity to defuse suspicions of identity fabrication. Trends of postwar realism in feature filmmaking, the breakdown of the studio system's publicity machine, the rise of gossip and scandal-obsessed tabloids like *Confidential*, and changes in dominant social discourses have all been pointed to as reasons for the decline in glamour and stardom's cultural capital since the 1940s. But I believe that an overlooked yet crucial catalyst in this demythologizing of stardom was the phenomenon of film stars on 1950s television.[12]

As such, perhaps Norma Desmond was right after all: the pictures truly got small. But early television's demand for the distinctive qualities that only Hollywood talent could provide did give film stars a uniquely prominent position on the new medium. And such prominence, to borrow again from Norma Desmond, is what makes one a star.

APPENDIX: ESTABLISHED FILM ACTOR APPEARANCES ON FIRST-RUN PRIME-TIME TELEVISION, 1948–61

I. MALE FILM ACTORS WITH CONTINUING ROLES ON TELEVISION SERIES

Actor	Series	Genre	Year(s)*	Network†
Bud Abbott	*The Colgate Comedy Hour*	variety	51–54	NBC
	The Abbott and Costello Show	comedy	52	SYN
Walter Abel	*Suspicion*	anthology	57–58	NBC
Eddie Albert	*Leave it to Larry*	comedy	52	CBS
	Nothing But the Best	variety	53	NBC
	The Eddie Albert Show	variety	53	CBS
Robert Alda	*By Popular Demand*	quiz/panel	50	CBS
	Personality Puzzle	quiz/panel	53	ABC
	Secret File U.S.A	adventure	55	SYN
	Can Do	quiz/panel	56	NBC
Ben Alexander	*Party Time at Club Roma*	variety	50–51	NBC
	Dragnet	crime drama	53–59	NBC
	Take a Good Look	quiz/panel	60	ABC
Don Ameche	*Take a Chance*	quiz/panel	50	NBC
	Holiday Hotel	variety	50–51	ABC
	Don Ameche's Musical Playhouse	variety	51	ABC
	Coke Time	variety	53	NBC
	The Jack Carson Show	variety	54–55	NBC
	Don Ameche Theater	anthology	58	SYN
Leon Ames	*Life with Father*	comedy	53–55	CBS
	Frontier Judge	Western	56	SYN
	Father of the Bride	comedy	61–62	CBS
Sig Arno	*My Friend Irma*	comedy	52–53	CBS
Edward Arnold	*Edward Arnold Theater*	anthology	54	SYN
	Strange Stories	anthology	56	SYN
Roscoe Ates	*The Marshal of Gunsight Pass*	Western	50	ABC
Gene Autry	*The Gene Autry Show*	Western	50–56	CBS
Lew Ayres	*Frontier Justice*	anthology	58	CBS

* "Year(s)" refers to the span of time across which the star appeared on the particular program, not the years of the program's entire run.

† SYN = syndicated programming; DUM = DuMont

Actor	Series	Genre	Year(s)*	Network†
Jim Backus	*I Married Joan*	comedy	52–55	NBC
	The Adventures of Champion	adventure	55–56	CBS
Noah Beery, Jr.	*Circus Boy*	adventure	56–58	NBC/ABC
	Riverboat	adventure	60–61	NBC
Ed Begley	*Leave it to Larry*	comedy	52	CBS
Rex Bell	*Cowboys and Injuns*	children's	50	ABC
Ralph Bellamy	*Man Against Crime*	crime drama	49–54	CBS/DUM/NBC
	To Tell the Truth	quiz/panel	57–59	CBS
William Bendix	*Life of Riley*	comedy	53–58	NBC
	The Overland Trail	Western	60	SYN
Willie Best	*The Trouble with Father/ The Stu Erwin Show*	comedy	50–55	ABC
	My Little Margie	comedy	52–53	NBC
	Waterfront	adventure	53–56	SYN
Charles Bickford	*The Man Behind the Badge*	anthology	53–55	CBS/SYN
William Bishop	*It's a Great Life*	comedy	54–56	NBC
Ray Bolger	*Where's Raymond?*	com/variety	53–55	ABC
Ward Bond	*Wagon Train*	Western	57–61	NBC
Lee Bowman	*The Adventures of Ellery Queen*	crime drama	51–52	ABC
	What's Going On?	quiz/panel	54	ABC
William Boyd	*Hopalong Cassidy*	Western	49–53	NBC/SYN
Charles Boyer	*Four Star Playhouse*	anthology	52–56	CBS
	The Charles Boyer Theater	anthology	53	SYN
Eddie Bracken	*Make the Connection*	quiz/panel	55	NBC
	Masquerade Party	quiz/panel	57	NBC
Walter Brennan	*The Real McCoys*	comedy	57–63	ABC/CBS
George Brent	*Wire Service*	adventure	56–57	ABC
David Brian	*Mr. District Attorney*	crime drama	54	SYN
Lloyd Bridges	*Sea Hunt*	adventure	57–61	SYN
Tom Brown	*Gunsmoke*	Western	55–75	CBS
	Mr. Lucky	adventure	59–60	CBS
Edgar Buchanan	*Hopalong Cassidy*	Western	49–51	NBC
	Judge Roy Bean	Western	56	SYN
Smiley Burnette	*Ozark Jubilee*	music	59	ABC
Raymond Burr	*Perry Mason*	legal drama	57–66	CBS
Ralph Byrd	*Dick Tracy*	crime drama	50–51	ABC
Rory Calhoun	*The Texan*	Western	58–60	CBS
Rod Cameron	*City Detective*	crime drama	53	SYN
	State Trooper	crime drama	57	SYN
	Coronado 9	crime drama	59	SYN

Actor	Series	Genre	Year(s)*	Network†
Eddie Cantor	The Eddie Cantor Comedy Theatre	variety	55	SYN
Macdonald Carey	Dr. Christian	medical	56	SYN
	Lock Up	crime drama	59–60	SYN
Richard Carlson	I Led Three Lives	spy drama	53–56	SYN
Leo Carrillo	Cisco Kid	Western	50–56	SYN
Leo G. Carroll	Topper	comedy	53–55	CBS/ABC/NBC
Jack Carson	All Star Revue	variety	50–52	NBC
	The Jack Carson Show	comedy	54	NBC
Chick Chandler	Soldiers of Fortune	adventure	55–56	SYN
George Chandler	Lassie	adventure	58–59	CBS
Dane Clark	Justice	legal drama	54–55	NBC
	Wire Service	adventure	56–57	ABC
	Bold Venture	adventure	59	SYN
Andy Clyde	The Real McCoys	comedy	57–62	ABC
	Lassie	adventure	58–64	CBS
Ray Collins	The Halls of Ivy	comedy	54–55	CBS
	Perry Mason	legal drama	57–66	CBS
Ronald Colman	The Halls of Ivy	comedy	54–55	CBS
Hans Conreid	Make Room For Daddy	comedy	56–65	CBS
	Take a Good Look	quiz/panel	59–61	ABC
	Take a Guess	quiz/panel	53	CBS
	What's It For?	quiz/panel	57–58	NBC
Tom Conway	Mark Saber/Inspector Mark Saber—Homicide Squad	crime drama	51–54	ABC
	The Betty Hutton Show	comedy	59–60	CBS
Jackie Coogan	Pantomime Quiz	quiz/panel	50–55	CBC/NBC/DUM
	Cowboy G-Men	Western	52	SYN
Jackie Cooper	The People's Choice	comedy	55–58	NBC
	Hennesey	comedy/drama	59–62	CBS
Melville Cooper	I've Got a Secret	quiz/panel	52	CBS
Wendell Corey	Harbor Command	crime drama	57	SYN
	Peck's Bad Girl	comedy	59	CBS
	Yes, Yes, Nanette	comedy	61	NBC
Ray Corrigan	Crash Corrigan's Ranch	children's	50	ABC
Lou Costello	The Colgate Comedy Hour	variety	51–54	NBC
	The Abbott and Costello Show	comedy	52	SYN
Joseph Cotten	The 20th Century–Fox Hour	anthology	55–56	CBS
	On Trial/ The Joseph Cotten Show	anthology	56–58	NBC
Broderick Crawford	Highway Patrol	crime drama	55–59	SYN

Actor	Series	Genre	Year(s)*	Network†
Hume Cronyn	*The Marriage*	comedy	54	NBC
Robert Cummings	*My Hero*	comedy	52–53	NBC
	The Bob Cummings Show	comedy	55–59	NBC/CBS
	The Bob Cummings Show	comedy	61–62	CBS
Jim Davis	*Stories of the Century*	Western	54	SYN
	Rescue 8	adventure	58	SYN
Gabriel Dell	*The Steve Allen Show*	variety	56–61	NBC
Andy Devine	*The Adventures of*			
	Wild Bill Hickok	Western	51–58	SYN
Richard Denning	*Mr. and Mrs. North*	mystery	52–54	CBS/NBC
	Michael Shayne	mystery/drama	60–61	NBC
Melvyn Douglas	*Hollywood Off Beat*	crime drama	52–53	SYN/DUM/CBS
	Blind Date	quiz/panel	53	ABC
	Frontier Justice	anthology	59	CBS
Charles Drake	*Robert Montgomery's*			
	Summer Stock	anthology	55–56	NBC
	Rendezvous	adventure	58	SYN
Dan Duryea	*China Smith*	adventure	52, 54	SYN
Stuart Erwin	*The Trouble with Father/*			
	The Stu Erwin Show	comedy	50–55	ABC
Tom Ewell	*The Tom Ewell Show*	comedy	60–61	CBS
Douglas Fairbanks, Jr.	*Douglas Fairbanks, Jr. Presents/*			
	Rheingold Theater	anthology	53–57	SYN
Charles Farrell	*My Little Margie*	comedy	52–55	CBS/NBC
	The Charlie Farrell Show	comedy	56	CBS
Frank Faylen	*Dobie Gillis*	comedy	59–63	CBS
Paul Fix	*The Rifleman*	Western	58–63	ABC
James Flavin	*Man with a Camera*	adventure	58–60	ABC
	The Roaring Twenties	crime drama	60–62	ABC
Errol Flynn	*Errol Flynn Theater*	anthology	57	SYN
Henry Fonda	*The Star and the Story*			
	/Rheingold Theater	anthology	55	SYN
	The Deputy	Western	59–61	NBC
Wallace Ford	*The Deputy*	Western	59–61	NBC
Preston Foster	*The Waterfront*	adventure	54–56	SYN
Douglas Fowley	*The Life and Legend*			
	of Wyatt Earp	Western	55–56	ABC
William Frawley	*I Love Lucy*	comedy	51–57	CBS
William Gargan	*Martin Kane, Private Eye*	crime drama	49–51	NBC
Kirby Grant	*Sky King*	Western	53–54	ABC
Reed Hadley	*Racket Squad*	crime drama	51–53	CBS
	The Public Defender	legal drama	54–55	CBS
Thurston Hall	*Topper*	comedy	53–55	CBS/ABC/NBC

Actor	Series	Genre	Year(s)*	Network†
Cedric Hardwicke	*Who Pays*	quiz/panel	59	NBC
	The Gertrude Berg Show	comedy	61–62	CBS
Louis Hayward	*The Lone Wolf*	adventure	55	SYN
Sterling Holloway	*The Life of Riley*	comedy	53–58	ABC
	Willy	comedy	55	CBS
Edward Everett Horton	*Holiday Hotel*	variety	50	ABC
Warren Hull	*A Couple of Joes*	variety	49–50	ABC
	The Ben Grauer Show	talk	50	NBC
	Cavalcade of Bands	variety	50	DUM
	Strike it Rich	quiz/panel	51–55	CBS
	Crawford Mystery Theatre	mystery/quiz	51–52	DUM
Sam Jaffee	*Ben Casey*	medical	61–66	ABC
Allen Jaffee	*The Duke*	comedy	54	NBC
	Hey, Jeannie	comedy	56–57	CBS
Frank Jenks	*Colonel Humphrey Flack*	comedy	53–54	DUM
Allyn Joslyn	*Where's Raymond?*	comedy	53–55	ABC
	The Eve Arden Show	comedy	57–58	CBS
Louis Jourdan	*Paris Precinct*	crime drama	55	SYN
Boris Karloff	*Starring Boris Karloff*	anthology	49	ABC
	Colonel March *of Scotland Yard*	mystery	54	SYN
	The Veil	anthology	58	SYN
	Thriller	anthology	60–62	NBC
Roscoe Karns	*Rocky King, Detective*	crime drama	50–54	DUM
	Hennesey	comedy/drama	59–62	CBS
Buster Keaton	*Life with Buster Keaton*	comedy	51	SYN
Robert Keith	*The Great Gildersleeve*	comedy	54–55	SYN
Tom Kennedy	*The Big Game*	quiz/panel	58	NBC
	The Gisele *Mackenzie Show*	variety	58	NBC
	Doctor I.Q.	quiz/panel	58–59	ABC
Otto Kruger	*The Lux Video Theatre*	anthology	55–56	NBC
Arthur Lake	*Blondie*	comedy	57	NBC
Jack Lambert	*Riverboat*	adventure	59–61	NBC
Charles Laughton	*This is Charles Laughton*	readings	53	SYN
Peter Lawford	*Dear Phoebe*	comedy	54–55	NBC
	The Thin Man	mystery	57–59	NBC
John Litel	*My Hero*	comedy	52–53	NBC
Gene Lockhart	*His Honor, Homer Bell*	comedy	55	SYN
Richard Long	*Bourbon Street Beat*	crime drama	59–60	ABC
	77 Sunset Strip	crime drama	60–61	ABC
Frank Lovejoy	*Man Against Crime*	crime drama	56	NBC
	Meet McGraw	crime drama	57–58	NBC

Actor	Series	Genre	Year(s)*	Network†
Robert Lowry	Circus Boy	adventure	56–58	NBC/ABC
William Lundigan	Climax!	anthology	54–58	CBS
	Shower of Stars	variety	54–58	CBS
	Men Into Space	sci-fi	59–60	CBS
Bert Lytell	Hollywood Screen Test	talent	48	ABC
	One Man's Family	soap opera	49–52	NBC
	The Orchid Award	variety	53	ABC
Fred MacMurray	My Three Sons	comedy	60–65	ABC
Hugh Marlowe	The Adventures of Ellery Queen	mystery	54	SYN
Herbert Marshall	The Unexpected	anthology	52	SYN
Chico Marx	The College Bowl	variety	50–51	ABC
Groucho Marx	You Bet Your Life	quiz	50–61	NBC
James Mason	The Lux Video Theatre	anthology	54–55	NBC
	The James Mason Show	readings	56	SYN
Raymond Massey	I Spy	anthology	56	SYN
	Dr. Kildare	medical	61–66	NBC
Francis McDonald	The Adventures of Champion	adventure	55–56	CBS
Charles McGraw	The Falcon	adventure	55	SYN
	Casablanca	intrigue	55–56	ABC
Horace McMahon	Martin Kane, Private Eye	crime drama	50–51	NBC
	Make Room for Daddy	comedy	53–54	ABC
	Naked City	crime drama	59–63	ABC
Adolphe Menjou	Favorite Story	anthology	53–54	SYN
	Target	anthology	57	SYN
Burgess Meredith	The Big Story	anthology	57	SYN
Gary Merrill	The Mask	crime drama	54	ABC
	Justice	legal drama	54–55	NBC
Ray Milland	The Ray Milland Show	comedy	53–55	CBS
	Trails West/ Death Valley Days	anthology	58	SYN
	Markham	crime drama	59–60	CBS
Thomas Mitchell	Mayor of the Town	comedy	54	SYN
	O. Henry Playhouse	anthology	57	SYN
George Montgomery	Cimarron City	Western	58–60	NBC
Robert Montgomery	Robert Montgomery Presents	anthology	50–57	NBC
Clayton Moore	The Lone Ranger	Western	49–57	ABC
Dennis Morgan	21 Beacon Street	crime drama	59–60	NBC/ABC
Harry Morgan	December Bride	comedy	54–59	CBS
	Pete and Gladys	comedy	60–62	CBS

Actor	Series	Genre	Year(s)*	Network†
Alan Mowbray	Colonel Humphrey Flack	comedy	53–54	DUM
	Hey Mulligan	comedy	54–55	NBC
	Colonel Humphrey Flack	comedy	58–59	SYN
	Dante	adventure	60–61	NBC
Jack Mulhall	The Ken Murray Show	variety	50–51	CBS
George Murphy	MGM Parade	documentary	55–56	ABC
Conrad Nagel	Celebrity Time	quiz/variety	49–50	CBS
	The Silver Theater	anthology	49–50	CBS
	The Conrad Nagel Show	interview	53	SYN
	Broadway to Hollywood Headline Clues	quiz/variety	53–54	DUM
	Where Were You?	interview	55	SYN
	The Conrad Nagel Theater	anthology	55	SYN
David Niven	Four Star Playhouse	anthology	52–56	ABC
	The David Niven Show	anthology	59	NBC
Lloyd Nolan	Martin Kane, Private Eye	crime drama	51–52	NBC
	Special Agent 7	crime drama	58	SYN
Hugh O'Brian	The Life and Legend of Wyatt Earp	Western	55–61	ABC
Edmond O'Brien	Johnny Midnight	crime drama	60	SYN
Pat O'Brien	Harrigan and Son	comedy	60–61	ABC
Arthur O'Connoll	Mr. Peepers	comedy	53–54	NBC
Donald O'Connor	The Colgate Comedy Hour	variety	51–54	NBC
	The Donald O'Connor Texaco Show	comedy/variety	54–55	NBC
Dennis O'Keefe	Suspicion	anthology	57	NBC
	The Dennis O'Keefe Show	comedy	59–60	CBS
Michael O'Shea	It's a Great Life	comedy	54–56	NBC
Frank Orth	Boston Blackie	crime drama	51–53	SYN
	The Brothers	comedy	56	CBS
Robert Paige	The Colgate Comedy Hour	variety	55	NBC
Willard Parker	Tales of the Texas Rangers	Western	58–59	ABC
John Payne	The Restless Gun	Western	57–59	NBC
Don Porter	Private Secretary	comedy	53–57	CBS
Dick Powell	Four Star Playhouse	anthology	52–56	CBS
	Dick Powell's Zane Grey Theater	anthology	56–62	CBS
	The Dick Powell Show	anthology	61–63	NBC
Robert Preston	Man Against Crime	crime drama	51	CBS
Vincent Price	Pantomime Quiz	quiz/panel	50–52	CBS/NBC/DUM
	E.S.P.	quiz/panel	58	ABC
George Raft	I'm the Law	crime drama	53	SYN
Basil Rathbone	Your Lucky Clue	quiz/panel	52	CBS

Actor	Series	Genre	Year(s)*	Network†
Gene Raymond	Fireside Theatre	anthology	53–55	NBC
Ronald Reagan	The Orchid Award	variety	53–54	ABC
	The General Electric Theater	anthology	53–62	CBS
Philip Reed	Ruthie on the Telephone	comedy	49	CBS
George Reeves	The Adventures of Superman	adventure	51–57	SYN
Duncan Renaldo	The Cisco Kid	Western	50–56	SYN
Roy Rogers	The Roy Rogers Show	Western	51–57	NBC
Cesar Romero	Passport to Danger	adventure	54–55	SYN
	Take a Good Look	quiz/panel	59–61	ABC
Mickey Rooney	Hey Mulligan/The Mickey Rooney Show	comedy	54–55	NBC
Charles Ruggles	The Ruggles	comedy	49–52	ABC
	The World of Mr. Sweeney	comedy	54–55	NBC
George Sanders	The George Sanders Mystery Theater	anthology	57	NBC
Dan Seymour	Sing It Again	quiz/variety	50–51	CBS
	Where Was I?	quiz/panel	52	DUM
Phil Silvers	The Phil Silvers Arrow Show	variety	48–49	NBC
	The Phil Silvers Show	comedy	55–59	CBS
Frank Sinatra	The Frank Sinatra Show	variety	50–52	CBS
	The Frank Sinatra Show	variety	57–58	ABC
Al (Fuzzy) St. John	Lash of the West	Western	53–54	ABC
Robert Stack	The Untouchables	crime drama	59–63	ABC
Robert Sterling	Topper	comedy	53–55	CBS/ABC/NBC
	Love That Jill	comedy	58	ABC
Craig Stevens	Peter Gunn	crime drama	58–61	NBC/ABC
Mark Stevens	Martin Kane, Private Eye	crime drama	53–54	NBC
	Big Town	crime drama	54–56	NBC
Onslow Stevens	This is the Life	drama	52–53	DUM/ABC
Paul Stewart	Top Secret	adventure	55	SYN
	Deadline	anthology	59	SYN
Milburn Stone	Gunsmoke	Western	55–75	CBS
Barry Sullivan	The Man Called X	spy drama	56	SYN
	Harbourmaster	adventure	57–58	CBS/ABC
Lyle Talbot	The Bob Cummings Show	comedy	55–59	NBC/CBS
	The Adventures of Ozzie and Harriet	comedy	56–66	ABC
Kent Taylor	Boston Blackie	crime drama	51–53	SYN
	The Rough Riders	Western	58–59	ABC
Robert Taylor	The Detectives	crime drama	59–62	ABC/NBC

Actor	Series	Genre	Year(s)*	Network†
Regis Toomey	Hey Mulligan	comedy	54–55	ABC
	Richard Diamond, Private Detective	crime drama	57–58	CBS
Arthur Treacher	Down You Go	quiz/panel	56	ABC/NBC
Forrest Tucker	Deep Sea Adventure	adventure	55	SYN
Johnny Weissmuller	Jungle Jim	adventure	55	SYN
Bill Williams	The Adventures of Kit Carson	Western	51–55	SYN
	Date with the Angels	comedy	57–58	ABC
Donald Woods	The Orchid Award	variety	53–54	ABC
	The Damon Runyon Theatre	anthology	55–56	CBS
Ed Wynn	The Ed Wynn Show	variety	49–50	CBS
	The Ed Wynn Show	comedy	58–59	NBC
Gig Young	Warner Bros. Presents	drama	55–56	ABC
Robert Young	Father Knows Best	comedy	54–62	CBS/NBC
	Window on Main Street	comedy	61–62	CBS

II. FEMALE FILM ACTORS WITH CONTINUING ROLES ON TELEVISION SERIES

Actress	Series	Genre	Year(s)*	Network†
June Allyson	The DuPont Show with June Allyson	anthology	59–61	CBS
Eve Arden	Our Miss Brooks	comedy	52–56	CBS
	The Eve Arden Show	comedy	57–58	CBS
Lucille Ball	I Love Lucy	comedy	51–57	CBS
	The Lucy-Desi Comedy Hour	comedy	57–60	CBS
Lynn Bari	The Detective's Wife	comedy	50	CBS
	Boss Lady	comedy	52	NBC
Tallulah Bankhead	All Star Revue	variety	52–53	NBC
Ethel Barrymore	The Ethel Barrymore Theater	anthology	53	SYN
Louise Beavers	Beulah	comedy	50–53	ABC
Joan Bennett	Too Young to Go Steady	comedy	59	NBC
Julie Bishop	My Hero	comedy	52–53	NBC
Mary Brian	Meet Corliss Archer	comedy	54–55	SYN
Barbara Britton	Mr. and Mrs. North	mystery	52–54	CBS/NBC
Hillary Brooke	The Abbott and Costello Show	comedy	51–53	SYN
	My Little Margie	comedy	52–55	CBS/NBC
Spring Byington	December Bride	comedy	54–59	CBS

Actress	Series	Genre	Year(s)*	Network†
Kitty Carlisle	I've Got a Secret	quiz/panel	52–53	CBS
	What's Going On?	quiz/panel	54	ABC
	To Tell the Truth	quiz/panel	56–57	CBS
Nancy Carroll	The Aldrich Family	comedy	50–51	NBC
Joan Caulfield	My Favorite Husband	comedy	53–55	CBS
	Sally	comedy	57–58	NBC
Lois Collier	Boston Blackie	crime drama	51–53	SYN
Arlene Dahl	Pepsi-Cola Playhouse	anthology	53–54	ABC
	Opening Night	anthology	58	NBC
Gail Davis	Annie Oakley	Western	53–56	SYN
Joan Davis	I Married Joan	comedy	52–55	NBC
Rosemary DeCamp	The Life of Riley	comedy	49–50	NBC
	Death Valley Days	anthology	52–65	SYN
	Love That Bob	comedy	55–59	NBC/CBS
Gloria DeHaven	The Gloria DeHaven Show	variety	53–54	ABC
	Make the Connection	quiz/panel	55	ABC
Jeff Donnell	The George Gobel Show	variety	54–58	NBC
Ann Doran	National Velvet	adventure	60–62	NBC
Joanne Dru	Guestward Ho!	comedy	60–61	ABC
Margaret Dumont	My Friend Irma	comedy	52–53	CBS
Irene Dunne	Schlitz Playhouse of Stars	anthology	52	CBS
Faye Emerson	Paris Cavalcade of Fashions	fashion	48–49	NBC
	The Faye Emerson Show/ Fifteen with Faye	talk	50–51	CBS/ABC/NBC
	Faye Emerson's Wonderful Town	variety	51–52	CBS
	Author Meets the Critics	talk	52	DUM
	I've Got a Secret	quiz/panel	52–58	CBS
	Quick as a Flash	quiz/panel	53–54	CBS
	Faye and Skitch	variety	53–54	NBC
	What's in a Word	quiz/panel	54	CBS
	Of All Things	variety	56	CBS
	Masquerade Party	quiz/panel	58–60	CBS/NBC
Dale Evans	The Roy Rogers Show	Western	51–57	NBC
Jinx Falkenburg	Tex and Jinx	talk	47–49	NBC/CBS
	Masquerade Party	quiz/panel	58	CBS/NBC
Betty Furness	Studio One	anthology	49–58	CBS
	Penthouse Party	variety	50–51	ABC
	Byline	mystery	51	ABC
	Westinghouse Desilu Playhouse	anthology	58–60	CBS
Mitzi Green	So This is Hollywood	comedy	55	NBC

Actress	Series	Genre	Year(s)*	Network†
Jean Hagen	Make Room for Daddy	comedy	53–56	ABC
Barbara Hale	Perry Mason	crime drama	57–66	CBS
June Havoc	Willy	comedy	54–55	CBS
Celeste Holm	Honestly, Celeste!	comedy	54	CBS
	Who Pays	quiz/panel	59	NBC
Rochelle Hudson	That's My Boy	comedy	54–59	CBS
Betty Hutton	The Betty Hutton Show	comedy	59–60	CBS
Frieda Inescort	Meet Corliss Archer	comedy	51	CBS
Anne Jeffreys	Topper	comedy	53–56	CBS/ABC/NBC
	Love that Jill	comedy	58	ABC
Adele Jergens	Pantomime Quiz	quiz/panel	50–52	CBS/NBC
Pert Kelton	Cavalcade of Stars	variety	50–52	DUM
	Henry Morgan's Great Talent Hunt	variety	51	NBC
Margaret Lindsay	Take a Guess	quiz/panel	53	CBS
June Lockhart	Who Said That?	quiz/panel	52–55	NBC/ABC
	Lassie	adventure	58–64	CBS
Anita Louise	My Friend Flicka	adventure	55–57	CBS
Ida Lupino	Four Star Playhouse	anthology	54–56	CBS
	The Ida Lupino Theater	anthology	56	SYN
	Mr. Adams and Eve	comedy	57–58	CBS
Enid Markey	Bringing Up Buddy	comedy	60–61	CBS
Hattie McDaniel	Beulah	comedy	52	ABC
Butterfly McQueen	Beulah	comedy	50–52	ABC
Patricia Medina	Tales of the 77th Bengal Lancers	adventure	56–57	NBC
Constance Moore	Window on Main Street	comedy	61–62	CBS
Ida Moore	The RCA Victor Show	comedy	53–54	NBC
Carmel Myers	The Carmel Myers Show	interview	51–52	ABC
Jane Nigh	Big Town	crime drama	52–53	CBS
Maureen O'Sullivan	The Children's Hour	variety	51	SYN
Merle Oberon	Assignment Foreign Legion	anthology	57	CBS
Lilli Palmer	Lilli Palmer Show	talk	51	CBS
	Lilli Palmer Theater	anthology	55–56	SYN
Lee Patrick	Boss Lady	comedy	52	NBC
	Topper	comedy	53–56	CBS/ABC/NBC
Zasu Pitts	Oh! Susanna	comedy	56–59	CBS
	The Gale Storm Show	comedy	59–60	ABC
Frances Rafferty	December Bride	comedy	54–59	CBS
Ella Raines	Janet Dean, Registered Nurse	medical	54	SYN
Lillian Randolph	Amos 'n' Andy	comedy	51–53	CBS
	The Great Gildersleeve	comedy	55	SYN

Actress	Series	Genre	Year(s)*	Network†
Martha Raye	All Star Revue	variety	51–53	NBC
	The Martha Raye Show	variety	54–56	NBC
Donna Reed	The Donna Reed Show	comedy	58–66	ABC
Debbie Reynolds	The Eddie Fisher Show	variety	57–59	NBC
Marjorie Reynolds	The Life of Riley	comedy	53–58	NBC
Ann Sothern	Private Secretary	comedy	53–57	CBS/NBC
	The Ann Sothern Show	comedy	58–61	CBS
Barbara Stanwyck	The Barbara Stanwyck Show	anthology	60–61	NBC
Gale Storm	My Little Margie	comedy	52–55	CBS/NBC
	Oh! Susanna	comedy	56–59	CBS
	The Gale Storm Show	comedy	59–60	ABC
Gloria Swanson	The Gloria Swanson Show	anthology	53	SYN
Jessica Tandy	The Marriage	comedy	54	NBC
Shirley Temple	Shirley Temple's Storybook	anthology	58–59	ABC
	The Shirley Temple Show	anthology	60–61	NBC
Audrey Totter	Cimarron City	Western	58–60	NBC
Mary Treen	Willy	comedy	54–55	CBS
Ethel Waters	Beulah	comedy	50–52	ABC
Mary Wickes	Inside U.S.A. with Chevrolet	variety	49–50	CBS
	The Peter Lind Hayes Show	comedy	50	NBC
	Bonino	comedy	53	NBC
	The Halls of Ivy	comedy	54–55	CBS
	The Danny Thomas Show	comedy	56–57	abc
	Dennis the Menace	comedy	59–61	CBS
Cara Williams	Pete and Gladys	comedy	60–62	CBS
Marie Wilson	My Friend Irma	comedy	52–54	CBS
Anna Mae Wong	The Gallery of Mme. Lui-Tsong	crime drama	51	DUM
Jane Wyatt	Father Knows Best	comedy	54–62	CBS/NBC
Jane Wyman	The Jane Wyman Theater	anthology	55–58	NBC
Loretta Young	Letter to Loretta	anthology	53–54	NBC
	The Loretta Young Show	anthology	54–61	NBC

III. MALE FILM ACTORS WITH ONLY EPISODIC APPEARANCES

Luther Adler	Brian Aherne	Frank Albertson
Dana Andrews	John Archer	Robert Armstrong
Fred Astaire	Nils Asther	Mischa Auer
Freddie Bartholomew	Alan Baxter	John Beal
Bruce Bennett	Clem Bevans	Theodore Bikel

Whit Bissell	Sidney Blackmer	Humphrey Bogart
Steve Brodie	Francis X. Bushman	Bruce Cabot
James Cagney	Lon Chaney, Jr.	Maurice Chevalier
Lee J. Cobb	Charles Coburn	Steve Cochran
Elisha Cook, Jr.	Gary Cooper	George Coulouris
Jerome Cowan	Buster Crabbe	Bing Crosby
Henry Daniell	Albert Dekker	Robert Donat
Brian Donlevy	Kirk Douglas	Tom Drake
Bobby Driscoll	James Dunn	William Eythe
Dick Foran	Glenn Ford	Eddie Foy, Jr.
Reginald Gardiner	Will Geer	James Gleason
Farley Granger	Alec Guinness	Edmund Gwenn
Jack Haley	Porter Hall	Billy Halop
Walter Hampden	Sterling Hayden	Richard Haydn
Russell Hayden	Sessue Hayakawa	Van Heflin
Paul Henreid	Russell Hicks	Halliwell Hobbes
John Hodiak	William Holden	Tim Holt
Skip Homeier	Oscar Homolka	Bob Hope
John Howard	Trevor Howard	John Hoyt
Rock Hudson	Henry Hull	Wilfred Hyde-White
Rex Ingram	John Ireland	Richard Jaeckel
Dean Jagger	Van Johnson	Ian Keith
Cecil Kellaway	Gene Kelly	Paul Kelly
Arthur Kennedy	Guy Kibbee	Terry Kilburn
Richard Kiley	Patric Knowles	Alan Ladd
Bert Lahr	Francis Lederer	Sam Levene
Richard Loo	Peter Lorre	James Lydon
Paul Lukas	Roddy McDowall	Frank McHugh
Victor McLaglen	Barton MacLane	Stephen MacNally
Joel McCrea	George Macready	Fredric March
Hugh Marlowe	Harpo Marx	Robert Mitchum
Victor Moore	Robert Morley	Robert Morse
Paul Muni	Jack Oakie	Edmund O'Brien
Dan O'Herlihy	Laurence Olivier	Robert Paige
Walter Pidgeon	Claude Rains	Erik Rhodes
Tex Ritter	Edward G. Robinson	Gilbert Roland
Robert Ryan	Randolph Scott	Red Skelton
Walter Slezak	Everett Sloane	Kent Smith
James Stewart	Dean Stockwell	Sheppard Strudwick
John Sutton	Akim Tamiroff	Franchot Tone
Richard Travis	Robert Warwick	John Wayne
Orson Welles	James Whitmore	Cornel Wilde
Ian Wolfe	Monty Wooley	Keenan Wynn
Roland Young		

Julie Adams	Dame Judith Anderson	Mary Astor
Lauren Bacall	Fay Bainter	Anne Baxter
Barbara Bel Geddes	Constance Bennett	Ingrid Bergman
Edna Best	Janet Blair	Joan Blondell
Ann Blyth	Mary Boland	Beulah Bondi
Geraldine Brooks	Virginia Bruce	Billie Burke
Madeleine Carroll	Marguerite Chapman	Cyd Charisse
Mae Clarke	Claudette Colbert	Patricia Collinge
Gladys Cooper	Ellen Corby	Joan Crawford
Pat Crowley	Linda Darnell	Jane Darwell
Bette Davis	Laraine Day	Yvonne DeCarlo
Frances Dee	Dolores Del Rio	Ellen Drew
Mildred Dunnock	Florence Eldridge	Madge Evans
Frances Farmer	Glenda Farrell	Edith Fellows
Betty Field	Gracie Fields	Rhonda Fleming
Nina Foch	Joan Fontaine	Sally Forrest
Anne Francis	Kay Francis	Mona Freeman
Judy Garland	Peggy Ann Garner	Greer Garson
Nancy Gates	Janet Gaynor	Virginia Gilmore
Dorothy Gish	Lillian Gish	Paulette Goddard
Betty Grable	Gloria Grahame	Bonita Granville
Coleen Gray	Kathryn Grayson	Jane Greer
Virginia Grey	Ethel Griffies	Nancy Guild
Margaret Hamilton	Ann Harding	Sara Haden
Susan Hayward	Irene Hervey	Judy Holliday
Miriam Hopkins	Mary Beth Hughes	Ruth Hussey
Rosalind Ivan	Glynis Johns	Leatrice Joy
Nancy Kelly	Evelyn Keyes	Andrea King
Veronica Lake	Dorothy Lamour	Hedy Lamarr
Elsa Lanchester	Angela Lansbury	Barbara Lawrence
Joan Leslie	Margaret Lindsay	Myrna Loy
Diana Lynn	Jeanette MacDonald	Dorothy McGuire
Aline MacMahon	Dorothy Malone	Virgina Mayo
Una Merkel	Ann Miller	Marilyn Monroe
Constance Moore	Terry Moore	Agnes Moorehead
Patricia Neal	Margaret O'Brien	Una O'Connor
Maureen O'Hara	Eleanor Parker	Elizabeth Patterson
Jane Powell	Luise Rainer	Paula Raymond
Irene Rich	Thelma Ritter	Lynne Roberts
Ginger Rogers	Ruth Roman	Jane Russell
Rosalind Russell	Ann Rutherford	Lizabeth Scott

Martha Scott   Ann Sheridan   Alexis Smith
Randy Stuart   Sylvia Sidney   Margaret Sullavan
Blanche Sweet   Phyllis Thaxter   Gene Tierney
Claire Trevor   Ruth Warrick   Lucille Watson
Arleen Whelan   Cara Williams   Esther Williams
Jane Withers   Cora Witherspoon   Natalie Wood
Teresa Wright

NOTES

INTRODUCTION (PAGES 1–15)

1. Christopher Anderson, *Hollywood TV: The Studio System in the Fifties* (Austin: University of Texas Press, 1994); Tino Balio, *Hollywood in the Age of Television* (Cambridge: Unwin Hyman, 1990); William Boddy, *Fifties Television* (Urbana: University of Illinois Press, 1990); Michele Hilmes, *Hollywood and Broadcasting: From Radio to Cable* (Urbana: University of Illinois Press, 1990).

2. John Langer, "Television's 'Personality System,'" *Media, Culture and Society* 4 (October 1981): 351–365; Jimmie Reeves, "Television Stardom: A Ritual of Social Typification and Individualization," in *Media, Myths and Narratives*, ed. James W. Carey (Newbury Park, Calif.: Sage Publications, 1988): 146–160; Richard Dyer, *Heavenly Bodies: Film Stars and Society* (London: MacMillan, 1986), 1–18; John Ellis, *Visible Fictions* (Boston: Routledge and Kegan Paul, 1982), 97–98.

3. Paul McDonald, *The Star System: Hollywood's Production of Popular Identities* (London: Wallflower Publishing, 2000), 2–14.

4. Susan Murray, "'Hitch Your Antenna to the Stars!' Early Television and the Renegotiation of Broadcast Stardom" (Ph.D. diss., University of Texas, 1999), 15.

5. Susan Murray, *'Hitch Your Antenna to the Stars!' Early Television and Broadcast Stardom* (New York: Routledge, 2005), 25–26.

6. Denise Mann, "The Spectacularization of Everyday Life," in *Private Screenings*, ed. Lynn Spigel and Denise Mann (Minneapolis: University of Minnesota Press, 1992), 41–69.

7. Diane Negra, "'Re-Made for Television: Hedy Lamarr's post-war star textuality," in *Small Screen, Big Ideas: Television in the 1950s*, ed. Janet Thumim (London: I. B. Tauris, 2002), 105–177; Mary Desjardins, "Maureen O'Hara's 'Confidential' Life: Recycling stars through gossip and moral biography," in Thumim, 118–130; Mary Desjardins, "'Marion Never Looked Lovelier': Hedda Hopper's Hollywood and the Negotiation of Glamour in Post-War Hollywood," *Quarterly Review of Film and Video* 16 (1999): 421–437.

8. Samantha Barbas, *Movie Crazy: Fans, Stars, and The Cult of Celebrity* (New York: Palgrave, 2001), 59.

9. Joshua Gamson, "The Assembly Line of Greatness: Celebrity in Twentieth-Century America," in *Popular Culture: Production and Consumption*, ed. C. Lee Harrington and Denise D. Bielby (Oxford: Blackwell, 2001), 269.

10. My methodology for identifying established Hollywood actors and the TV shows on which they appeared was as follows: my designation of an actor or actress as established in Hollywood relied on the information given in *Halliwell's Filmgoer's Companion* 11th ed. (New York: HarperCollins, 1995) and Ephraim Katz's *The Film Encyclopedia*, 2nd ed. (New York: HarperCollins, 1994). Based on the information contained there, if the actor had appeared as a leading player, character actor, or

second player in at least five films prior to an initial appearance on television in the 1950s, I considered him an established Hollywood actor. To determine TV appearances, I consulted the two volumes of *The Complete Actors TV Credits, 1948–1988* (Metuchen, N.J.: Scarecrow Press, 1990), which lists the actors who appeared on television during that period and the series and/or episodes on which they appeared. Initially going page by page through these volumes, I identified the names of established Hollywood actors who had appeared on television in at least one episode in the period from 1948 to 1961. For those names left out of *The Complete Actors TV Credits,* I relied on scanning the indexes of *Total Television,* 3rd ed. (New York: Penguin Books, 1991) and *The Complete Directory to Prime Time Network and Cable TV Shows, 1946–Present,* 6th ed. (New York: Ballantine Books, 1995), as well as the listings in *Television Drama Series Programming: A Comprehensive Chronicle* (Metuchen, N.J.: Scarecrow Press, 1992).

11. Cleveland Amory, transcript of interview with William Crawford (c. 1984), Faye Emerson Collection, Wisconsin Center for Film and Theater Research.

12. Boddy, *Fifties Television,* 8.

1. THE PRODUCTION OF NEW CAREERS (PAGES 16–68)

1. Thomas Schatz, *Boom and Bust: American Cinema in the 1940s* (Berkeley and Los Angeles: University of California Press, 1997); Peter Lev, *The Fifties: Transforming the Screen, 1950–59* (Berkeley and Los Angeles: University of California Press, 2003); Tino Balio, ed., *The American Film Industry,* 2nd ed. (Madison, Wis.: University of Wisconsin Press, 1985); Christopher H. Sterling and John M. Kittross, *Stay Tuned: A Concise History of American Broadcasting* (Belmont, Calif.: Wadsworth Publishing, 1990).

2. Thomas Harris, "The Building of Popular Images: Grace Kelly and Marilyn Monroe," in *Stardom: Industry of Desire,* ed. Christine Gledhill (London: Routledge, 1991), 40.

3. Cathy Klaprat, "The Star as Market Strategy: Bette Davis in Another Light," in Balio, *American Film Industry,* 351–376.

4. Douglas Gomery, *Shared Pleasures: A History of Movie Presentation in the United States* (Madison, Wis.: University of Wisconsin Press, 1992), 83–88; Kristin Thompson and David Bordwell, *Film History,* 2nd ed. (New York: McGraw-Hill, 2003), 328.

5. Janet Staiger, "The Package-Unit System: Unit Management After 1955," in *The Classical Hollywood Cinema: Film Style and Mode of Production to 1960,* ed. David Bordwell, Janet Staiger, and Kristin Thompson (New York: Columbia University Press, 1985), 330–337; Schatz, *Boom and Bust,* 463; Lev, *The Fifties,* 303; Paul Monaco, *The Sixties: 1960–69* (Berkeley and Los Angeles: University of California Press, 2001), 269.

6. Balio, *American Film Industry,* 402; Jane M. Gaines, *Contested Culture: The Image, the Voice, and the Law* (Chapel Hill: University of North Carolina Press, 1991), 150–152.

7. Blyth qtd. in Jack Holland, "What are a Newcomer's Chances in HW?" *Screenland,* May 1948, 43. The challenges that certain postwar stars experienced while going through scandals without the safety net of the studio system's publicity machinery are explored in numerous essays in Adrienne L. McLean and David A. Cook, *Headline Hollywood: A Century of Film Scandal* (New Brunswick, N.J.: Rutgers University Press, 2001).

8. Mickey Rooney, "Where Did the Loot Go?" *Cosmopolitan,* March 1966, 88.

9. Mary Astor, *A Life on Film* (New York: Delacorte Press, 1971), 194.

10. Michele Hilmes, *Hollywood and Broadcasting: From Radio to Cable* (Urbana: University of Illinois Press, 1990), 55–61; Richard B. Jewell, "Hollywood and Radio: Competition and Partnership in the 1930s," *Historical Journal of Film, Radio, and Television* 4, no. 2 (1984): 125–141.

11. Susan Murray, *"Hitch Your Antenna to the Stars!" Early Television and Broadcast Stardom* (New York: Routledge, 2005), 21; Andrews qtd. in Hal Humphrey, "TV is Like Working in a Store, Says Dana," *LA Mirror,* May 29, 1957. For future reference, all Humphrey articles referenced in this book were obtained from the Hal Humphrey Collection, Cinema-TV Library, University of Southern California.

12. Review of "The Thin Line," *The Star and the Story, Daily Variety,* June 21, 1954; unless otherwise noted, all program reviews from *Variety* were obtained from the multivolume compilation of reviews, *Variety Television Reviews, 1923–1988* (New York: Garland, 1989–91). Young qtd. in Jeff Kisseloff, *The Box: An Oral History of Television, 1920–1961* (New York: Penguin Books, 1995), 337; Bogart qtd. in "TV— Haven For Has-Beens?" *TV Guide,* July 24–30, 1954, 23; Max Wilk, *The Golden Age of Television* (New York: Delacorte Press, 1976), 119; Reeves qtd. in Tim Purtell, "The Death of a Superhero," *Entertainment Weekly,* June 13, 1997, 80.

13. Heflin qtd. in "Recruits From Hollywood," *Time,* October 5, 1953, http://www .time.com/time/archive; R. D. Heldenfels, *TV's Greatest Year: 1954* (New York: Continuum, 1994), 157; Fonda qtd. in Stan Optkowsky, *TV: The Big Picture* (New York: Dutton, 1961), 107.

14. Keenan Wynn, as told to James Brough, *Ed Wynn's Son* (Garden City, N.Y.: Doubleday, 1959), 225; "Coast-to-Coast Relay May Be Impetus to Studio and Stars Plunging into TV," *Variety,* January 24, 1951, 16; Wanger qtd. in Harriet Van Horne, "Some Actors Like Television," *Theatre Arts,* July 1952, 90.

15. "Fear that Film Stars May Flub TV Stunts Also Figures in Studio Bans," *Variety,* December 2, 1950, 2; Vernon Scott, "Joan to Make TV Comedienne Debut," *Hollywood Citizen-News,* October 11, 1958; Rahna Maugham, "Television Tremens," *Silver Screen,* March 1948, 29.

16. Hal Kanter, *An Oral History with Hal Kanter* (Beverly Hills, Calif.: Academy of Motion Picture Arts and Sciences, Oral History Program, 1996), 135; "TV's Bread and Butter Girl: It's the Randy Stuarts Who Keep the Camera Rolling," *TV Guide,* February 26–March 4, 1954, 10.

17. Hal Humphrey, "What's My Name," *LA Mirror,* August 12, 1961; Hal Humphrey, "TV, the Great Rejuvenator," *LA Mirror,* September 9, 1954; Val Adams, *New York Times,* March 1, 1956, 18; Hal Humphrey, "The Duffs Aren't Doing it for Junior," *LA Mirror,* May 24, 1957.

18. D. Jenkins, "June Allyson's Glamor Treatment for Her New Series," *TV Guide,* October 3–9, 1959, 9–13; "Dan Duryea," *TV,* January 1955, 61; Alyce Canfield, "They Shocked Hollywood," *TV Revue,* May 1954, 24–29.

19. "Web Execs See Top Pic Stars Making Break Into Video by Next Fall," *Variety,* February 20, 1952, 37; Ryan qtd. in Hank Grant, *Hollywood Reporter,* January 4, 1963, Robert Ryan clipping file, Margaret Herrick Library, Academy of Motion Pictures Arts and Sciences.

20. Ronald L. Davis, *Arlene Dahl: Reminiscences* (Sanford, N.C.: Microfilming Corp. of America, 1978), 25–26.

21. "Tele Follow-Up Comment," *Variety,* January 14, 1953; James Baughman, "Nice Guys Last Fifteen Seasons," *Film and History* 30, no. 2 (2000): 29–40.

22. Fellows qtd. in Hal Humphrey, *LA Mirror,* May 6, 1953; "Tele Follow-Up Comment," *Variety* August 24, 1955.

23. "'Toast of Town' Deals with 20th, M-G," *Variety,* March 11, 1953, 4; Sullivan qtd. in "50% of 'Toast' Fans Burn at Loss of 'Live' Talent; Sullivan Drops Pix," *Variety,* June 24, 1953, 1; "TV—Just a Big Trailer Camp," *Variety,* July 13, 1955, 25; "TV Wants Film Stars in Person," *Variety,* October 21, 1953, 2.

24. Sinatra qtd. in "Sinatra Says SAG Should Clamp Down on Those Cuffo TV Shots," *Variety,* April 20, 1955, 31; "Cuffo Interviews On Com'l Telepix Banned by SAG," *Variety,* April 27, 1955, 26.

25. Derek Kompare, *Rerun Nation: How Repeats Invented American Television* (New York: Routledge, 2005), 44–46; Hilmes, *Hollywood and Broadcasting,* 156–167; Verna Scott, "Dick Powell Warbles Again," *Hollywood Citizen-News,* November 23, 1957, Dick Powell clipping file, Herrick Library.

26. Hilmes, *Hollywood and Broadcasting,* 152–56; Christopher Anderson, *Hollywood TV: The Studio System in the Fifties* (Austin: University of Texas Press, 1994).

27. "WB and RKO, Last Major Film Holdouts, to be 'Toasted' by Sullivan," *Variety,* April 8, 1953, 1; *Broadcasting,* May 18, 1953, 38; Fonda qtd. in Jack Holland, "Henry Fonda Speaks His Mind," *TV-Radio Life,* August 27, 1954, 40; Thomas M. Pryor, "Film Star Traffic to Increase," *New York Times,* December 25, 1954, 7; Betty Hutton as told to Carl Bruno, telephone interview with author, October 23, 2005; Young qtd. in "Loretta Young in Ham, Pure Ham," *TV Guide,* October 19–25, 1957, 18.

28. "TV Film Employment: It's Going Up From Coast to Coast, Screen Actors Report," *Broadcasting,* December 13, 1954, 44.

29. Manulis qtd. in Kisseloff, *The Box,* 262.

30. "Stars in Your Eyes: Whole Constellations Gleam in TV Dramas This Season," *TV Guide,* November 6–12, 1954, 11; William K. Hawes, Jr., "A History of Anthology Television Drama Through 1958" (Ph.D. diss., University of Michigan, 1960), 231; Eric Barnouw, *The Image Empire: A History of Broadcasting in the United States From 1953* (New York: Oxford University Press, 1970), 7; Powell qtd. in "Better-Written Scripts Attracting Top Stars into Vidpix," *Daily Variety,* May 6, 1955, Dick Powell clipping file, Herrick Library.

31. "H'Wood Vidpic Edge—Top Stars," *Variety*, July 9, 1952, 21–22; *Television Digest*, June 22, 1957, 7; Coyne Steven Sanders and Tom Gilbert, *Desilu: The Story of Lucille Ball and Desi Arnaz* (New York: Morrow, 1993), 95–101.

32. Ommerle qtd. in B. Stahl, "Studio One Goes West," *TV Guide*, December 28–January 3, 1957, 5; George Rosen, "Decline and Fall of the East," *Variety*, October 16, 1957, 25.

33. "Weaver Scans the Way Ahead," *Broadcasting*, February 28, 1955, 42; NBC publicity qtd. in Kenneth Michael Mashon, "NBC, J. Walter Thompson, and the Evolution of Prime-Time Television Programming and Sponsorship, 1946–1958" (Ph.D. diss., University of Maryland, 1996), 196; "Film Stars' 'Love That TV,'" *Variety*, March 2, 1955, 25. For comparison, the average one-hour drama in 1955 had a budget of $55,900, according to "Network TV Costs," *Sponsor*, September 5, 1955, 49; "Spectaculars Mean New Horizons," *TV Guide*, August 28–September 3, 1954, 5–7.

34. Thomas DeLong, *Quiz Craze: America's Infatuation with Game Shows* (New York: Praeger, 1991), 168, 176; Jack Gould, "Superfluous Plugs," *New York Times*, March 4, 1956, II: 9.

35. "Sometimes You Think You're in the Middle of a Movie," *Washington Post*, November 15, 1953, http://www.proquest.com; George Rosen, "Pix Holdouts on TV— No More," *Variety*, June 13, 1956, 3.

36. "War of Two Worlds: TV and Movie Stars Battle for Dramatic Parts," *TV Guide*, March 12–18, 1954, 5.

37. Fortune qtd. in Frank Rose, *The Agency: William Morris and the Hidden History of Show Business* (New York: HarperCollins, 1995), 69; ibid., 218.

38. Anderson, *Hollywood TV*, 262; Rose, *The Agency*, 88; Dennis McDougal, *The Last Mogul: Lew Wasserman, MCA, and the Hidden History of Hollywood* (New York: Crown, 1998), 109.

39. "Talent Agents: what's the alternative to paying their price?," *Sponsor*, February 7, 1955, 109.

40. Stewart qtd. in Gary Fishgall, *Pieces of Time: The Life of Jimmy Stewart* (New York: Scribner, 1997), 252.

41. Holm qtd. in Val Adams, "Celeste Holm: TV Cub Reporter," *New York Times*, October 10, 1954, http://www.proquest.com.

42. Taylor qtd. in "Robert Taylor on *The Detectives*," *TV Guide*, October 10–16, 1959, 25.

43. Laurence Laurent, "Next, the Comics'll Be Doing Gobel Impressions," *Washington Post*, November 30, 1954, http://www.proquest.com.

44. Rooney qtd. in Dan Jenkins, "Mickey Rooney Has Come of Age," *TV Guide*, May 11, 1957, 10.

45. Thomas McNultey, *Errol Flynn: The Life and Career* (Jefferson, N.C.: McFarland, 2004), 262; Allen qtd. in McNulty, 276; review of "The Red Skelton Show," *Daily Variety*, October 1, 1959.

46. Hal Erickson, *Syndicated Television: The First 40 Years, 1947–87* (Jefferson, N.C.: McFarland, 1989), 67.

47. Astor, *Life on Film,* 204.

48. Linda J. Alexander, telephone interview with author, June 12, 2007.

49. Anderson, *Hollywood TV,* 57–68.

50. Tony Thomas, *The Dick Powell Story* (Burbank, Calif.: Riverwood Press, 1992), 15. Soon-to-be Four Star partner David Niven jokingly said of McCrea, "He was too rich or busy or something." See Cecil Smith, "Film Stars Take Over TV Show," *Los Angeles Times,* March 27, 1955, http://www.proquest.com; "Joel McCrea Signed for 4-Star Series," *Variety,* August 6, 1952, 21; Bud Goode, "Four Star Triple Threat," *Radio-TV Mirror,* May 1955, 74.

51. "Four Star Playhouse," *TV-Radio Life,* December 10, 1954, 4; Niven qtd. in D. Jenkins, "David Niven Balks at Live TV," *TV Guide,* February 22–28, 1958, 23; for claims of the stars' production control, see articles such as Smith, "Film Stars"; "David Niven, Rogue," *TV Guide,* October 10–16, 1964, 17; "Four Star Playhouse," *TV-Radio Life,* December 10, 1954, 3–5; Lloyd Shearer, "Hollywood's Three Wise Men," *Detroit Free Press,* March 15, 1959, 22.

52. David Niven, *The Moon's a Balloon* (London: Hamish Hamilton, 1971), 287.

53. Goode, "Four Star Triple Threat," 74; "4 Star Playhouse's Hiatus; Stars Busy," *Variety,* October 19, 1955, 31; *Variety,* September 7, 1955, 38.

54. John Crosby, "Says You Ought to Catch This Prize-Winning Drama," *Washington Post,* March 24, 1954, 43; Hal Humphrey, "Dick Powell Isn't Retiring, But Just Relaxing His Stomach a Bit," *LA Mirror,* October 5, 1960.

55. McDougal, *Last Mogul,* 229–230; Anderson, *Hollywood TV,* 260. Under antitrust pressure, MCA dissolved its talent agency in 1962.

56. Thomas, *Dick Powell Story,* 15. See also Bill Davidson, "Dick Powell, Part II," *TV Guide,* March 31–April 6, 1962, 25.

57. Powell qtd. in Hal Humphrey, "Powell Knows How to Duck," *LA Mirror,* December 15, 1951; Bill Davidson, "Dick Powell, Part I" *TV Guide,* March 24–30, 1962, 9; Powell qtd. in Hal Humphrey, "Assortment of Televiews," *LA Mirror,* February 20, 1953, 69; "Powell Plans Vidpix Exit," *Variety,* November 10, 1954, 47; "If 'Conqueror' Clicks, Powell Will Kiss-Off TV," *Daily Variety,* October 1, 1957). Sadly, a large number of *The Conqueror*'s cast and crew were later stricken with cancer, including Powell and stars John Wayne, Susan Hayward, and Agnes Moorehead. The location shoot at a former atomic bomb testing site in Utah has been blamed for these illnesses.

58. Burt Rosen, telephone interview with author, June 29, 2000; Mark Alvey, "Dick Powell," in *The Encyclopedia of Television,* 2nd ed., ed. Horace Newcomb (New York: Fitzroy Dearborn, 2004), 1803.

59. Sheridan Morley, *The Other Side of the Moon: The Life of David Niven* (London: Weidenfeld and Nicolson, 1985), 182–183; Niven qtd. in Cecil Smith, "Niven's Series May Be a Sparkler on a Dusty Menu," *Los Angeles Times,* April 12, 1959, G5.

60. Niven qtd. in Cecil Smith, "Film Stars Take Over TV Show," *Los Angeles Times,* March 27, 1955, IV:4.

61. David Niven, "An Englishman Gives Up Tea and Duchesses!" unidentified and undated periodical, David Niven clipping file, Wisconsin Center for Film and Theater Research (emphasis in original).

62. Smith, "Niven's Series."

63. Bacall qtd. in Morley, *Other Side of the Moon*, 183.

64. "Ten to Tune In," *Newsweek*, May 16, 1960, 76; "Four Star's Gross Net Up for 1960," *Variety*, November 30, 1960, 26; "Four Star Ties Revue for Volume," *Television Digest*, May 30, 1960, 11; Lyn Tornabene, "June Allyson and Dick Powell," *Cosmopolitan*, January 1961, 11; "Stockpile of Danny Thomas Segs, 'Real McCoys' Sold to Four Star," *Variety*, August 30, 1961, 27.

65. Mark Alvey, "The Independents: Rethinking the Television Studio System," in *Television: The Critical View*, 6th ed., ed. Horace Newcomb (New York: Oxford University Press, 2000), 34–51; Burt Rosen (see note 58); June Allyson, *June Allyson* (New York: Putnam, 1982), 230; Boyer qtd. in Digby Diehl, "Q&A: Charles Boyer," *Los Angeles Times*, September 24, 1972, N18. In 1967, a group of investors bought Four Star Productions and sustained it mainly as a syndication distributor, with only a handful of shows and features under subsequent production.

66. "Dick Powell Estate," *New York Times*, January 11, 1963, 5:2.

67. Susan Hayward, *Key Concepts in Cinema Studies* (New York: Routledge, 1996), 340.

68. MCA representative qtd. in Dan Moldea, *Dark Victory: Ronald Reagan, MCA and the Mob* (New York: Viking, 1986), 150; producer qtd. in Dwight Whitney, "Bette Davis Serves Notice," *TV Guide*, May 31–June 6, 1958, 18; "Is Hollywood Doomed?" *Radio Stars and Television*, January 1949, 26.

2. FAYE EMERSON AND THE EARLY TELEVISION PERSONALITY (PAGES 69–104)

1. Susan Murray, *Hitch Your Antenna to the Stars* (New York: Routledge, 2005), 129–130, 132; Leo Bogart, *The Age of Television*, 3rd ed. (New York: Ungar, 1972), 31.

2. Murray, *Hitch Your Antenna*, 117–137; quote, 121 (emphasis in original).

3. Ibid, 67.

4. "Personality," *Time*, December 31, 1951, http://www.time.com/time/archive; Stefan Kanfer, ed., *The Essential Groucho* (New York: Vintage Books, 2000), 209.

5. Lynn Spigel, *Make Room for TV: Television and the Family Ideal in Postwar America* (Chicago: University of Chicago Press, 1992), 84.

6. Harry Conover, "Glamour is the Bunk!" *Radio Stars and Television*, January 1949, 46–47; Anonymous, "Is Hollywood Doomed?," *Radio Stars and Television*, January 1949, 29; Harry Conover, "TV's Cover Girl," *Variety*, January 4, 1950, 113.

7. "The Quick Queen of Television," *Newsweek*, July 19, 1954, 50.

8. Lola Clare Bratten, "Nothing Could Be Finah: The Dinah Shore Chevy Show," in *Small Screens, Big Ideas: Television in the 1950s*, ed. Janet Thumim (London: I. B. Tauris, 2002), 98, 100.

9. Banner and Asher qtd. in "Dinah Shore—An Exception," *TV Guide Roundup*, ed. Editors of *TV Guide* (New York: Holt, Rinehart and Winston, 1960), 44; Pete Martin, "I Call On Dinah Shore," *Saturday Evening Post*, October 19, 1957, http://ejournals.ebsco.com.

10. Mimi White and Marsha Cassidy, "Innovating Women's Television in Local and National Networks: Ruth Lyons and Arlene Francis," *Camera Obscura* 17, no. 3 (2002): 41, 52; "The Quick Queen of Television," 50.

11. Marsha Cassidy, *What Women Watched: Daytime Television in the 1950s* (Austin: University of Texas Press, 2005), 145–146.

12. Arlene Francis, *Arlene Francis: A Memoir* (New York: Simon and Schuster, 1978), 198.

13. William Crawford, Faye Emerson biography draft (c. 1984), located in the Faye Emerson Collection, Wisconsin Historical Society (WHS).

14. Pressbooks for *Find the Blackmailer* and *Secret Enemies*, "The Pressbooks for United Artists, 1919–1949; Warner Bros., 1922–1949; and Monogram Pictures, 1937–1946," Primary Source Microfilm, 2001, WHS.

15. Pressbooks for *The Very Thought of You, Hotel Berlin,* and *Uncertain Glory;* Jerry Asher, "Fabulous Fayezie!" unidentified and undated periodical, Faye Emerson clipping file, Wisconsin Center for Film and Theater Research (WCFTR); "Quiet Life, Aim of Faye Emerson," *Los Angeles Times,* October 7, 1945, B1.

16. "Faye Emerson Quits Films to be With Elliott," *Los Angeles Times,* March 4, 1946, 2; Crawford, Faye Emerson biography draft; Sam Zolotow, "'Play's The Thing' at Booth Tonight," *New York Times,* April 28, 1948, 31.

17. Crawford, Faye Emerson biography draft.

18. "Not Too Heavy," *Time,* April 24, 1950, 57.

19. Fred Wayfield, "Faye Emerson Fills Saturday Night with 'Wonderful Town,'" *New York Compass,* June 18, 1951, Emerson Clipping File, WCFTR.

20. Hal Humphrey, "Some Have It, Some Don't," *LA Mirror,* June 25, 1951; Joan King Flynn, "How Faye Emerson got into Television," unidentified and undated periodical, Emerson Clipping File, WCFTR; Val Adams, "Glamor Girl of the Television Screen," *New York Times,* February 19, 1950, 11; Debs Myers, "Faye Emerson," *Cosmopolitan,* August 1950, 34.

21. Pete Martin, "The Blonde Bombshell," *Saturday Evening Post,* June 30, 1951, Emerson Clipping File, WCFTR; Adams, "Glamor Girl of the Television Screen;" Jimmy Durante, "Faye Emerson's Got Glamor," *TV Screen,* August 1951, Emerson Clipping File, WCFTR; Harris, "Young Lady in a Hurry," *Look,* August 15, 1950, 74.

22. Faye Emerson, "Just Be Natural," *Movie Stars Parade,* July 1950, 77; Harriet Van Horne, "Faye Sketches Boston's Broad A-ppeal In First of TV's 'Wonderful Town' Series," *New York World Telegram and Sun,* June 18, 1951, Emerson Clipping File, WCFTR; Harris, "Young Lady in a Hurry," 74; Myers, "Faye Emerson," 109; Judith Cortada, "Closeup of a Star . . . Faye Emerson," *Radio Best,* October 1950, 11–13, 63–64; Nathalie Fredrik, "Faye Emerson's Recipe for Happiness," *TV Show,* May 1951, 42; Sonia Stein, "Faye Has Lots of the Denim-Type Virtues," *Washington Post,* August 17, 1952, L1.

23. John Crosby, *New York Herald Tribune,* January 23, 1950, n.p., Emerson Collection; Earl Wilson, untitled, unidentified periodical, September 15, 1952, Emerson Collection.

24. "Not Too Heavy," 56; "Tele's 'Let's Keep it Clean,'" *Variety,* March 29, 1950, 33.

25. Bert Briller, "TV Code Has Upped Necklines, But Long Plugs, Beer Blurbs, Violence, Race Carbons Still Pose Problems," *Variety*, December 31, 1952, 20; Skitch Henderson, personal interview with author, New York City, New York, October 14, 1999.

26. John Crosby, transcript of interview with William Crawford, c. 1984, n.p., Emerson Collection; Harriet Van Horne, audiotaped interview with William Crawford, February 24, 1984, Emerson Collection; Henderson, personal interview.

27. Christopher H. Sterling and John M. Kittross, *Stay Tuned: A Concise History of American Broadcasting* (Belmont, Calif.: Wadsworth Publishing, 1990), 324; Rex Reed, audiotaped interview with William Crawford, c. 1984, Emerson Collection.

28. Eleanor Harris, "Young Lady in a Hurry," 74; Myers, "Faye Emerson," 109; American Hair Design Institute press release, March 5, 1952, n.p., Emerson Collection; Karal Ann Marling, *As Seen on TV: The Visual Culture of Everyday Life in the 1950s* (Cambridge, Mass.: Harvard University Press, 1994), 28.

29. Untitled articles in unidentified periodicals, Emerson Collection; *Guilty Bystander* contract, located in Emerson Collection; Henderson, personal interview.

30. Untitled article in unidentified periodical, Emerson Collection. See also Pete Martin, "The Blonde Bombshell;" Cleveland Amory, transcript of interview with William Crawford, c. 1984, Emerson Collection; Val Adams, "Glamor Girl of the Television Screen," 11.

31. Skitch Henderson; "Weekly Program Costs," *Variety*, November 15, 1950, 35, and "Weekly Program Costs," *Variety*, November 14, 1951, 26.

32. Fred Rayfield, "Faye Emerson Fills Saturday Night with 'Wonderful Town,'" *New York Compass*, June 18, 1951; Janet Kern, "Fine Job as 'Author' Moderator Booms Faye Emerson's Stock," *Chicago Herald American*, February 3, 1952, Emerson Clipping File, WCFTR.

33. Shayon qtd. in Cary O'Dell, *Woman Pioneers in Television: Biographies of Fifteen Industry Leaders* (Jefferson, N.C.: McFarland, 1997), 88.

34. "What Happened to the V?" *TV Forecast*, November 17, 1951, Emerson Clipping File, WCFTR; Stein, "Faye Has Lots of the Denim-Type Virtues;" Kern, "Fine Job."

35. "Faye's Pepsi Fade; May Give Up Time," *Variety*, April 9, 1952, 45; "Faye, Robert Q. Rating Causalities?" *Variety*, October 3, 1951, 29.

36. "Pepsi-Emerson Tie Balks CBS-TV Big Sat. Night Plans," *Variety*, November 28, 1951, 24; Stein, "Faye Has Lots of the Denim-Type Virtues;" "Ponder Fall Status of Emerson Show," *Variety*, August 15, 1951, 25.

37. *Radio and Television Life*, March 21, 1953, n.p., Emerson Collection; *Cincinnati Enquirer*, July 25, 1952, n.p., Emerson Collection; "Faye Emerson to Hostess Pepsi Show," *Variety*, May 13, 1953, 20; Maggie Newhouse, audiotaped interview with William Crawford, c. 1984, Emerson Collection.

38. Henderson, personal interview. Many press accounts and interviews back up Skitch Henderson's personal account that Emerson's "rage was unbound" and that this, combined with alcoholism, hindered her career. See Faye Emerson, autobiography notes, Emerson Collection; Jean Andrews, audiotaped interview with William Crawford, c. 1984, Emerson Collection; Pete Martin, "The Blonde Bombshell."

NOTES

39. Untitled article, *Valley Times*, June 30, 1953, n.p., Emerson Collection; Hal Humphrey, "TV is No Maker of Stars," *Los Angeles Mirror*, January 15, 1953; *Gotham Guide*, February 19, 1955, n.p.; untitled article, *TV Star Parade*, December 1956, Emerson Collection; Doris Lilly, audiotaped interview with William Crawford, c. 1984, Emerson Collection.

40. John Lester, "Faye Emerson Will Moderate 'Women' Show," *Long Island Press*, May 8, 1956, Emerson Clipping File, WCFTR.

41. Kenneth Michael Mashon, "NBC, J. Walter Thompson, and the Evolution of Prime-Time Television Programming and Sponsorship, 1946–1958" (Ph.D. diss., University of Maryland, 1996), 174–175; Jay Nelson Tuck, "On the Air," *New York Post*, April 18, 1957, Emerson Clipping File, WCFTR. For more on the gendered split between daytime and prime time, see Michele Hilmes, *Radio Voices: American Broadcasting, 1922–1952* (Minneapolis: University of Minnesota Press, 1997), and for an extensive discussion of the role of both female and male hosts in daytime television, see Cassidy, *What Women Watched*.

42. Faye Emerson, untitled column manuscript, n.p., Emerson Collection. While Emerson had an earlier gossip column that was ghostwritten, these later articles were indeed written by her, as confirmed by Emerson's personal files located in the Emerson Collection, which contain handwritten versions of the articles that nearly match the final published versions.

43. Supposedly, Emerson's public displays of intelligence were also behind her 1950 divorce from Elliot Roosevelt. Gossip columns even pinpointed a television appearance that represented the beginning of the end of their relationship. During a December 18, 1948, appearance on the NBC quiz show *Who Said That?* Emerson guest-starred on the program with her husband and handily answered question after question as he merely watched in stony silence. The final indignity for Roosevelt came when he was unable to identify a quote from his own book on his father, and Emerson quickly chimed in with the answer. The publicity that followed the event revealed her earnest attempts to defend her husband; she was quoted as telling one reporter, "He's busy and I have plenty of time to read the papers." But the couple separated and ultimately divorced in 1950, with Emerson explaining, "I was bad for his ego." See Martin, "The Blonde Bombshell;" Flynn, "How Faye Emerson got into Television." Dichter qtd. in C. Robert Jennings, "Quiz Shows: The Woman Question," *New York Times Magazine*, February 9, 1958, 16, 65.

44. Adams, "Glamor Girl of the Television Screen," 11; Myers, "Faye Emerson," 37.

45. Emerson qtd. in Myers, "Faye Emerson," 37.

46. Henderson, personal interview; Rita Morley Harvey, *Those Wonderful, Terrible Years: George Heller and the American Federation of Television and Radio Artists* (Carbondale: Southern Illinois University Press, 1996), 180–191; Crawford, Faye Emerson biography draft.

47. Mitch Erickson, audiotape interview with William Crawford, March 7, 1984; "Faye Emerson: Happy Anonymity," *New York Post*, August 25, 1963; anonymous letter to the editor, *New York Journal-American* (January 8, 1957). Each item from the Emerson Collection.

48. Dane Harris, "Faye Emerson Pleads for More Women in Television," *Atlanta Journal,* October 29, 1957, Emerson Collection; Charles S. Aaronson, "In Our View," *Motion Picture Daily,* May 21, 1956, Emerson Collection.

49. Garry Moore, audiotape interview with William Crawford, March 8, 1984, Emerson Collection.

50. "If Faye Emerson Were President," *TV Guide,* June 3–9, 1950, 9, 12.

51. Dennis Patrick, audiotape interview with William Crawford, c. 1984, Emerson Collection; Faye Emerson, "Eggheads Make the Best Lovers." *Esquire,* November 1957, 66.

52. Gil Cates, audiotaped interview with William Crawford, c. 1984, Emerson Collection; "Faye Emerson: Happy Anonymity," *New York Post,* August 25, 1963. Photographs in subsequent *National Inquirer* "Where Are They Now" reports from the 1970s and 1980s indicate that she did exactly as she said she would, growing her grey hair out fully and putting on considerable weight.

53. Garrick Utley, audiotaped interview with William Crawford, c. 1984, Emerson Collection.

54. Amory, interview with William Crawford.

3. THE STAR AND THE STORY (PAGES 105–145)

1. Cotten qtd. in Bib Thomas, "Joseph Cotten's Toughest TV Role is Playing a Guy Named Joseph Cotten," *Chicago Tribune,* May 19, 1956, D5. The original quote used the British variant of clue: "clew."

2. William Boddy, *Fifties Television: The Industry and Its Critics* (Urbana: University of Illinois Press, 1990), 85; Jack Gould, "A Plea for Live Video," *New York Times,* December 7, 1952, http://www.proquest.com; Jack Gould, "Radio and Television," *New York Times,* June 30, 1952, http://www.proquest.com.

3. "Death of the Salesmen," *Time,* January 31, 1955, http://www.time.com/time /archive; Michele Hilmes, *Radio Voices: American Broadcasting, 1922–1952* (Minneapolis: University of Minnesota Press, 1997), 214–218; Cotton qtd. in "The Hosts: Open House on TV," *TV Guide,* February 4–10, 1956, 21.

4. Kruger qtd. in "The Hosts: Open House on TV;" Hal Humphrey, "Assortment of Televiews," *LA Mirror,* February 20, 1953; review of "Double Exposure," *Variety,* August 20, 1952; Wes D. Gehring, *Irene Dunne: First Lady of Hollywood* (Lanham, Md.: Scarecrow, 2003), 168–176; Margie Schultz, *Irene Dunne: A Bio-Bibliography* (New York: Greenwood, 1991), 18–24, 152–169.

5. Review of "To Each His Own," *Daily Variety,* August 27, 1954; review of "The Mansion," *Daily Variety,* October 13, 1954; Kevin Sweeney, *James Mason: A Bio-Bibliography* (Westport, Conn.: Greenwood, 1999), 22–29, 202–205; Sheridan Morley, *James Mason: Odd Man Out* (New York: Harper and Row, 1989), 96–116.

6. Mason qtd. in "James Mason Will Produce and Be Star in Jane Eyre," *Los Angeles Times,* October 2, 1955, http://www.proquest.com; Laurence Laurent, "10 Programs the New Year Might Be Happier Without," *Washington Post,* December 26, 1954, http://www.proquest.com; John Crosby, "He's Surprised to Find This One on the TV Cable," *Washington Post,* January 21, 1955, http://www.proquest.com; Fonda qtd. in

Cecil Smith, "Fonda Saddles Up for Bright Series," *Los Angeles Times*, August 2, 1959, http://www.proquest.com.

7. George Frazier, "Nobody Pushes Bob Around," *Colliers*, June 4, 1949; Pete Martin, "Fightin' Bob—The Hollywood Crusader," *Saturday Evening Post*, October 7, 1950; Sam Boal, "Robert Montgomery Presents," *Coronet*, September 1954; articles located in Robert Montgomery Clipping File, Herrick Library; Jeanine Basinger, "Robert Montgomery," in *International Dictionary of Films and Filmmakers*, 3rd ed. (Detroit, Mich.: St. James Press, 1997), 841. Frank Sturcken claims an anonymous source indicated that Montgomery actually had no production control over the show and that he was merely a publicity figurehead for the show. However, I can find no other sources to back up this claim. See Frank Sturcken, *Live Television: The Golden Age of 1946–58 in New York* (Jefferson, N.C.: McFarland, 1990), 56.

8. Madelyn Ritrosky-Winslow, "Transforming Stardom: Loretta Young's Journey From Film to Television" (Ph.D. diss., Indiana University, 1997), 105–130.

9. Ibid, 107.

10. Michele Hilmes, *Radio Voices*, 151–182; review of "Katy," *Daily Variety*, October 25, 1955; review of "Take Care of My Child," *Daily Variety*, November 12, 1956; review of "A Dollar's Worth," *Daily Variety*, October 22, 1957; review of "Rummage Sale," *Daily Variety*, April 16, 1957.

11. Cecil Smith, "Jane Wyman Launches Her Own TV Show," *Los Angeles Times*, August 28, 1955, Jane Wyman Clipping File, Herrick Library; James Bawden, "Jane Wyman: American Star Par Excellence," *Films in Review* (April 1975), 193–208; Lawrence J. Quirk, *Jane Wyman: The Actress and the Woman: An Illustrated Biography* (New York: Dembner Books, 1986); Edward Z. Epstein and Joseph Morella, *Jane Wyman: A Biography* (Boston: G. K. Hall, 1986).

12. Review of "The Barbara Stanwyck Show," *Daily Variety*, September 21, 1960; review of "The Tender Shoot," *Daily Variety*, October 23, 1959; Allyson qtd. in Ritrosky-Winslow, "Transforming Stardom," 137; Ritrosky-Winslow, "Transforming Stardom," 164.

13. Cecil Smith, "Shirley Temple to Open Fairytale Series Tonight," *Los Angeles Times*, January 13, 1958, http://www.proquest.com; Army Archerd, "Shirley Temple: A Selfish Mother?" *Washington Post* , September 18, 1960, http://www.proquest.com; Patsy Guy Hammontree, *Shirley Temple: A Bio-Bibliography* (Westport, Conn.: Greenwood, 1998), 141–146; "Return of the Blue Bird," *Time*, January 17, 1958, http://www.time.com /time/archive; Lester David and Irene David, *The Shirley Temple Story* (New York: Putnam, 1983), 156–158.

14. Earl B. Dunckel, "Ronald Reagan and the General Electric Theater," an oral history conducted by Gabrielle Morrison, Regional Oral History Office, The Bancroft Library, University of California, Berkeley, 1982, 3; Ronald Reagan, *Where's the Rest of Me?* (New York: Duell, Sloan and Pearce, 1965), 230–246; Dan Moldea, *Dark Victory: Ronald Reagan, MCA and the Mob* (New York: Viking, 1986), 107.

15. Stephen Vaughn, *Ronald Reagan in Hollywood* (Cambridge: Cambridge University Press, 1994), 233–236; "Ronald Reagan—Actor, Host, Public Relations Man," *TV Guide*, November 22–28, 1958, 17–18.

16. Vaughn, *Ronald Reagan*; Reagan, *Where's the Rest of Me?*; Dunckel, "Ronald Reagan," 2, 7–8.

17. Reagan qtd. in "Hey Ronnie," 17; Reagan, *Where's the Rest of Me?*; 251; Dunckel, "Ronald Reagan," 12, 30.

18. Adolphe Menjou and M. M. Musselman, *It Took Nine Tailors* (New York: Whittlesey House, 1948), 39, 179.

19. "The Pressbooks for United Artists, 1919–1949; Warner Bros., 1922–1949; and Monogram Pictures, 1937–1946," Primary Source Microfilm, 2001, Wisconsin Historical Society.

20. Ibid.

21. Menjou and Musselman, *It Took Nine Tailors*, 136, 174, 181, 215; ad located in unidentified periodical, Menjou Clipping File, Wisconsin Center for Film and Theater Research (WCFTR); Kent B. Stiles, "News From the World of Stamps," *New York Times*, mentions of Menjou found on April 17, 1949, April 29, 1949, November 25, 1956, and February 24, 1957.

22. Hal Erickson, *Syndicated Television: The First Forty Years, 1947–1987* (Jefferson, N.C.: McFarland, 1989), 67; Frederic Ziv, personal interview with author, Cincinnati, Ohio, January 15, 1999.

23. Ziv qtd. in Morleen Getz Rouse, personal notes from interview of Frederic Ziv, September 4, 1975.

24. Barbara Wilinsky, "First and Finest: British Films on U.S. Television in the Late 1940s," *The Velvet Light Trap* (Fall 1997): 21.

25. Jeff Kisseloff, *The Box: An Oral History of Television, 1920–1961* (New York: Penguin Books, 1995), 272; Ziv qtd. in Kisseloff, 285.

26. Ziv qtd. in Rouse, September 4, 1975 interview; Morleen Getz Rouse, personal notes from interview of Leon Benson, October 1, 1975; Ziv qtd. in Morleen Getz Rouse, "A History of the F. W. Ziv Radio and Television Syndication Companies: 1930–1960" (Ph.D. diss., University of Michigan, 1976), 120.

27. Jerome Lawrence and Robert Lee, memo to Harry Tattleman, dated June 11, 1948; this and subsequent memos located in Lawrence and Lee Papers, New York Public Library for the Performing Arts.

28. Review of "The Gold Bug," *Variety*, February 13, 1953; Ziv, personal interview.

29. According to *Time* magazine, Colman was guaranteed $150,000 a year. See "Open-Ended Game," *Time*, April 28, 1947, 66–67. Considering that the show had amassed $675,000 in sales by February 1950, this was a major investment in one figure. Ziv qtd. in Morleen Getz Rouse, personal notes from interview of Frederic Ziv, August 6, 1975.

30. Menjou qtd. in "Worse and Worse: Menjou Foresees Early End of US Under Current Rule," *Los Angeles Times*, April 4, 1952, B1; Stanley Kramer with Thomas M. Coffey, *A Mad, Mad, Mad, Mad World: A Life in Hollywood* (New York: Harcourt Brace, 1997), 97.

31. Bob Lee, memo to Jerome Lawrence, May 1, 1952; Menjou qtd. in "Menjou Says Anti-Reds Can't Get Jobs in Pix," *Variety*, February 2, 1952; Adolphe Menjou, personal letter to J. Edgar Hoover, July 23, 1956. Letter received in response to an FBI Freedom of Information Act inquiry.

32. Jerome Lawrence and Robert Lee, memo to John Sinn, April 25, 1952; emphasis in original.

33. Jerome Lawrence and Robert Lee, memo to John Sinn, May 1, 1952.

34. Lawrence and Lee, May 1, 1952; Ziv interview.

35. "Cantor Pricing a Test," *Billboard*, November 27, 1954, 4.

36. All scripts are located in the Frederic Ziv Production Files, WCFTR.

37. Hilmes, *Radio Voices*, 217. There is no evidence in production files that Menjou had any other function on the show besides as a performer, and story selection generally came from Lawrence and Lee or other figures employed as writers. Production files do indicate that for the radio version, host Ronald Colman had some measure of input on which tales would be adapted and how they would be adapted, particularly for those episodes in which he would appear.

38. *TV Guide*, July 24–30, 1954, A-10 (New England edition).

39. "Favorite Story," *TV Guide*, May 21–27, 1954, 15.

40. Jack Gould, "Tolstoy Tale of Human Greed Opens NBC TV's 'Favorite Story,' but Oh, Those Commercials," *New York Times*, January 14, 1953, 37; Harriet Van Horne, *World Telegram and Sun*, January 23, 1953, Lawrence and Lee Papers.

41. Review of "Diamond Lens," *Variety*, July 17, 1953; review of "Story of Two Lives," *Variety*, July 26, 1953.

42. Review of "The Lady and the Law," *Variety*, April 17, 1954; *Broadcasting*, December 13, 1954, 39–40.

43. Erickson, *Syndicated Television*, 68.

44. Charles Mercer, "Menjou Very Proud of Target's TV Success, *Los Angeles Times*, April 1, 1958, Adolphe Menjou Clipping File, Herrick Library.

45. "Counterfeit Coin" review, *Variety*, December 18, 1958.

46. Menjou, personal letter to J. Edgar Hoover, August 19, 1960, FBI Freedom of Information Act Files.

4. STARDOM AND THE SITCOM (PAGES 146–188)

1. Judith Roof, *All About Thelma and Eve: Sidekicks and Third Wheels* (Urbana: University of Illinois Press, 2002), 20, 161.

2. Arden qtd. in Val Adams, "A Recruit Discourses on Acting," *New York Times*, September 14, 1952, sec, 10, p. 11.

3. Review of "Our Miss Brooks," *Variety*, February 15, 1956.

4. William A. Henry III, *The Great One* (New York: Doubleday, 1992); W. J. Weatherby, *Jackie Gleason* (New York: Pharos Books, 1992); David Marc, "Jackie Gleason," in *The Encyclopedia of Television*, 2nd ed., ed. Horace Newcomb (New York: Fitzroy Dearborn, 2004), 989–990. William Bendix later went on to star in a second, very successful television version of *Life of Riley* (NBC, 1953–58)

5. Susan Murray, *"Hitch Your Antenna to the Stars": Early Television and Broadcast Stardom* (New York: Routledge, 2005), 154.

6. Phil Silvers, *The Laugh is On Me: The Phil Silvers Story* (Englewood Cliffs, N.J.: Prentice-Hall, 1973), 117, 202.

7. Ibid., 203.

8. Review of "Meet Mr. McNutley," *Variety*, September 23, 1953; Jon Bruce, "It Got Its Face Lifted," *TV-Radio Life*, November 19, 1954, Ray Milland Clipping File, Herrick Library; John Crosby, "He Calls the Milland Series 'An Unqualified Disaster,'" *Washington Post*, September 30, 1953, http://www.proquest.com; Tugend qtd. in Bruce, "It Got Its Face Lifted"; Milland qtd. in "*Markham*, Ray Milland is a Cultured Private Eye," *TV Guide*, June 6–12, 1959, 11.

9. Young qtd. in Sonia Stein, "Boyer Will Soon Make With Romance on Radio," *Washington Post*, March 12, 1950, http://www.proquest.com; James Robert Parish with Gregory W. Mank, *The Hollywood Reliables* (Westport, Conn.: Arlington House Publishers, 1980), 285.

10. Jack Gould, "'Father Knows Best' is Translated to Video," *New York Times*, October 6, 1954, http://www.proquest.com; Young qtd. in *TV Guide Roundup* (New York: Holt, Rinehart and Winston, 1960), 63 (emphasis in original).

11. Eve Arden, *The Three Phases of Eve* (New York: St. Martin's, 1985), 78; Cummings qtd. in Philip K. Scheuer, "Busy Bob Cummings Finds Some Time for Campaigning," *Los Angeles Times*, April 3, 1955, http://www.proquest.com.

12. Michele Hilmes, "Femmes Boff Program Toppers: Women Break Into Prime Time, 1943–1948," in *Transmitting the Past: Historical and Cultural Perspectives on Broadcasting*, eds. Susan Brinson and J. E. Winn (Tuscaloosa: University of Alabama Press, 2005), 153.

13. Alexander Doty, "The Cabinet of Lucy Ricardo: Lucille Ball's Star Image," *Cinema Journal* 29 no. 4 (Summer 1990): 8.

14. Ibid., 10–16.

15. "Radio Comedienne," *Life*, October 1, 1945, Joan Davis Clipping File, Herrick Library; David G. Tucker, *The Women Who Made Television Funny: Ten Stars on 1950s Sitcoms* (Jefferson, N.C.: McFarland, 2007), 75–91.

16. Heather Osborne-Thompson, "Routine Adjustments: Re-viewing Women's Television Comedy Genres, 1950–1969" (Ph.D. diss., University of Southern California, 2004), 57–70, quote on p. 63.

17. Osborne-Thompson, 70–75. For a typical article detailing Davis's exhaustive work habits, see John Maynard, "TV's 2-D Gal," *Pictorial Review*, October 25, 1953, 4.

18. Jeanine Basinger, "The Lady Who Was Maisie," *Film Comment* 35, no. 6 (November–December 1999): 24–26, 30–32; Margie Schultz, *Ann Sothern: A Bio-Bibliography* (New York: Greenwood, 1990), 6–10.

19. "If You Knew Suzie . . . ," *TV Time*, c. 1953, Ann Sothern Clipping File, Herrick Library; Lisa Parks, "Watching the 'Working Gals': Fifties Sitcoms and the Repositioning of Women in Postwar American Culture," *Critical Matrix* 11, no. 2 (1999): 60.

20. "If You Knew Suzie . . ."

21. Sothern qtd. in "Don Porter's Back, and Ann Sothern's Got Him," *TV Guide*, April 16–22, 1960, 14; Sothern qtd. in Hal Humphrey, "Is Ann Sothern the Last of the TV Comediennes?" *LA Mirror*, February 18, 1960.

22. Tucker, *Women Who Made Television Funny*, 90.

23. Richard Gehman, "Indestructible Donna," *The American Weekly*, January 7, 1962, 6–7.

24. Jay Fultz, *In Search of Donna Reed* (Iowa City: University of Iowa Press, 1998), 117.

25. Val Adams, "Television in Review: Betty Hutton," *New York Times*, September 13, 1954, 31.

26. Kelcy L. Morgan, "What Makes Betty Hutton Bothered?" *Uncensored*, May 1955, 16.

27. Ben Carbonetto, telephone interview with author, October 25, 2005.

28. Bob Johnson, "Betty Hutton Rules the Roost," *TV Guide*, November 21–27, 1959, 10.

29. Judith M. Redding, *Film Fatales: Independent Women Directors* (Seattle, Wash.: Seal Press, 1997), 25, 28; Lupino qtd. in untitled newspaper article, c. 1965, Ida Lupino Clipping File, USC Cinema-TV Library; Jerry Vermilye, "Ida Lupino," *Films in Review*, May 1959, 266; Peter Bart, "Lupino, the Dynamo," *New York Times*, March 7, 1965, sec. 2, p. 7.

30. Molly Haskell, *From Reverence to Rape: The Treatment of Women in the Movies* (Chicago: University of Chicago Press, 1987), 201; Claire Johnston, "Women's Cinema as Counter-Cinema," in *Movies and Methods*, ed. Bill Nichols (Berkeley and Los Angeles: University of California Press, 1976), 1:216; Annette Kuhn, ed., *Queen of the "B"s: Ida Lupino Behind the Camera* (Westport, Conn.: Praeger, 1995).

31. Lupino qtd. in Francine Parker, "Discovering Ida Lupino" *Action* (May–June 1967), 21; Lupino qtd. in Louise Heck-Rabi, *Women Filmmakers: A Critical Reception* (Metuchen, N.J.: Scarecrow, 1984), 245. See similarly submissive comments attributed to Lupino in Freda Balling, "Where Adam is King," *Radio-TV Mirror*, August 1957, 50, 68–70, and Ida Lupino, "Me, Mother Directress," *Action*, May–June 1967, 14.

32. Mary Celeste Kearney and James Moran, "Ida Lupino as Director of Television," in Kuhn, *Queen of the "B"s*, 143.

33. Review of "Stand-In," *Variety*, July 23, 1956.

34. "Mother Lupino," *Time*, February 8, 1963, 42.

35. Robert Johnson, "*Mr. Adams and Eve* Modeled After Stars Duff and Lupino," *TV Guide*, June 1–7, 1957, 18 (emphasis in original); Hal Humphrey, " . . . And Come Out Fighting," *LA Mirror*, May 25, 1955. See also "Mr. Adams and Eve," *TV Guide*, April 20–26, 1957, 26. Numerous articles on the program insist that Lupino and Duff lugged a pair of large candlesticks from their home to the set every day.

36. Patricia Mellencamp, "Situation Comedy, Feminism, and Freud: Discourses of Lucy and Gracie," in *Feminist Television Criticism: A Reader*, ed. Julie D'Acci and Lynn Spigel (Oxford: Clarendon Press, 1997), 72–73.

37. Balling, "Where Adam is King," 50.

38. Ibid., 68; *Family Circle*, March 1958, Ida Lupino Clipping File, Herrick Library; Ally Acker, *Reel Women: Pioneers of the Cinema 1896 to Present* (New York: Continuum, 1991), 76.

39. The actual Oscar ceremony was televised live only five days after this episode aired, and it wasn't much less silly than *Mr. Adams and Eve* depicted. This was the

year that Dalton Trumbo won posing as Robert Rich, one of the nominated screen-
writers went unnamed because of the writer's past connections with the blacklist, and
Jean-Paul Sartre was nominated for best motion picture story, initially competing
against a Bowery Boys picture titled *High Society* that was mistakenly nominated by
Academy members who confused it with the Bing Crosby musical of the same name.
And while a twelve-year-old boy did not win for Best Actor, an eleven-year-old girl,
Patty McCormack, was nominated for Best Supporting Actress.

40. There were apparently rumors, which grew stronger in the wake of the quiz
show scandals, that *Person to Person*'s guests were actually coached by producers and
press agents on what sorts of answers to give, to assure that an image of a contented,
"normal" home life was presented. See Richard Bartone, "Person to Person," in *The
Encyclopedia of Television*, ed. Newcomb, 1748.

41. Dwight Whitney, "Ida Lupino, Director" *TV Guide*, October 8–14, 1966, 18;
Review of "Mr. Adams and Eve," *Variety*, January 16, 1957; "Mr. Adams and Eve," *TV
Guide*, April 20–26, 1957. A total of sixty-six episodes of the show were shot across its
run.

42. Jerry Herndon is played by Hollywood character actor Jerome Cowan, who actually appeared with Ida Lupino in *High Sierra* (1941).

5. THE STAR IN THE STORY (PAGES 189–220)

1. Richard Jewell, "Hollywood and Radio," *Historical Journal of Film, Radio and
Television* 4, no.2 (1984): 125–141.

2. Worthington J. Miner and Franklin J. Schaffner, *Worthington Miner: A Directors
Guild of America Oral History* (Metuchen, N.J.: The Directors Guild of America and
Scarecrow Press, 1985), 207; Wright qtd. in "Recruits From Hollywood," *Time*, Octo-
ber 5, 1953, http://www.time.com/time/archive.

3. Hill qtd. in Ira Skutch, ed., *The Days of Live: Television's Golden Age as Seen by
21 Directors Guild of America Members* (Lanham, Md.: The Scarecrow Press; Los Angeles: Directors Guild of America, 1998), 144.

4. Michael Munn, *Charlton Heston* (New York: St. Martin's, 1986); Heston qtd. in
Bob Thomas, "Charlton Heston Should Avoid TV, It Says Here," *Hollywood Citizen
News*, February 13, 1958, Charlton Heston Clipping File, Herrick Library.

5. Daniels qtd. in William Hawes, "A History of Anthology Television Drama
Through 1958" (Ph.D. diss., University of Michigan, 1960), 10; Rice qtd. in William I.
Kaufman, ed., *Best Television Plays* (New York: Merlin Press, 1950), 94.

6. Fred Coe, "TV Drama's Declaration of Independence," *Theatre Arts*, June 1954, 31.

7. Review of "Welcome Stranger," *Daily Variety*, September 7, 1954; review of
"Christmas in July," *Daily Variety*, September 13, 1954.

8. *General Electric Theater* advertisement, *Variety*, November 6, 1957, 28–29;
Thomas M. Pryor, "Film Star Traffic to TV on Increase," *New York Times*, December
25, 1954, 7.

9. John Dullard, "Report #6," c. 1955, n.p., DuPont Advertising Files, Hagley Museum and Library.

10. Freddie Fields, memo to Jock Elliot, May 1, 1956, DuPont Files (emphasis in original); "Recommendation for DuPont's Continued Use of Television," March 29, 1956, DuPont Files; Jock Elliot, letter to R. M. DeGraff, June 27, 1956, DuPont Files. The resulting altered program did not present many A-list stars, but star caliber certainly increased over that found in the previous incarnation of the show, with Walter Brennan, Maureen O'Sullivan, Ann Harding, Dan Duryea, Lew Ayres, and Frank Lovejoy appearing during the 1956–57 season.

11. Manulis qtd. in Jeff Kisseloff, *The Box: An Oral History of Television, 1920–1961* (New York: Penguin Books, 1995), 262; "Actors Themselves Abet Type-Casting," *Variety*, December 28, 1955, 4; Allyson qtd. in D. Jenkins, "June Allyson's Glamor Treatment for Her New Series," *TV Guide*, October 3–9, 1959, 12; *New York World-Telegram and Sun*, October 29, 1955, Esther Williams Clipping File, Herrick Library.

12. Laraine Day and Barbara Hall, *An Oral History with Laraine Day* (Beverly Hills, Calif.: Academy of Motion Picture Arts and Sciences, Oral History Program, 1998), 224, 229; Wright qtd. in Lowell E. Redelings, "The Hollywood Scene," *Hollywood Citizen-News*, September 24, 1953, Teresa Wright Clipping File, Herrick Library.

13. "Spectaculars Mean New Horizons," *TV Guide*, August 28-September 3, 1954, 6; Vance Kepley, Jr., "From 'Frontal Lobes' to the 'Bob-and-Bob' Show: NBC Management and Programming Strategies, 1949–65," in *Hollywood in the Age of Television*, ed. Tino Balio (Cambridge: Unwin Hyman, 1990), 46–48; James Baughman, *Television's Guardians: The FCC and the Politics of Programming, 1958–1967* (Knoxville: University of Tennessee Press, 1985), 98–102.

14. "TV is Rocking with Specials," *Sponsor*, July 18, 1959, 69–70.

15. Stanton qtd. in "Stanton, Shriner, Winchell Talk About Programs That Start This Week," *New York Times*, September 30, 1956, sec. 10, p. 13.

16. "Inside Playhouse 90," *Newsweek*, November 5, 1956, 106; Jack Gould, "Uphill Fight: Playhouse 90 Lacking Sponsorship," *New York Times*, January 18, 1959, 15; "Playhouse 90's Got a Spec-Size Sponsor Problem on Its Hands," *Variety*, August 29, 1956, 27; "TV Playhouse 90 in Dual-Producer Setup; Dicker Coe," *Variety*, December 4, 1957, 29. Fred Coe, John Houseman, Arthur Penn, Gordon Duff, and Herbert Brodkin were brought in to replace Manulis.

17. Winant qtd. in Kisselhoff, *The Box*, 230; *Playhouse 90* publicity pamphlet, released by CBS Television in 1957, Library of American Broadcasting, University of Maryland at College Park. All of the subsequent publicity quotes are from this pamphlet.

18. William Boddy, *Fifties Television: The Industry and Its Critics* (Urbana: University of Illinois Press, 1990), 163–164.

19. Penn qtd. in Gorham Kindem, *The Live Television Generation of Hollywood Film Directors: Interviews with Seven Directors* (Jefferson, N.C.: McFarland, 1994), 70; "CBS's Playhouse 90," *Time*, October 22, 1956, 87; Ethel Winant, telephone interview with author, March 23, 2000.

20. Frankenhiemer qtd. in Skutch, *Days of Live*, 131; Winant interview; Ethel Winant, letter to Fred Coe, August 3, 1959, Fred Coe Papers, Wisconsin Historical Society.

21. Kisselhoff, *The Box*, 261.

22. "On *Playhouse 90* Martin Manulis Aims to Please Adults," *TV Guide*, October 12–18, 1957, 19.

23. Review of "Forbidden Area," *Daily Variety*, October 5, 1956; review of "Portrait of a Murderer," *Daily Variety*, March 3, 1958; Hunter qtd. in Hedda Hopper, "Will It Last? Tab Wonders," *Chicago Sunday Tribune Magazine*, May 12, 1957, Tab Hunter Clipping File, Herrick Library.

24. Gordon F. Sander, *Serling: The Rise and Twilight of Television's Last Angry Man* (New York: Plume, 1994), 118; Keenan Wynn, as told to James Brough, *Ed Wynn's Son* (Garden City, N.Y.: Doubleday, 1959), 220.

25. Jack Gould, *New York Times*, October 21, 1956, sec. 2, p. 11; review of "Requiem of a Heavyweight," *Daily Variety*, October 15, 1956; Wynn, *Ed Wynn's Son*, 222. Interestingly, this experience itself became the topic for a later drama. A *Westinghouse Desilu Playhouse* episode called "The Man in the Funny Suit," which aired on April 15, 1960, dramatized Wynn's "Requiem" experience. Ed, Keenan, and Rod Serling played themselves.

26. Review of "Sizemore and Son," *Daily Variety*, October 22, 1956; review of "Sincerely, Willis Wayde," *Daily Variety*, December 17, 1956.

27. Mickey Rooney, *I.E.: An Autobiography* (New York: Putnam, 1965), 202–226; review of "The Comedian," *Daily Variety*, February 18, 1957; "The Remarkable Comeback of Mickey Rooney," *McCall's*, September 1957, Mickey Rooney Clipping File, Herrick Library.

28. Review of "A Sound of Different Drummers," *Variety*, October 9, 1957.

29. Lorre qtd. in "Peter Lorre is a Gentle Soul," *TV Guide*, November 2–8, 1957, 28.

30. *Playhouse 90* publicity pamphlet; "Turn the Other Profile," *TV-Radio Mirror*, May 1957, 15.

31. William Boddy, "'The Shining Centre of the Home': Ontologies of Television in the 'Golden Age,'" in *Television in Transition: Papers From the First International Television Studies Conference*, ed. Phillip Drummond and Richard Paterson (London: BFI, 1985), 126.

32. "Turn the Other Profile," *TV-Radio Mirror*, 57; Boddy, *Fifties Television*, 191–192.

33. "Playhouse 90's Got a Spec-Size Sponsor Problem on Its Hands," 27; "Singer Pulls Out of Playhouse 90," *Variety*, February 27, 1957, 23; "Marlboro Iffy on Playhouse 90," *Variety*, February 12, 1958, 29; Jack Gould, "Uphill Fight," 15; Della Cioppa qtd. in Alex C. MacKenzie, Jr., "Descriptive Analysis of the Factors that Influenced the Creation, Introduction, and Impact of Selected Television Programs of the Years, 1946–1976" (Ph.D. diss., Case Western Reserve University, 1979), 269. For a typical negative review of an episode, see Jack Gould, "A Sorry Contrast," *New York Times*, June 12, 1958, sec. 2, p. 13.

34. "It Takes More Than a Star," *Variety*, August 31, 1960, 23. See also "Stars Asking (and Getting) Higher Fees as TV Dramas Feel Pinch," *Variety*, August 25, 1954, 23; George Rosen, "TV's Half-Billion $ Talent Tap," *Variety*, July 27, 1955, 1; Jack Hellman, "'59-'60 TV Spec Roster in Nutshell," *Variety*, July 15, 1959, 37.

35. Cowdin qtd. in Stanley Frank, "TV's Most Provocative Show," *Saturday Evening Post*, February 13, 1960, 56.

36. Abrahams qtd. in "'Do or Die' on 90 Minute Shows," *Variety*, July 4, 1956, 23.

37. "CBS-To-Theaters 'Features,'" *Variety*, February 27, 1957, 21; "SG Repacted for Playhouse 90," *Variety*, March 6, 1957, 23.

38. Weaver qtd. in Boddy, *Fifties Television*, 252.

39. Lemmon qtd. in "Jack Lemmon Not on News Payrolls, But Still Pans TV," *Beverly Hills Citizen*, April 15, 1960, Jack Lemmon Clipping File, Herrick Library.

40. Robert Montgomery, *Open Letter From a Television Viewer* (New York: James H. Heineman, 1968), 14.

41. Review of "A Dream of Treason," *Variety*, January 27, 1960.

42. "Robert Montgomery's Secret Weapon: Stars," *TV Guide*, November 17–23, 1956, 20; "How Much TV is Too Much for Star?" *Variety*, July 25, 1956, 20.

CONCLUSION (PAGES 221–237)

1. "The Great Bull Market—Stacks of Guest Stars Soar Almost Out of Sight," *TV Guide*, December 14–20, 1957, 12; Hal Humphrey, *LA Mirror*, September 21, 1953; Ben Bodec and Alfred J. Jaffee, "Talent Agents: What's the Alternative to Paying Their Price?" *Sponsor*, February 7, 1955, 36; "Review of *The June Allyson Show*," *TV Guide*, October 31–November 6, 1959, 30.

2. "TV Teletype," *TV Guide*, August 29–September 4, 1959, 2; George Rosen, "TV's 'Hero': Cost-Accountant," *Variety*, June 8, 1960, 1.

3. George Rosen, "TV's Very Special Regret," *Variety*, November 25, 1959, 53; "TV's New Faces," *Television Digest*, June 22, 1959, 15; anonymous industry observer qtd. in John Bartlow Martin, "Television USA, Part III: The Master Planners," *Broadcasting*, November 4, 1961, 37.

4. "Strategy for a Program Battle," *Broadcasting*, August 17, 1959, 27–37; Goldensen qtd. in "The abc of ABC," *Forbes*, June 15, 1959, 15.

5. Christopher Anderson, *Hollywood TV: The Studio System in the Fifties* (Austin: University of Texas Press, 1994), 140; Bob Stahl, "The Men Who Run ABC," *TV Guide*, August 1–7, 1959, 6; Goldensen qtd. in "The abc of ABC," 15. Because of the outrage of many critics, viewers, and even Congresspeople, the show survived continual threats of cancellation until finally ending in 1963.

6. Hal Humphrey, *LA Mirror*, July 12, 1961.

7. "Metro To Build Stars—Again," *Variety*, December 12, 1960, 5, 71; "'Future Stars on Rolls,' Eddie Kafafian," *Variety*, January 25, 1956, 3; Wald qtd. in Hal Humphrey, "TV Replaces Movie Scouts," *LA Mirror*, March 30, 1956; "Turn the Other Profile," *TV-Radio Mirror*, May 1957, 15.

8. Ed Robertson, *Maverick: Legend of the West* (Beverly Hills, Calif.: Pomegranate Press, 1994), 31–35; Anderson, *Hollywood TV*, 252–253, 273–278; Garner qtd. in untitled article, *Hollywood Citizen*, November 22, 1961, James Garner Clipping File, Herrick Library.

9. Hal Humphrey, *LA Mirror,* August 21, 1961; Andrews qtd. in Hal Humphrey, *LA Mirror,* April 4, 1963.

10. Stanwyck qtd. in Jane Ellen Wayne, *Stanwyck* (New York: Arbor House, 1985), 158; "Loretta Young: Queen of TV Actresses," *Chicago Tribune,* August 28, 1960, Loretta Young Clipping File, Herrick Library.

11. "How Much TV is Too Much for Star?" *Variety,* July 25, 1956, 21; Ziv qtd. in *Television Digest,* August 13, 1955, 5; Garner qtd. in Pete Martin, "I Call on Bret Maverick," *Saturday Evening Post,* October 11, 1958, 21.

12. Daniel J. Boorstin, *The Image: A Guide to Pseudo-Events in America* (New York: Atheneum, 1961); Richard Schickel, *Intimate Strangers: The Culture of Celebrity* (Garden City, N.Y.: Doubleday, 1985); Leo Braudy, *The Frenzy of Renown: Fame and Its History* (New York: Oxford University Press, 1986); Jeannette Walls, *Dish: The Inside Story on the World of Gossip* (New York: Spike, 2000); Joshua Gamson, *Claims to Fame: Celebrity in Contemporary America* (Berkeley and Los Angeles: University of California Press, 1994); Mary Desjardins, "'Marion Never Looked Lovelier': Hedda Hopper's Hollywood and the Negotiation of Glamour in Post-war Hollywood," *Quarterly Review of Film & Video* 16, nos. 3–4 (Summer 1999): 421–437; Mary Desjardins, "Systematizing Scandal: *Confidential* Magazine, Stardom, and the State of California," in *Headline Hollywood,* ed. Adrienne L. McLean and David A. Cook (New Brunswick, N.J.: Rutgers University Press, 2001), 206–231.

BIBLIOGRAPHY

BOOKS AND ARTICLES

Acker, Ally. *Reel Women: Pioneers of the Cinema 1986 to Present.* New York: Continuum, 1991.

Allyson, June. *June Allyson.* New York: Putnam, 1982.

Alvey, Mark. "The Independents: Rethinking the Television Studio System." In *Television: The Critical View,* 6th edition, edited by Horace Newcomb, 34–51. New York: Oxford University Press, 2000.

Anderson, Christopher. *Hollywood TV: The Studio System in the Fifties.* Austin: University of Texas Press, 1994.

Arden, Eve. *The Three Phases of Eve.* New York: St. Martin's, 1985.

Astor, Mary. *A Life on Film.* New York: Delacorte Press, 1971.

Balio, Tino, ed. *Hollywood in the Age of Television.* Cambridge: Unwin Hyman, 1990.

Barbas, Samantha. *Movie Crazy: Fans, Stars, and the Cult of Celebrity.* New York: Palgrave, 2001.

Barnouw, Eric. *The Golden Web: A History of Broadcasting in the United States, 1933 to 1953.* New York: Oxford University Press, 1968.

———. *The Image Empire: A History of Broadcasting in the United States From 1953.* New York: Oxford University Press, 1970.

———. *The Sponsor: Notes on a Modern Potentate.* Oxford: Oxford University Press, 1978.

———. *Tube of Plenty: The Evolution of American Television.* New York: Oxford University Press, 1990.

Basinger, Jeanine. "Robert Montgomery." In *International Dictionary of Films and Filmmakers.* 3rd ed. Detroit, Mich.: St. James Press, 1997.

Baughman, James. "Nice Guys Last Fifteen Seasons: Jack Benny on Television, 1950–1965." *Film and History* 30, no. 2 (2000): 29–39.

———. *Same Time, Same Station: Creating American Television, 1948–1961.* Baltimore, Md.: Johns Hopkins University Press, 2007.

———. *Television Guardians: The FCC and the Politics of Programming, 1958–1967.* Knoxville: University of Tennessee Press, 1985.

Berenstein, Rhona J. "Acting Live: TV Performance, Intimacy, and Immediacy (1945–1955)." In *Reality Squared: Televisual Discourse on the Real,* edited by James Friedman, 25–49. New Brunswick, N.J.: Rutgers University Press, 2002.

Bilby, Kenneth. *The General: David Sarnoff and the Rise of the Communications Industry.* New York: Harper and Row, 1986.

Boddy, William. *Fifties Television: The Industry and Its Critics.* Urbana: University of Illinois Press, 1990.

———. "Operation Frontal Lobes Versus the Living Room Toy: The Battle Over Programme Control in Early Television." *Media, Culture and Society* 9 (1987): 347–368.

———. "'The Shining Centre of the Home': Ontologies of Television in the 'Golden Age.'" In *Television in Transition: Papers From the First International Television Studies Conference,* edited by Phillip Drummond and Richard Paterson, 125–134. London: BFI Publishing, 1985.

———. "The Studios Move Into Prime Time: Hollywood and the Television Industry in the 1950s." *Cinema Journal* 24, no. 4 (Summer 1985): 23–37.

Bogart, Leo. *The Age of Television.* 3rd ed. New York: Ungar, 1972.

Boorstin, Daniel J. *The Image: A Guide to Pseudo-Events in America.* 1962. Reprint, New York: Vintage Books, 1992.

Braudy, Leo. *The Frenzy of Renown: Fame and Its History.* New York: Oxford University Press, 1986. Reprint, Vintage Books, 1997.

Bordwell, David, Janet Staiger, and Kristin Thompson, eds. *The Classical Hollywood Cinema: Film Style and Mode of Production to 1960.* New York: Columbia University Press, 2001.

Brough, James. *Ed Wynn's Son.* Garden City, N.Y.: Doubleday, 1959.

Buscombe, Edward. "Thinking it Differently: TV and Film Industry." *Quarterly Review of Film Studies* 9, no. 3 (Summer 1984): 196–203.

Butler, Jeremy, ed. *Star Texts: Image and Performance in Film and Television.* Detroit, Mich.: Wayne State University Press. 1991.

Cassidy, Marsha. *What Women Watched: Daytime Television in the 1950s.* Austin: University of Texas Press, 2005.

Cassidy, Marsha, and Mimi White, "Innovating Women's Television in Local and National Networks." *Camera Obscura* 17, no. 3 (2002): 31–69.

Castleman, Harry, and Walter J. Podrazik. *Watching TV: Four Decades of American Television.* New York: McGraw-Hill, 1982.

Clark, Danae. *Negotiating Hollywood: The Cultural Politics of Actors' Labor.* Minneapolis: University of Minnesota Press, 1995.

Cook, Bruce. "Why TV Stars Don't Become Movie Stars (and Vice Versa)." *American Film* 1, no. 8 (June 1976): 58–61.

D'Acci, Julie, and Lynn Spigel, eds. *Feminist Television Criticism: A Reader.* Oxford: Clarendon Press, 1997.

David, Lester, and Irene David. *The Shirley Temple Story.* New York: Putnam, 1983.

Davis, Ronald L. *Arlene Dahl: Remembrances.* Sanford, N.C.: Microfilming Corp. of America, 1978.

Day, Laraine, and Barbara Hall. *An Oral History with Laraine Day.* Beverly Hills, Calif.: Academy of Motion Picture Arts and Sciences, Oral History Program, 1998.

DeLong, Thomas. *Quiz Craze: America's Infatuation with Game Shows.* New York: Praeger, 1991.

Desjardins, Mary. "'Marion Never Looked Lovelier': Hedda Hopper's Hollywood and the Negotiation of Glamour in Post-War Hollywood." *Quarterly Review of Film and Video* 16 (1999): 421–437.

Doherty, Thomas. *Cold War, Cool Medium: Television, McCarthyism, and American Culture.* New York: Columbia University Press, 2003.

Dominick, Joseph R., and Millard C. Pearce. "Trends in Network Prime-Time Programming, 1953–74." *Journal of Communication* 26 (Winter 1976): 70–80.

Doty, Alexander. "The Cabinet of Lucy Ricardo: Lucille Ball's Star Image." *Cinema Journal* 29, no. 4 (Summer 1990): 3–22.

Drummond, Phillip, and Richard Patterson, eds. *Television in Transition: Papers From the First International Television Studies Conference.* London: BFI, 1985.

Dyer, Richard. *Heavenly Bodies: Film Stars and Society.* London: MacMillan, 1986.

———. *Stars.* London: BFI, 1979.

Ellis, John, *Visible Fictions: Cinema, Television, Video.* Boston: Routledge and Kegan Paul, 1982. (Rev. ed., New York: Routledge, 1992).

Epstein, Edward Z., and Joseph Morella. *Jane Wyman: A Biography.* Boston: G. K. Hall, 1986.

Erickson, Hal. *Syndicated Television: The First 40 Years, 1947–87.* Jefferson, N.C.: McFarland, 1989.

Foley, Karen Sue. *The Political Blacklist in the Broadcast Industry: The Decade of the 1950s.* New York: Arno, 1979.

Francis, Arlene. *Arlene Francis: A Memoir.* New York: Simon & Schuster, 1978.

Fultz, Jay. *In Search of Donna Reed.* Iowa City: University of Iowa Press, 1998.

Gaines, Jane M. *Contested Culture: The Image, the Voice, and the Law.* Chapel Hill: University of North Carolina Press, 1991.

Gamson, Joshua. *Claims to Fame: Celebrity in Contemporary America.* Berkeley and Los Angeles: University of California Press, 1994.

Gehring, Wes D. *Irene Dunne: First Lady of Hollywood.* Lanham, Md.: Scarecrow, 2003.

Gledhill, Christine, ed. *Stardom: Industry of Desire.* London: Routledge, 1991.

Goldensen, Leonard H., with Marvin J. Wolf. *Beating the Odds: The Untold Story Behind the Rise of ABC.* New York: Scribner, 1991.

Gomery, Douglas. "Failed Opportunities: The Integration of the U.S. Motion Picture and Television Industries." *Quarterly Review of Film Studies* (Summer 1984): 219–227.

———. *Shared Pleasures: A History of Movie Presentation in the United States.* Madison, Wis.: University of Wisconsin Press, 1992.

Hammontree, Patsy Guy. *Shirley Temple: A Bio-Bibliography.* Westport, Conn.: Greenwood, 1998.

Harrington, C. Lee, and Denise D. Bielby, eds. *Popular Culture: Production and Consumption.* Oxford: Blackwell, 2001.

Harvey, Rita Morley. *Those Wonderful, Terrible Years: George Heller and the American Federation of Television and Radio Artists.* Carbondale: Southern Illinois University Press, 1996.

Haskell, Molly: *From Reverence to Rape: The Treatment of Women in the Movies.* Chicago: University of Chicago Press, 1987.

Havig, Alan. "Fred Allen and Hollywood." *Journal of Popular Film and Television* 7, no. 3 (1979): 273–291.

Hawes, William. "A History of Anthology Television Drama Through 1958." Ph.D. diss., University of Michigan, 1960.

BIBLIOGRAPHY

———. *Live Television Drama, 1946–1951.* Jefferson, N.C.: McFarland, 2001.

Hayward, Susan. *Key Concepts in Cinema Studies.* New York: Routledge, 1996.

Heck-Rabi, Louise. *Women Filmmakers: A Critical Reception.* Metuchen, N.J.: Scarecrow, 1984.

Heldenfels, R. D. *TV's Greatest Year: 1954.* New York: Continuum, 1994.

Henry, William A., III. *The Great One.* New York: Doubleday, 1992.

Hill, John, and Martin McLoone. *Big Picture, Small Screen: The Relations Between Film and Television.* Luton, Bedfordshire, England: University of Luton Press, 1996.

Hilmes, Michele. "The 'Ban' That Never Was: Hollywood and the Broadcasting Industry in 1932." *The Velvet Light Trap,* no. 23 (Spring 1989): 39–48.

———. "Femmes Boff Program Toppers: Women Break Into Prime Time, 1943–1948." In *Transmitting the Past: Historical and Cultural Perspectives on Broadcasting,* edited by Susan Brinson and J. E. Winn, 137–160. Tuscaloosa: University of Alabama Press, 2005.

———. *Hollywood and Broadcasting: From Radio to Cable.* Urbana: University of Illinois Press, 1990.

———. *Radio Voices: American Broadcasting, 1922–1952.* Minneapolis: University of Minnesota Press, 1997.

Holmes, Su. "'As They Really Are and in Close-up': Film Stars on 1950's British Television." *Screen* 42, no. 2 (Summer 2001): 167–187.

Jewell, Richard. "Hollywood and Radio: Competition and Partnership in the 1930s." *Historical Journal of Film, Radio and Television* 4, no.2 (1984): 125–141.

Kahn, Gordon. *Hollywood on Trial: The Story of the 10 Who Were Indicted.* 1948. Reprint, New York: Arno Press and the New York Times, 1972.

Kanter, Hal. *An Oral History with Hal Kanter.* Beverly Hills, Calif.: Academy of Motion Picture Arts and Sciences, Oral History Program, 1996.

Kaufman, William I., ed. *Best Television Plays.* New York: Merlin Press, 1950.

Kindem, Gorham. *The Live Television Generation of Hollywood Film Directors: Interviews with Seven Directors.* Jefferson, N.C.: McFarland, 1994.

Kisseloff, Jeff. *The Box: An Oral History of Television, 1920–1961.* New York: Penguin Books, 1995.

Klaprat, Cathy. "The Star as Market Strategy: Bette Davis in Another Light." In *The American Film Industry,* edited by Tino Balio, 351–376. Madison: University of Wisconsin Press, 1985.

Kompare, Derek. *Rerun Nation: How Repeats Invented American Television.* New York: Routledge, 2005.

Kramer, Stanley, with Thomas M. Coffey. *A Mad, Mad, Mad, Mad World: A Life in Hollywood.* New York: Harcourt Brace, 1997.

Krampner, Jon. *The Man in the Shadows: Fred Coe and the Golden Age of Television.* New Brunswick, N.J.: Rutgers University Press, 1997.

Kuhn, Annette, ed. *Queen of the "B"s: Ida Lupino Behind the Camera.* Westport, Conn.: Praeger, 1995.

Lafferty, William. "Film and Television." In *Film and the Arts in Symbiosis: A Resource Guide,* edited by Gary R. Edgerton, 273–309. New York: Greenwood Press, 1988.

———. "'A New Era in TV Programming' Becomes 'Business as Usual': Videotape Technology, Local Stations, and Network Power, 1957–1961." *Quarterly Review of Film and Video* 16 (1999): 405–419.

———. "'No Attempt at Artiness, Profundity, or Significance': Fireside Theater and the Rise of Filmed Programming." *Cinema Journal* 27, no. 1 (Fall 1987): 23–46.

Langer, John. "Television's 'personality system.'" *Media, Culture and Society* 4 (October 1981): 351–365.

Lev, Peter. *The Fifties: Transforming the Screen, 1950–59.* Berkeley and Los Angeles: University of California Press, 2003.

MacDonald, J. Fred. *Don't Touch that Dial: Radio Programming in American Life, 1920–1960.* Chicago: Nelson-Hall, 1979.

———. *One Nation Under Television: The Rise and Decline of Network TV.* New York: Pantheon Books, 1990.

MacKenzie, Alex C. Jr. "Descriptive Analysis of the Factors that Influenced the Creation, Introduction, and Impact of Selective Television Programs of the Years, 1946–1976." Ph.D. dissertation, Case Western Reserve University, 1979.

Marling, Karal Ann. *As Seen on TV: The Visual Culture of Everyday Life in the 1950s.* Cambridge, Mass.: Harvard University Press, 1994.

Mashon, Kenneth Michael. "NBC, J. Walter Thompson, and the Evolution of Prime-Time Television Programming and Sponsorship, 1946–1958." Ph.D. dissertation, University of Maryland, 1996.

McDonald, Paul. "I'm Winning on a Star: The Extraordinary Ordinary World of Stars in Their Eyes." *Critical Survey* 7, no. 1 (1995): 59–66.

———. *The Star System: Hollywood's Production of Popular Identities.* London: Wallflower Publishing, 2000.

McDougal, Dennis. *The Last Mogul: Lew Wasserman, MCA, and the Hidden History of Hollywood.* New York: Crown, 1998.

McLean, Adrienne L., and David A. Cook, *Headline Hollywood: A Century of Film Scandal.* New Brunswick, N.J.: Rutgers University Press, 2001.

McNulty, Thomas. *Errol Flynn: The Life and Career.* Jefferson, N.C.: McFarland, 2004.

Mellencamp, Patricia. "Situation and Simulation." *Screen* 26, no. 2 (April 1985): 30–40.

Menjou, Adolphe, and M. M. Musselman. *It Took Nine Tailors.* New York: Whittlesey House, 1948.

Metz, Robert. *CBS: Reflections in a Bloodshot Eye.* Chicago: Playboy Press, 1975.

Miner, Worthington J., and Franklin J. Schaffner. *Worthington Miner: A Directors Guild of America Oral History.* Metuchen, N.J.: The Directors Guild of America and Scarecrow Press, 1985.

Moldea, Dan. *Dark Victory: Ronald Reagan, MCA and the Mob.* New York: Viking, 1986.

Monaco, Paul. *The Sixties: 1960–69.* Berkeley and Los Angeles: University of California Press, 2001.

Montgomery, Robert. *An Open Letter From a Television Viewer.* New York: James E. Heineman, 1968.

Morley, Sheridan. *The Other Side of the Moon: The Life of David Niven.* London: Weidenfeld and Nicolson, 1985.

Murray, Lawrence L. "Complacency, Competition, Cooperation: The Film Industry Responds to the Challenge of Television." *Journal of Popular Film* 6, no. 1 (1977): 47–68.

Murray, Susan. *"Hitch Your Antenna to the Stars!" Early Television and Broadcast Stardom.* New York: Routledge, 2005.

Newcomb, Horace, ed. *Television: The Critical View.* 6th ed. New York: Oxford University Press, 2000.

Niven, David. *The Moon's a Balloon.* London: Hamish Hamilton, 1971.

O'Dell, Cary. *Women Pioneers in Television: Biographies of Fifteen Industry Leaders.* With a foreword by Sally Jessy Raphael. Jefferson, N.C.: McFarland, 1997.

Optowsky, Stan. *TV: The Big Picture.* New York: Dutton, 1961.

Osborne-Thompson, Heather Kathryn. "Routine Adjustments: Re-viewing Women's Television Comedy Genres, 1950–1969." Ph.D. diss., University of Southern California, 2004.

Paper, Lewis J. *Empire: William S. Paley and the Making of CBS.* New York: St. Martin's, 1987.

Parish, James Robert, with Gregory W. Mank. *The Hollywood Reliables.* Westport, Conn.: Arlington House Publishers, 1980.

Parks, Lisa. "'Watching the 'Working Gals': Fifties Sitcoms and the Repositioning of Women in Postwar American Culture." *Critical Matrix* 11, no. 2 (Winter 1999): 42–66.

Quirk, Lawrence J. *Jane Wyman: The Actress and the Woman: An Illustrated Biography.* New York: Dembner Books, 1986.

Reagan, Ronald, with Richard G. Hubler. *Where's the Rest of Me?* New York: Duell, Sloan and Pearce, 1965.

Redding, Judith M. *Film Fatales: Independent Women Directors.* Seattle, Wash.: Seal Press, 1997.

Reel, Frank A. *The Networks: How They Stole the Show.* New York: Scribner, 1979.

Reeves, Jimmie L. "Television Stardom: A Ritual of Social Typification and Individualization." In *Media, Myths and Narratives: Television and the Press,* edited by James W. Carey, 146–160. Newbury Park, Calif.: Sage Publications, 1988.

Ritrosky-Winslow, Madelyn. "Transforming Stardom: Loretta Young's Journey From Film to Television." Ph.D. diss., Indiana University, 1997.

Robertson, Ed. *Maverick: Legend of the West.* Beverly Hills, Calif.: Pomegranate Press, 1994.

Roof, Judith. *All About Thelma and Eve: Sidekicks and Third Wheels.* Urbana: University of Illinois Press, 2002.

Rooney, Mickey. *I. E.: An Autobiography.* New York: Putnam, 1965.

Rose, Frank. *The Agency: William Morris and the Hidden History of Show Business.* New York: HarperCollins, 1995.

Rouse, Morleen Getz. "A History of the F. W. Ziv Radio and Television Syndication Companies, 1930–1960." Ph.D. diss., University of Michigan, 1976.

Sander, Gordon F. *Serling: The Rise and Twilight of Television's Last Angry Man.* New York: Plume, 1994.

Sanders, Coyne Steven, and Tom Gilbert. *Desilu: The Story of Lucille Ball and Desi Arnaz.* New York: Morrow, 1993.

Schatz, Thomas. *Boom and Bust: American Cinema in the 1940s.* Berkeley and Los Angeles: University of California Press, 1997.

———. "Desilu, I Love Lucy, and the Rise of Network TV." In *Making Television: Authorship and the Production Process,* edited by Robert J. Thompson and Gary Burns, 117–136. New York: Praeger, 1990.

Schickel, Richard. *Intimate Strangers: The Culture of Celebrity in America.* Garden City, N.Y.: Doubleday, 1985. Reprint, with a new afterword by the author, Chicago: Ivan R. Dee, 2000.

Schultz, Margie. *Irene Dunne: A Bio-Bibliography.* New York: Greenwood, 1991.

Schwoch, James. "A Failed Vision: The Mutual Television Network." *The Velvet Light Trap,* no. 33 (Spring 1994): 3–13.

———. "Selling the Sight/Site of Sound: Broadcast Advertising and the Transition From Radio to Television." *Cinema Journal* 30, no. 1 (Fall 1990): 55–66.

Seagrave, Kerry. *Movies at Home: How Hollywood Came to Television.* Jefferson, N.C.: McFarland, 1999.

Siepmann, Charles Arthur. *Radio, Television and Society.* New York: Oxford University Press, 1950.

Silvers, Phil. *The Laugh Is on Me: The Phil Silvers Story.* Englewood Cliffs, N.J.: Prentice-Hall, 1973.

Skutch, Ira, ed. *Five Directors: The Golden Years of Radio. Based on Interviews with Himan Brown, Axel Gruenberg, Fletcher Markle, Arch Oboler, Robert Louis Shayon.* Lanham, Md: Scarecrow Press; Los Angeles: Directors Guild of America, 1998.

———. *Ira Skutch: I Remember Television: A Memoir.* With a foreword by Delbert Mann. Metuchen, N.J.: Scarecrow Press; Hollywood, Calif.: Directors Guild of America, 1989.

———, ed. *The Days of Live: Television's Golden Age as Seen by 21 Directors Guild of America Members.* Lanham, Md.: Scarecrow Press; Los Angeles: Directors Guild of America, 1998.

Slide, Anthony, ed. *Selected Radio and Television Criticism.* Metuchen, N.J.: Scarecrow Press, 1987.

Smith, Sally Bedell. *In All His Glory: The Life of William S. Paley.* New York: Simon and Schuster, 1990.

Smoodin, Eric. "Motion Pictures and Television: 1930–45." *Journal of UFVA.* 34, no. 3 (Summer 1982): 3–8.

Smulyan, Susan. *Selling Radio: The Commercialization of American Broadcasting, 1920–1934.* Washington, D.C.: Smithsonian Institution Press, 1994.

Spigel, Lynn. *Make Room for TV: Television and the Family Ideal in Postwar America.* Chicago: University of Chicago Press, 1992.

Spigel, Lynn, and Michael Curtin. *The Revolution Wasn't Televised: Sixties Television and Social Conflict.* New York: Routledge, 1997.

Spigel, Lynn, and Denise Mann, eds. *Private Screenings: Television and the Female Consumer.* Minneapolis: University of Minnesota Press, 1992.

Sterling, Christopher H., and John M. Kittross. *Stay Tuned: A Concise History of American Broadcasting.* Belmont, Calif.: Wadsworth Publishing, 1990.

Sturcken, Frank. *Live Television: The Golden Age of 1946–1958 in New York.* Jefferson, N.C.: McFarland, 1990.

Thomas, Tony. *The Dick Powell Story.* Burbank, Calif.: Riverwood Press, 1992.

Thompson, Kristin, and David Bordwell. *Film History.* 2nd ed. New York: McGraw-Hill, 2003.

Thumim, Janet, ed. *Small Screens, Big Ideas: Television in the 1950s.* London: I. B. Tauris, 2002.

Tucker, David C. *The Women Who Made Television Funny: Ten Stars on 1950s Sitcoms.* Jefferson, N.C.: McFarland, 2007.

Vaughn, Stephen. *Ronald Reagan in Hollywood.* Cambridge: Cambridge University Press, 1994.

Vianello, Robert. "The Power Politics of Live Television." *Journal of Film and Video* (Summer 1985): 26–40.

———. "The Rise of the Telefilm and the Network's Hegemony over the Motion Picture Industry." *Quarterly Review of Film Studies* 9 (Summer 1984): 204–218.

Walls, Jeannette. *Dish: The Inside Story on the World of Gossip.* New York: Spike, 2000.

Wayne, Jane Ellen. *Stanwyck.* New York: Arbor House, 1985.

Weatherby, W. J. *Jackie Gleason.* New York: Pharos Books, 1992.

Wertheim, Arthur Frank. "The Rise and Fall of Milton Berle." In *American History, American Television,* edited by John O'Connor, 55–77. New York: Ungar, 1983.

Wilk, Max. *The Golden Age of Television.* New York: Delacorte Press, 1976.

ARCHIVAL MATERIAL

DuPont Advertising Files, Hagley Museum and Library, Wilmington, Delaware.

Early Television Collection, University of California–Los Angeles.

Margaret Herrick Library, Academy of Motion Picture Arts and Sciences, Los Angeles, California.

Hal Humphrey Collection, Cinema-TV Library, University of Southern California.

Jerome Lawrence and Robert Lee Papers, New York Public Library for the Performing Arts.

Library of American Broadcasting, University of Maryland at College Park.

Museum of Television and Radio, Beverly Hills, California, and New York, New York.

Photofest, New York.

Russel B. Nye Popular Culture Collection, Michigan State University.

Warner Bros. Archives, University of Southern California.

Wisconsin Center for Film & Theater Research and Wisconsin Historical Society, Madison, Wisconsin.

Frederic Ziv Radio Collection, Electronic Media Division, College Conservatory of Music, University of Cincinnati.

INDEX

Page numbers in *italics* represent illustrations.

ABOUT THE AUTHOR

Christine Becker is an associate professor in the Department of Film, Television, and Theatre at the University of Notre Dame, where she teaches courses on such subjects as television criticism and aesthetics, film history, and media stardom.